Napoleon's Expedition to Russia

Napoleon's Expedition to Russia

General Count Philippe de Ségur

Edited by

CHRISTOPHER SUMMERVILLE

> It was here that we have inscribed with the sword and blood one of the most memorable pages of our history.
>
> Philippe-Paul de Ségur

ROBINSON
London

Constable & Robinson Ltd
3 The Lanchesters
162 Fulham Palace Road
London W6 9ER
www.constablerobinson.com

First published in the UK by Robinson
an imprint of Constable & Robinson Ltd 2003

A copy of the British Library Cataloguing in Publication Data is available from the British Library

ISBN 1–84119–454–9

Printed and bound in the EU

10 9 8 7 6 5 4 3 2 1

Contents

Editor's Preface

'Comrades, I have undertaken the task of retracing the history of the Grand Army and its leader during the year 1812. I address it to such of you as the ices of the north have disarmed and who can no longer serve their country but by the recollections of their misfortunes and their glory.'[1] With this dedication, General Count Philippe-Paul de Ségur began what is, perhaps, the most compelling account of the greatest catastrophe in military history. First published in Paris in December 1824 (some three and a half years after Napoleon's death), de Ségur's book caused an immediate sensation among a public hungry for information on a war which, within the space of six months, claimed 1,000,000 lives and set in motion the chain of events responsible for the fall of France's First Empire. By 1827, de Ségur's work – entitled *History of the Expedition to Russia, Undertaken by the Emperor Napoleon in the Year 1812* – had been reprinted at least eight times, with editions appearing in every major European language. In Great Britain, endorsement came from no less a source than the Duke of Wellington, who declared, 'Ségur's work has drawn the public's attention to the most extraordinary and stupendous transactions and events of modern times, and of which no times have produced a parallel.'[2]

Despite such accolades, de Ségur's epic has, nevertheless, drifted out of print in recent years: a fact largely explained by its sheer size; for, sprawling over two volumes in its original form, the book necessarily demands serious commitment, in terms of both time and money. It remains, however, a tour de force and provides a fascinating window on a gloriously heroic, yet breathtakingly tragic, slice of history. Ransacked by generations of historians eager for graphic source material, it is no dry military debrief but a work of imagination and drama; and contains some of the most striking and poignant descriptions of war ever written. In catering for the general public rather than a military elite, de Ségur has left behind an accessible account of a momentous series of events: a kind of elegant nightmare, whose chief somnambulist is Napoleon himself, wading through gore and seeing only glory. Aware of the weight of his subject and, as a survivor, still in awe of the ordeal, de Ségur prefaced his tale with a quotation from Virgil: 'Although my soul dreads remembrance and has left me grieving, I shall begin . . .'[3]

Determined, therefore, to let de Ségur tell his story to a new generation of readers, I felt that the time was ripe to revisit his text. It occurred to me that, as a portion of the original is concerned with the political build-up to, and consequent fall-out from, Napoleon's invasion of Russia (not to mention a lengthy biographical sketch of the author in my copy of the English translation of 1827), the book could be cropped without losing the basic framework of its military narrative. In fact, by concentrating on the campaign's key events and paraphrasing everything else, a tighter, more compact single-volume edition might be produced: still containing essential background information and retaining all the power and drama of the original. The present volume, then, is the result of this concept: a plan which, from the beginning, was intended to satisfy both general reader and aficionado alike – a book to be read in both the study and on the subway. More importantly, it gets de Ségur back on the bookshelves, where he belongs.

H.A. Patchett-Martin, the English translator of de Ségur's memoirs, informs us that 'Count Philippe de Ségur, general of division, peer of France, academician, was born in 1780 and died in 1873. He lived for the greater part of a century and cut a brilliant figure in war, politics and letters. A private in 1800, he became a general in February 1812 and fought continuously up to the end of the imperial era. He served through all the wars of the Empire on the staff of Napoleon or at the head of picked troops. With an equal passion for literary and for military glory, he occupied his leisure after the peace in writing numerous works, and published in 1824 his famous narrative of the campaign in Russia, which was talked of all over Europe.'[4] Despite de Ségur's assertion that, as a young man, he was 'not fit for anything, not even to be a clerk in an office, for my writing was too bad',[5] it is for his extraordinary account of catastrophe in Russia that he will be forever remembered.

De Ségur was an aristocrat who, like so many other young men of his time, was captivated by the charisma of Napoleon Bonaparte. Renouncing his family's Royalist sympathies, he embraced the Revolution and enlisted as a cavalry trooper: 'I had found my vocation; from that moment I was a soldier, I only dreamt of combats and disdained any other career.'[6] And yet de Ségur had long entertained literary ambitions: in 1802 he published an account of his first campaign, fought two years previously in the Grisons, during which he had served as General MacDonald's aide-de-camp. But it was to be Napoleon's colossal invasion of Russia which would furnish de Ségur with the necessary raw material for a virtuoso performance in descriptive prose. The historian Edward Foord once observed that Napoleon's career 'resembles the fateful development of a Greek tragedy'[7] and one might add that its theme was hubris. Nowhere is this theme more dramatically exposed than in the expedition to Russia; and nowhere is this débâcle more vividly described than in de Ségur's celebrated account.

What makes de Ségur's narrative especially valuable, however, is his proximity to the Emperor: for by 1812, having been promoted to general, he was serving as *maréchal-des-logis*[8] on Napoleon's staff, a situation which allowed him to study the Emperor at close quarters. It was an opportunity not to be missed and – as the editor of the English translation of 1827 points out – the secret of de Ségur's success 'is undoubtedly to be found, independently of the inherent importance of the subject, in the . . . graphic and dramatic sketches of the "Great Captain" of modern times . . . and in the conscientious manner in which, notwithstanding his sincere and unaffected admiration of Napoleon, he has admitted of his errors and given merited praise to the perseverance, constancy and magnanimity of the Russians and their emperor.'[9]

Not everyone was happy, however, with de Ségur's description of a French military effort gone wrong; or his self-imposed brief to 'avail myself of the privilege, sometimes painful, sometimes glorious, of telling what I have seen'.[10] According to Baron de Marbot, the celebrated Napoleonic memoirist, some veterans were 'distressed by the spirit of the work'[11] – which dared to portray Napoleon as a mere mortal, subject to errors of judgement, just like everyone else. The exiled Emperor had recently died, leaving behind him a legacy of glory unsurpassed in the annals of military history: de Ségur's decision not to conceal what he witnessed 'in the persuasion that truth is of all attributes that which alone is worthy of a great man',[12] did not, therefore, go down well in some of the more sensitive Bonapartist circles. Marbot continues: 'the old officers of the Empire, feeling that they were attacked, charged General Gourgaud to reply. He did it successfully but in too bitter a fashion and a duel resulted between him and M. de Ségur, who was wounded.'[13] However, the *rencontre* with Gourgaud – a fanatical disciple of Napoleon and a notorious duellist – merely served to heighten public interest in his book and by 1827 de Ségur's literary credentials were well and truly established.

The text which I have used for this present edition of de Ségur's classic is that published by Treuttel, Wurz, Treuttel Jnr and Richter in 1827 and, unless otherwise stated, all quotations by de Ségur are taken from this source. However, in the interests of clarity, I have included additional material for the benefit and convenience of the modern reader. Accompanying de Ségur's narrative, therefore, are the following extras: a map; a short introduction, giving the political background to the military action; chapter titles and opening quotations from other contemporary sources, plus a brief introduction of the action to come; and at the end, a brief biographical list of the Grand Army's principal personalities; a chronology of major events; an epilogue, giving the conclusion to de Ségur's story; a glossary of specialist terms; notes to the text plus the sources of all quotations; and finally, a full bibliography.

In the interests of fluency and consistency, I have found it necessary to make the following changes to the original text: distances are now given exclusively in French leagues (approximately equivalent to three English miles); on the whole, I have favoured proper names over titles in order to identify individuals (e.g. Murat, rather than the King of Naples, etc.); Russian place-names have been rendered consistently (I have relied upon Edward Foord's *Napoleon's Russian Campaign of 1812*, as a guide: his system appearing both straightforward and logical to English eyes); dates and numerals have been rendered consistently; obsolete words replaced by their modern equivalents; and the punctuation completely revised. I have also found it necessary, on occasion, to crop repetitive and unnecessarily verbose passages, in order to create a sharper, crisper text with added pace and momentum. Finally, I have taken the liberty of shortening de Ségur's original title to *Napoleon's Expedition to Russia*.

Working on a new edition of de Ségur has been both demanding and rewarding; and I would like to take this opportunity to express my gratitude to all those who have encouraged, helped and supported me in this project: special thanks are due to Laurence Cornhill, Antonia Evans, Ewa Haren, Roger and Ileana McMeeking.

C.J. Summerville

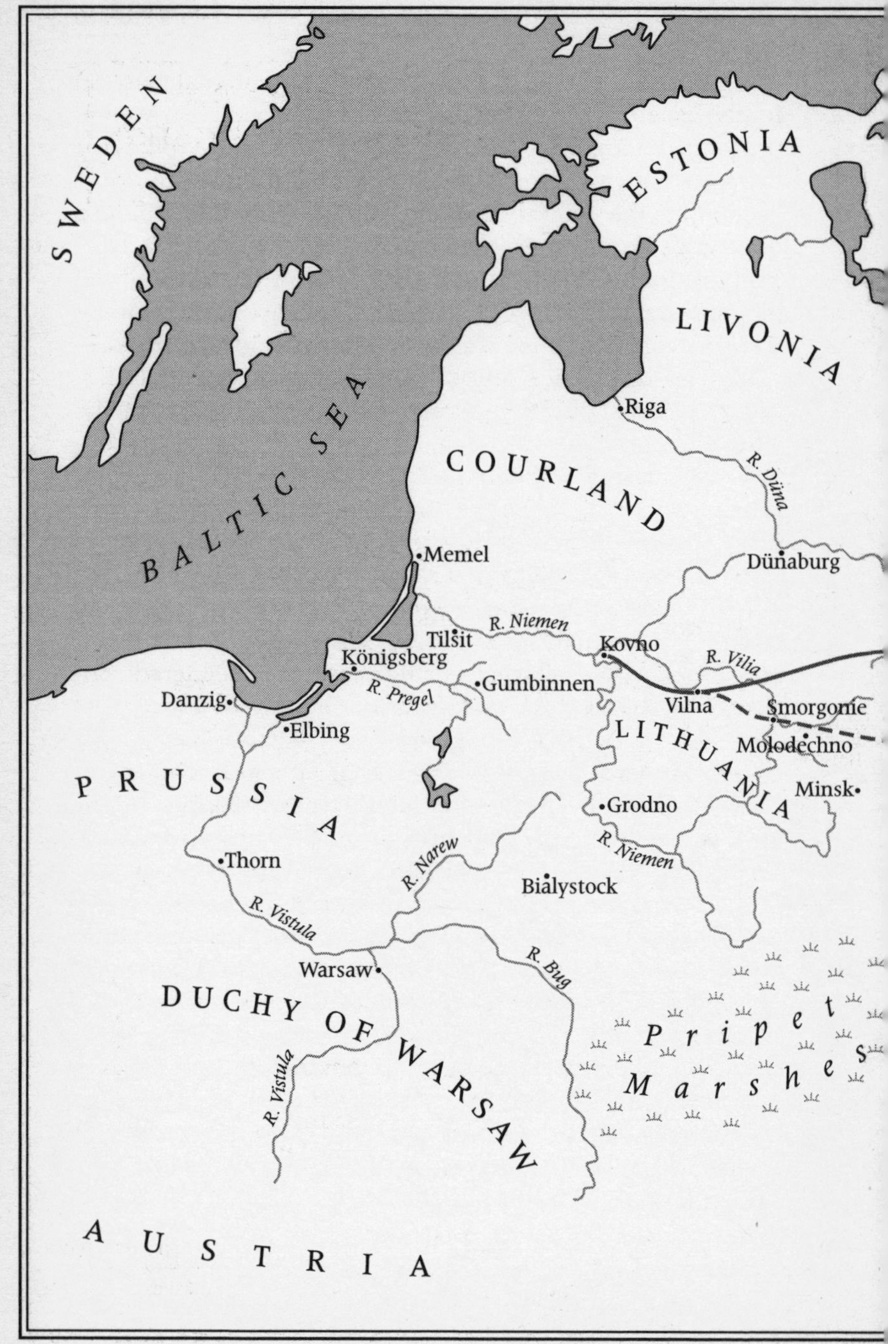

SWEDEN
ESTONIA
LIVONIA
BALTIC SEA
COURLAND
Riga
R. Düna
Memel
Dünaburg
R. Niemen
Tilsit
Kovno
Königsberg
R. Vilia
Gumbinnen
R. Pregel
Danzig
Elbing
Vilna
Smorgonie
LITHUANIA
Molodechno
PRUSSIA
Minsk
Grodno
Thorn
R. Narew
R. Niemen
Bialystock
R. Vistula
R. Bug
Warsaw
DUCHY OF WARSAW
Pripet Marshes
R. Vistula
AUSTRIA

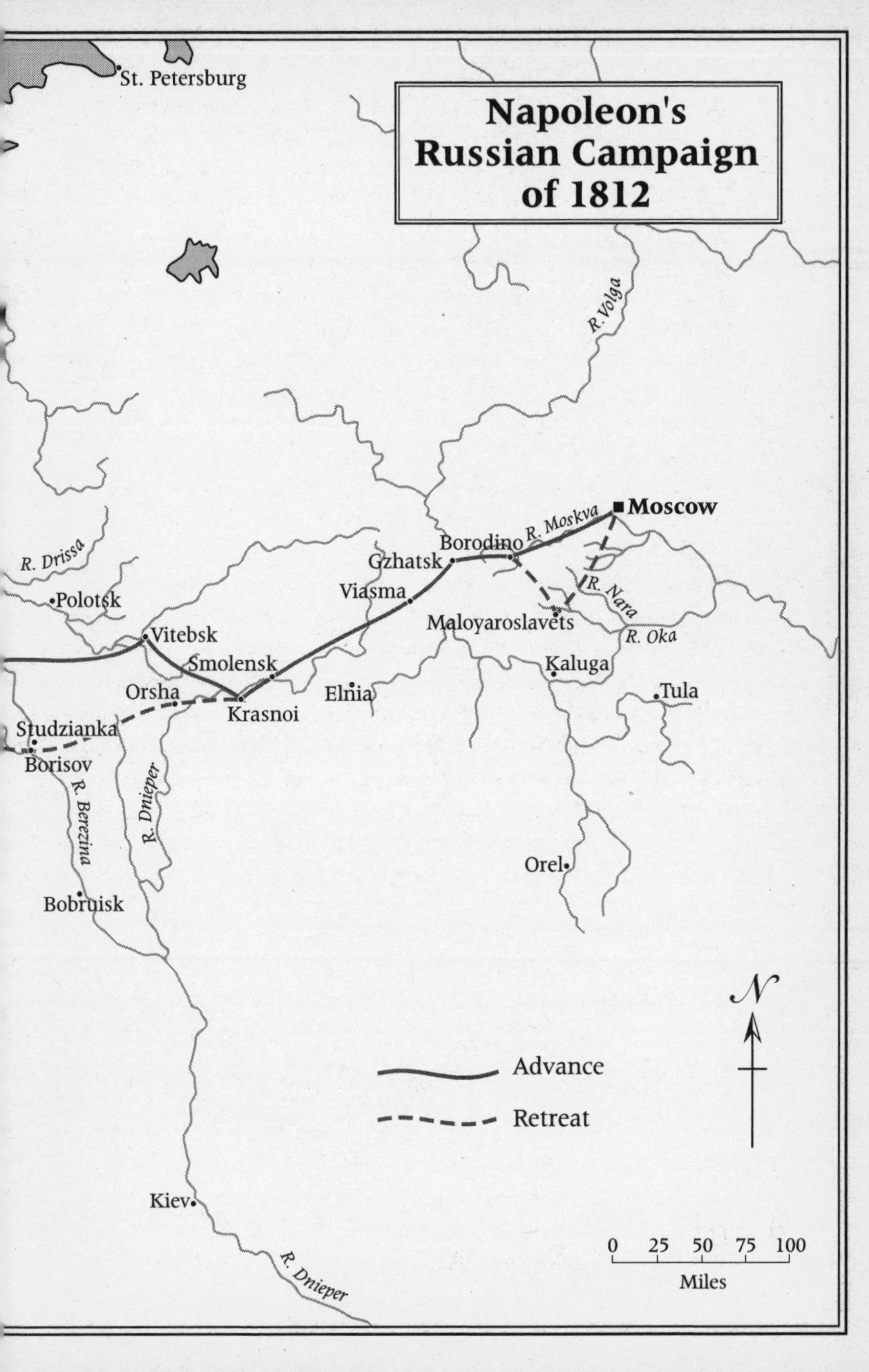
Napoleon's Russian Campaign of 1812
St. Petersburg
R. Volga
Moscow
R. Moskva
Borodino
Gzhatsk
Viasma
R. Nara
Maloyaroslavets
R. Oka
Kaluga
Tula
R. Drissa
Polotsk
Vitebsk
Smolensk
Orsha
Krasnoi
Elnia
Studzianka
Borisov
R. Berezina
R. Dnieper
Bobruisk
Orel
N
Advance
Retreat
Kiev
R. Dnieper
0 25 50 75 100
Miles

Introduction

To negotiate is not to do as one likes.

Napoleon[1]

'Another three years and I am master of the universe!'[2] *declared a triumphant Napoleon Bonaparte in 1811. With Europe at his feet and his arch-enemy England teetering on the brink of ruin as economic warfare with France began to bite, few would have questioned the Emperor's euphoria. And yet Napoleon's prediction could not have been more unfortunate, for by 1814 he had lost everything: crown, dynasty, empire – almost his very life, in a botched suicide attempt following the fall of Paris to the allies of the Sixth Coalition, and his subsequent enforced abdication. This spectacular reversal of fortune, which turned the political map of Europe on its head, was like a great avalanche: awe-inspiring in its destructiveness, cataclysmic and inexorable. What is more, its onset may be precisely dated: 24 June 1812, the day Napoleon led the largest army the world had yet witnessed, across the Rubicon of the River Niemen, into the domain of Alexander of Russia.*

Napoleon's coronation as Emperor of the French on 2 December 1804 was the catalyst for an intensification of a conflict begun in 1791, when the absolute monarchies of the Ancien Régime sought to stifle the violent and destabilizing energies unleashed by the French Revolution. Destined to last until the Emperor's swansong at Waterloo in 1815, this original Great War took the form of a series of campaigns, fought by successive European coalitions (funded by British cash), against the militancy of a French superpower animated by revolutionary zeal and dreams of foreign conquest. Underlying this ideological conflict was the economic rivalry between France and Great Britain: emerging industrial giants, eager to dominate the markets of the Old and New Worlds.

Although Britain quickly established mastery of the seas – gaining a decisive victory at Trafalgar on 21 October 1805 – a series of startling victories on land gave France dominion over most of Europe and confirmed Napoleon's reputation as a commander of genius. In fact, by June 1807 Bonaparte had defeated every army sent against him: an Austro-Russian force had been humbled at Austerlitz on 2 December 1805; the Prussian military machine crushed in a single day at the Battle of Jena-Auersädt on 14 October 1806; and the recalcitrant Russians given yet another drubbing eight months later at the Battle of Friedland. Only Britain remained in the ring and yet – protected by the English Channel and the wooden walls of the Royal Navy – frustratingly out of reach. 'Perfidious Albion' would have to be brought low by other means.

Napoleon's response to Britain's bellicosity was the Continental System. The idea was simple: to close down all continental ports – by fair means or foul – to British shipping, thereby enforcing a crippling blockade which would bring the 'nation of shopkeepers' to its knees via economic ruin. Britain replied with her own seaborne blockade of French ports and soon all trading nations – whether neutral or partisan – were caught in the crossfire, as both powers sought to starve each other of mercantile lifeblood. Although Napoleon knew from the outset that his system would result in economic hardship for both sides, he calculated that Britain would crack first; for the Continental System to work effectively, however, it would be essential to seal off the whole European coastline to British merchantmen. Achieving this goal became Napoleon's number one priority.

Bonaparte's ambitions took a huge stride forward when, within days of victory at Friedland, Alexander sued for peace. A parley between the two emperors was arranged for 25 June at Tilsit, a town on the border between East Prussia and Russian Courland.

The meeting, which took place aboard a raft moored midstream of the River Niemen, represented the pinnacle of Napoleon's career: 'suddenly I found myself victorious, laying down the law, courted by emperors and kings.'[3] *As for Alexander (a dreamy, fanciful, romantic character, always susceptible to a new guru), seven years Napoleon's junior and completely bowled over by sudden proximity to the greatest captain of the age, he was instantly spellbound by the Bonaparte charisma.*

Having annihilated the Russian field army at Friedland, Napoleon might have been expected to impose a harsh peace upon Alexander: instead, he was careful to cultivate him and made him the object of a charm offensive. The reasoning behind Napoleon's apparent consideration for a conquered enemy was simple, as de Ségur himself explains: 'As his great object was the extension of the Continental System and to make it surround Europe, the co-operation of Russia would complete its development.' Taken in by Napoleon's display of deference, the impressionable Alexander unhesitatingly committed his country to economic ruin in the cause of France. 'How I loved that man!' he later recalled, ruefully.[4]

The peace settlement which Napoleon obtained at Tilsit was a highly favourable one, which allowed him to continue redesigning the map of Europe. He had already dismantled the Habsburg-controlled Holy Roman Empire, following Austria's defeat at Austerlitz: replacing it with a patchwork of German puppet-states loyal to France, dubbed the Confederation of the Rhine. Now the work of empire-building could continue: Prussia was to be dismembered, losing half its territory to two new Napoleonic creations, the Kingdom of Westphalia and the Grand Duchy of Warsaw. The former, Bonaparte gave as a gift to his playboy brother, Jérôme, who was proclaimed king on 7 July 1807; the latter, a new French satellite, was to be a kind of mini Polish state, perched – much to St Petersburg's chagrin – on Russia's front doorstep. Thus, Napoleon emerged from Tilsit having extended his empire and the influence of the Bonaparte clan, cowed Prussia, and bound Alexander to pledge his full support in the economic war with Britain. The latter left Tilsit happy at finding a powerful partner, friend and mentor; but Napoleon regarded Alexander merely as a promising protégé and willing disciple: the honeymoon of the two emperors was to be short-lived.

In fact, the ink was hardly dry on the treaty which declared 'Complete and perfect peace and amity'[5] *between France and Russia, before the first cracks appeared in the new entente. Once out of range of Napoleon's magnetic personality, Alexander fell prey to the opinions of his family and advisers, all of whom detested Napoleon and saw Tilsit as a pact with the devil. Moreover, a cool-headed, objective appraisal of the situation brought to light a number of stumbling blocks which, in the event, would prove to be insurmountable obstacles to a lasting peace.*

Firstly, commitment to Napoleon's Continental System meant losing lucrative trade with Britain, a major destination for Russian wheat, timber, hemp and tallow. Without any kind of compensation for lost revenue, Russian merchants faced financial ruin: a fact not lost on Alexander's anti-French ministers. Secondly, Alexander's major ambition of acquiring Constantinople through conquest appeared to be a move which Napoleon – fearing Russian interference in the Mediterranean – was determined to block. Lastly, there was the matter of Polish independence, an idea which Napoleon had flirted with, but which was anathema to St Petersburg. The old Kingdom of Poland had been partitioned and swallowed up by Russia, Prussia and Austria between 1772 and 1795; but Napoleon's creation of the Grand Duchy of Warsaw awakened Russian fears of a full reconstitution of Polish lands and national identity: despite declarations to the contrary, Napoleon was perceived by St Petersburg – with much bitterness – as meddling in Russian affairs.

Relations had thus noticeably deteriorated when the two emperors met again at Erfurt, on 14 October 1808. The extension of the Continental System had led Napoleon to invade first Portugal and then Spain earlier in the year and – much to everyone's surprise – his armies had received one setback after another. Meanwhile, seeking revenge for Austerlitz and heartened by French reversals in the Peninsula, Austria was preparing a blitzkrieg of her own: Napoleon called the meeting at Erfurt, therefore, to bolster rela-

tions with Alexander and gain assurances of Russian support should Austria attack while war still raged in the Peninsula. However, a subtle shift in position had taken place since Tilsit as Napoleon, beset by difficulties, no longer looked quite so omnipotent.

Although the Conference of Erfurt passed off peaceably enough, with Napoleon approving in theory Alexander's desire for territorial gains in the Balkans and Alexander committing himself – again, in theory – to intervene in the event of war with Austria, astute onlookers noticed that a shift had occurred: Alexander was now in the ascendant, as Napoleon's star, almost imperceptibly, began to wane. The latter, however, remained confident of his hold over the Tsar and in a letter to Josephine, joked, 'I am satisfied with Alexander . . . If he were a woman, I think I would make him my mistress!'[6] But in truth, Alexander had begun to realize that the interests of Russia and France were diametrically opposed; and that friendship with Napoleon was a one-way street he was better out of.

In 1809 began the countdown to the inevitable war between Napoleon and Alexander. On 10 April Austria invaded Bavaria, Napoleon's ally, thus launching the War of the Fifth Coalition. Alexander, contrary to the spirit of Erfurt, remained an onlooker, doing virtually nothing to prevent Austrian mobilization. Napoleon – who was forced to abandon his subjugation of Spain in order to meet this new threat – once again demonstrated his mettle by scoring a decisive victory against Austria's generalissimo, Archduke Charles, at Wagram on 5 July. Although the Austrians were crushed, Vienna occupied and the Fifth Coalition smashed, Alexander's lack of support was not lost on Napoleon.

The following year, in an atmosphere of smouldering grudges and gathering mistrust, a series of unfortunate diplomatic gaffes prodded the two emperors closer to open conflict. Firstly, there was the matter of Napoleon's replacement for the Empress Josephine – his 'lucky star' – who had been ditched the previous year for dynastic reasons. Napoleon's first choice for a brood mare had fallen on Alexander's youngest sister, Grand Duchess Anna Pavlovna. However, given the fact that the girl's mother, the

Dowager Empress Marie Feodorovna, considered Napoleon to be the devil incarnate, a match was never on the cards and negotiations for Anna's hand became bogged down. Impatient to bed a new empress, Napoleon promptly dropped the idea of a Romanov bride and settled instead on Marie-Louise, daughter of his erstwhile enemy, Francis of Austria. The Russian court, though no doubt relieved by this development, chose to react with outrage at what they deemed a public insult.

The next upset occurred on 21 August 1810, when General Jean-Baptiste Bernadotte, one of Napoleon's marshals, was selected by the Swedish government to become Crown Prince to the ailing and heirless King Charles XIII. Although Napoleon thought Bernadotte's accession laughable, the Russians saw it as an act of provocation on his part and – bringing up the vexed issue of the Grand Duchy of Warsaw once more – accused Napoleon of surrounding them with enemies.

Bonaparte blundered even further into Alexander's bad books on 13 December when, in a bid to close completely Europe's North Sea coastline to British shipping, he blithely annexed the Duchy of Oldenburg. The son of the reigning Duke happened to be married to Alexander's sister, Catherine Pavlovna, and the territory itself was regarded in St Petersburg as a virtual Russian dependant. Despite offers of compensation from the French, Alexander was mortified by Napoleon's high-handedness and took the incident as a personal affront. By the end of the month, the final breakdown occurred when Alexander pointedly threw down the gauntlet by imposing high tariffs on French merchandise and opening Russia's ports to neutral shipping: the British, sailing under the flag of the non-aligned United States, were back in business.

Throughout 1811 both sides indulged in public accusations and counter-accusations, while privately preparing for war. On 5 June Napoleon gave his recently returned ambassador to St Petersburg, Armand de Caulaincourt, a grilling over Alexander's intentions. Caulaincourt spent five hours trying to dissuade Napoleon from a campaign which, in his opinion, could never be won. He informed his emperor of Alexander's admiration of the Spanish, who, although constantly beaten by the French, doggedly refused to surrender; of his vow never to accept a dictated peace; of the power of Russia's greatest ally, her ferocious winter, which never failed to fight on her side; and of the Tsar's promise that, 'I shall not be the first to draw my sword, but I shall be the last to sheathe it.'[7] *Dismissing Alexander as 'fickle and feeble', Napoleon silenced Caulaincourt by reeling off a list of the troops and resources at his disposal: at this point the diplomat's heart sank, as he realized war was inevitable. In fact, as Napoleon's biographer Bourrienne points out, 'The two emperors equally wished for war; the one with the view of consolidating his power, the other in the hope of freeing himself from a yoke which had become a species of vassalage.'*[8]

Early 1812 saw both emperors fishing for allies in the coming conflict. On 24 February, Bonaparte bullied Prussia into supplying him with 20,000 troops for his Grand Army of Russia; following this up on 14 March with an alliance with Austria, designed to supply him with 30,000 more. Ten days later, Alexander concluded a secret treaty with Bernadotte (Napoleon, in yet another diplomatic blunder inspired by the relentless logic of the Continental System, had managed to alienate his ex-colleague by occupying Swedish Pomerania on 10 January), whereby the latter promised to help Russia in return for a free hand in conquering Norway.

On 27 April Alexander offered an ultimatum to Napoleon – intended to be unacceptable – outlining his conditions for rejoining the Continental System: these included French evacuation of Prussia, compensation for the loss of Oldenburg and the creation of a neutral buffer zone between the two empires. Napoleon's response was to pack his entire court into 300 carriages and head for Dresden, where he ordered his allies to rally in a show of strength. In the words of de Ségur, 'The time for deliberation had passed and that for action at last arrived. On 9 May 1812 Napoleon, hitherto always triumphant, quitted a palace which he was destined never again to enter victorious.'

He arrived at the Saxon capital on 16 May – his march from Paris being one long triumphal procession – and held court for two weeks, while the crowned heads of Europe toadied up to him. Designed as a shameless propaganda exercise, Napoleon pulled out all the stops in an effort to demonstrate the hopelessness of Alexander's position in the face of a Europe united under his eagles. At Dresden, the Napoleonic circus became the biggest show on earth, with the Emperor himself as its main attraction: 'Whole nations had quitted their homes to throng his path,' writes de Ségur, 'rich and poor, nobles and plebeians, friends and enemies, all hurried to the scene . . . They wished to be able to tell their less fortunate countrymen and Posterity, that they had seen Napoleon.' In the words of Edward Foord, however, Bonaparte's propaganda coup was to be 'a memorable example of pride preceding a fall'.

As for Alexander, he remained unshaken: he knew that, although Napoleon's Austrian and Prussian allies publicly kowtowed before their imperial master, in private, neither power was seriously committed to war with Russia. His confidence increased on 28 May when, to Napoleon's astonishment, he successfully concluded peace with Turkey, for many years Russia's bitterest enemy. He was now free to redeploy troops from the Balkan theatre to meet the Napoleonic threat. The Tsar's final diplomatic coup came on 20 June when the Sixth Coalition came into being: once again, British capital was to finance war with Napoleon, and Alexander – a nominal enemy during his honeymoon with Bonaparte – was welcomed back into the fold with the promise of substantial aid.

Napoleon quit Dresden on 29 May, eager for action, and marched his Grand Army to the Russian frontier via Thorn, Danzig and Königsberg: arriving at Kamen, on the banks of the Niemen, on 23 June. De Ségur, deeply moved like so many other eyewitnesses at the awesome and novel sight of half a million men under arms, sets the scene: 'We were about to reach the extremity of Europe, where never European army had been before! We were about to erect new columns of Hercules. The grandeur of the enterprise, the agitation of co-operating Europe, the imposing spectacle of an army of 400,000 foot and 80,000 horse, so many warlike reports and martial clamours, kindled the minds of veter-

ans themselves. It was impossible for the coldest to remain unmoved amid the general impulse, to escape from the universal attraction. In conclusion: the composition of the army was good and every good army is desirous of war . . .'

1 An Expedition of an Almost Fabulous Nature

The gigantic enterprise being now resolved on, preparations were made as if for the conquest of the world.

Louis-Antoine Fauvelet de Bourrienne

Napoleon took to the road in 1812 like some ageing rock star embarking on a farewell tour: overweight and out of condition; prone to tantrums and surrounded by sycophants; his self-belief bloated by sixteen years of success. Having reached the pinnacle of power and with a continent at his feet, many believed this to be his last campaign: a final flourish from a satiated god of war. Thus, no soldier of ambition wished to be left behind: for glory, promotion, plunder were in the offing and victory was a foregone conclusion. In de Ségur's own words, the campaign 'promised to be nothing but a military march to Petersburg and Moscow'.

Napoleon's strategy aimed at the early annihilation of the Russian field army in order to bully Alexander back into line. He calculated that the Russians would be forced to stand and fight on their frontier or risk losing their Polish and Lithuanian provinces. In fact, Napoleon's whole plan rested on the assumption that Alexander would oblige him with an early battle. He did not envisage a war of conquest, but of swift victory: a short, sharp shock to the Russian system, which would scare St Petersburg into submission. The campaign was not designed to last longer than three weeks.

In order to achieve this rapid victory, Napoleon had assembled the largest host the world had yet seen: he marched into Russia at the head, not so much of an army, as the population of some cosmopolitan European capital; a city on the move. Half a million men, culled from every corner of Europe, constituted a Grand Army which, resplendent in the gorgeous, gaudy uniforms of the period, was designed to dismay the Tsar and decide the victory within twenty days. The trump card in Napoleon's pack was the Imperial Guard – his 'bulwark of granite' – a kind of army-within-an-army, composed, for the most part, of veterans loyal to his person alone. Feared throughout Europe, the mere threat of the Guard's deployment had won for Napoleon many a hard-fought field. This celebrated corps was divided into Young, Middle and Old units, depending upon length of service, and was a force of all arms: infantry, cavalry, and artillery. The elite of this elite were the grenadiers and chasseurs of the Old Guard: Napoleon's beloved grognards, or 'grumblers', of whom he frequently expected miracles.

Yet for all its pomp and spectacle, the Grand Army would prove to be something of a liability. For a start, its unprecedented size worked against it, confounding contemporary methods of command and control and a commissariat which, from the very outset, struggled in vain to keep the soldiers fed. There was also a question mark set against the army's quality; for, unlike the Emperor's earlier campaigns, the war in Russia was to be waged with a largely green crop of conscripts (many French veterans being bogged down in the Iberian Peninsula, combating their master's 'Spanish ulcer'). Then there was the matter of loyalty, for less than half of the Grand Army's troops were actually French: the remainder consisting of a bewildering assortment of allies, both willing and otherwise. Thus, although it threw a terrifyingly long shadow and the ground trembled beneath its feet, the Grand Army of Russia was, in fact, a military babel of mixed quality and confused loyalties.

The troops were accompanied by 150,000 horses, pulling 30,000 wagons, 1,200 cannon and providing mounts for a cavalry force of 36,000 troopers. Officers travelled in style with wives, servants, grooms and possessions packed into numerous carts and carriages. While Napoleon (no longer the youthful republican hero but a middle-aged imperial majesty) sallied forth like some oriental warlord, his headquarters crammed into fifty wagons and requiring some 650 horses to transport it. As for Murat, Napoleon's brother-in-law and King of Naples, he went to war with a personal military staff, his royal Neapolitan household and an army of cooks, commanded by a famous Paris chef. He demanded sixty horses for his personal use alone and his baggage required a fleet of carriages. Little wonder then, that the memoirist, Baron Lejeune, later described the sight of this remarkable pageant as, 'the most extraordinary and magnificent spectacle . . . one which could not but have an intoxicating effect on a conqueror'.[1]

Napoleon had chosen a northerly route into Russia in order to anchor his army on the Grand Duchy of Warsaw – a trusted ally – and also to take possession of the roads leading to St Petersburg and Moscow. He deployed his host thus: the main column, under his direct control, formed the central spearhead; flanking this force to the right, came troops under the command of his stepson Eugène and his younger brother Jérôme; the right (southern) wing was secured by a 30,000-strong Austrian corps under Prince Schwarzenberg; while the left was held by Marshal MacDonald, aided by 20,000 Prussians.

'To sum it up,' Napoleon had announced to his generals on the eve of hostilities, 'a battle is my plan of campaign and success is my whole policy.' And it was in search of this single decisive clash that the Grand Army invaded Russian territory on 24 June. The Russians, however, found themselves so heavily outnumbered that the only sensible thing to do was retreat; and this they did, drawing the Grand Army after them like some breathless, overweight brute, scenting blood.

When Napoleon crossed the Niemen, Alexander was a mere seventy-five miles away at Vilna. It was here, at the ancient capital of Lithuania, that he had established his headquarters.[2] *His short residency had been marked by a round of festivities, as the local nobles hobnobbed with St Petersburg high society, willing the war-clouds to disperse. Alexander received the news of invasion in an aside from his aide-de-camp, General Balashov, while attending a moonlit ball. He kept the revelation temporarily under his hat, so as not to spoil the dancing. Next day, before quitting Vilna, he despatched Balashov with a letter for Napoleon, declaring that it was not too late to avoid war, provided that he evacuate Russian territory forthwith; for, as long as a single French soldier stood on Russian soil, he would refuse to negotiate. Napoleon's promising protégé and willing disciple, fit – apparently – merely to be his 'mistress', was set to become his master.*

NAPOLEON ADDRESSED his army thus: 'Soldiers,' said he, 'the second Polish war is commenced. The first was concluded at Friedland and at Tilsit. At Tilsit, Russia swore eternal friendship with France and war with England. She now violates her oaths. She will give no explanation of her capricious conduct until the French eagles have repassed the Rhine, by that means leaving our allies at her mercy. Russia is hurried away by fatality; her destiny must be accomplished. Does she then believe us to be degenerated? Are we not still the soldiers of Austerlitz? She places us between war and dishonour: the choice cannot be doubtful. Let us advance then, let us cross the Niemen and carry the war into her territory! The second Polish war will be as glorious for French arms as the first; but this time, the peace we shall conclude will carry with it its own guarantee; it will put an end to the fatal influence which Russia for the last fifty years has exercised over the affairs of Europe.'[3]

This tone, which at the time was deemed prophetic, befitted an expedition of an almost fabulous nature. It was quite necessary to invoke Destiny and give credit to its dominion, when the fate of so many human beings and so much glory were about to be consigned to its mercy.

The Emperor Alexander also harangued his army but in a very different manner. The differences between the two nations and the two sovereigns were conspicuous in these proclamations. In fact, the one which was defensive was unadorned and moderate; the other, offensive, was flushed with audacity and the confidence of victory. The first appealed to religion, the other to fate; the one to love of country, the other to love of glory: but neither of them referred to the liberation of Poland, which was the real object of the war.[4]

The Grand Army marched to the Niemen in three separate masses: Jérôme Bonaparte, King of Westphalia, with 80,000 men, moved upon Grodno; Eugène de Beauharnais, Viceroy of Italy, with 75,000 men, upon Pilony; Napoleon with 220,000 men, upon Nogaraiski, a farm situated three leagues[5] before Kovno. On 23 June, before daylight, the imperial column reached the Niemen but without seeing it: the borders of the great Prussian forest of Pilwisky and the hills which line the river concealed the colossal army which was about to cross it.

Napoleon, who had travelled in a carriage thus far, mounted his horse at two o'clock in the morning. He reconnoitred the Russian river without disguising himself – as has been falsely asserted – but under cover of night crossed that frontier which five months later he was only able to repass under cover of the same shade. When he came up to the bank, his horse suddenly fell and threw him on the sand. A voice exclaimed, 'This is a bad omen, a Roman would recoil!' It is not known whether it was himself or one of his retinue who pronounced these words.[6]

His task of reconnoitring concluded, he gave orders that, at the close of the following day, three bridges should be thrown over the river near the village of Poniémen. He then retired to his headquarters where he passed the whole day: sometimes in his tent, sometimes in a Polish house, listlessly reclined in the midst of a breathless atmosphere and a suffocating heat, vainly courting repose.

On the return of night he again made his approach to the river. The first who crossed it were a few sappers in a small boat. They approached the Russian side with some degree of apprehension but found no obstacle to oppose their landing. There they found peace (the war was entirely on their own side). All was tranquil on this foreign soil, which had been described to them as so menacing. A subaltern officer of Cossacks, however, commanding a patrol, presented himself to their view. He was alone and appeared to consider himself in full peace and to be ignorant that the whole of Europe in arms was at hand. He enquired of the strangers who they were. 'Frenchmen!' they replied. 'What do you want?' rejoined the officer. 'For what reason do you come into Russia?' A sapper briskly replied, 'To make war upon you; to take Vilna; to deliver Poland!' The Cossack then withdrew. He disappeared into the woods, into which three of our soldiers – giving vent to their enthusiasm and with a view to sound the forest – discharged their firearms.

Thus it was that the feeble report of three muskets (to which there was no reply) informed us of the opening of a new campaign and the commencement of a great invasion.

Either from a feeling of prudence or from presentiment, this first signal of war threw the Emperor into a state of violent irritation. Three hundred *voltigeurs* immediately passed the river in order to cover the building of the bridges.

The French columns then began to issue from the valleys and the forest. They advanced in silence to the river, under cover of darkness. It was necessary to touch them in order to recognize their presence. Fires, even sparks, were forbidden. They slept with weapons in hand, as if in presence of the enemy. The crops of green rye, moistened with dew, served as beds for the men and food for the horses.

The night (its coolness preventing sleep, its darkness prolonging the hours) and the dangers of the following day combined to give solemnity to the situation; but the expectation of a great battle supported our spirits. The proclamation of Napoleon had just been read; the most memorable passages of it were repeated in a whisper; and the genius of conquest kindled our imaginations.

Before us was the Russian frontier. Our eager gaze already sought to invade the promised land of our glory across the shades of night. We seemed to hear the joyful shouts of the Lithuanians at the approach of their deliverers. We pictured to ourselves the river lined with their outstretched hands. Here, we were in want of everything; there, everything would be lavished upon us! The Lithuanians would hasten to supply our wants; we were about to be encircled by love and gratitude! What mattered one unpleasant night? The day would shortly appear and with it its warmth (and all its illusions).

The day did appear and revealed to us dry desert sands and dark, gloomy forests. Our eyes then reverted sadly upon ourselves; but we were again inspired by pride and hope, on seeing the imposing spectacle of our united army.[7]

Three hundred yards from the river, on the most elevated height, the tent of the Emperor was visible. Around it the hills and valleys were covered with men and horses. As soon as the earth presented to the sun those moving masses, clothed with glittering arms, the signal was given and instantly the multitudes began to file off in three columns towards the bridges. They were seen to take a winding direction as they descended the narrow plain which separated them from the Niemen; to approach it, to reach the three bridges, to compress and prolong their columns in order to cross them; and at last reach that foreign soil which they were about to devastate (and which they were destined to cover with their own dreadful wreckage).

So great was their enthusiasm that two divisions of the advanced guard disputed for the honour of being the first to pass and were near coming to blows, some exertions being necessary to quiet them. Napoleon hastened to plant his foot on Russian territory. He took this first step towards his ruin without hesitation. At first, he stationed himself near the bridge, encouraging the soldiers with his looks. The latter all saluted him with their accustomed cries. They appeared, indeed, more animated than he was: whether it was that he felt oppressed by the weight of so great an invasion, or that his enfeebled frame could not support the

of Pilony. The army of the King of Westphalia did not enter Grodno till the 30th.

From Kovno Napoleon proceeded in two days as far as the defiles which defended the plain of Vilna. He waited to make his appearance there for news from his advanced posts. He was confident that Alexander would fight for the possession of that capital (the sound of some musketry encouraged him in that hope), when news was brought him that the city was undefended. Thither he advanced, ruminating and dissatisfied. He accused his generals of the advanced guard of suffering the Russian army to escape. It was the most active of them, Montbrun,[10] whom he reproached and against whom his anger rose to the point of menace. A menace without effect, a violence without a result!

In the midst of his anger his dispositions for entering Vilna displayed tact: he caused himself to be preceded and followed by Polish regiments. But more occupied by the retreat of the Russians than the grateful and admiring acclamations of the Lithuanians, he rapidly passed through the city and hurried to the advanced posts. Several of the best hussars of the 8th Regiment, having ventured themselves in a wood without proper support, had just perished in an action with the Russian Guard. De Ségur,[11] who commanded them, after a desperate defence had fallen covered with wounds. The enemy had burnt his bridges and his stores and was flying by different roads: but all in the direction of Drissa.

2 A Flag of Truce

> For days past the French army had left a swath of pillage and destruction in its wake as it moved through a friendly territory. Heaven only knew what it would do on enemy soil!
>
> Heinrich Vossler[1]

On the eve of invasion, Alexander's forces were scattered the length of Russia's western frontier: there were troops far to the north, in Finland; troops in the Balkans; and troops stationed to the south of Russia's great natural barrier to invading armies, the Pripet Marshes. Facing the Napoleonic juggernaut, however, were the First and Second Armies of the West: the former, 126,000 strong and commanded by Barclay de Tolly, was concentrated around Vilna; while the latter, 60,000 strong and led by Prince Bagration, was concentrated some 100 miles to the south at Volkovysk. Napoleon's spear-like thrust had driven a wedge between these two armies. His plan – if the Russians would not oblige him with immediate battle – was to keep Barclay and Bagration apart, cut them off from their supports, and destroy them at his leisure.

The Russians, however, were withdrawing in accordance with the first phase of a plan devised by the Prussian émigré, *Colonel von Pfuel, Alexander's principal adviser.*[2] *The plan – conceived several months before – centred around an allegedly impregnable camp which von Pfuel had caused to be built at Drissa, approximately 100 miles east of Vilna. His idea, based on the assumption (erroneous as it turned out) that the Russians had at least as many troops in the field as the French, was for Barclay to lure Napoleon to Drissa where, according to von Pfuel, he would be stopped in his tracks; while Bagration, attacking from the south, took the Grand Army in flank: thus catching Bonaparte between two fires.*

But Napoleon's army vastly outnumbered Alexander's and on the day it took Vilna, Alexander received the disastrous news that the Drissa fort was, in fact, anything but impregnable: not only was it barely finished, it was also too small and had been built in the wrong place! Having soaked up the labour of several thousand serfs over a period of six months, the fort was simply an expensive folly. Strategically, von Pfuel's idea was unsound anyway, as Napoleon could simply bypass the camp and march on Moscow or St Petersburg unhindered. Although the retreat on Drissa continued (for want of a better plan), the denouement of von Pfuel's hare-brained stratagem was never realized.

Meanwhile, the Grand Army had begun to fall apart a mere seventy-five miles inside Russian territory. The young recruits, unused to the rigours of campaign, consumed their five-day rations within the first twenty-four hours of the invasion, only to faint from hunger on the ensuing days. There was a lack of fresh water (the retreating Russians having poisoned the wells) and no forage for the horses. Meanwhile the weather – intense heat followed by freezing rain – was, according to Baron Lejeune, 'a veritable disaster to our troops'. To cap it all, the supply system had broken down completely, the wagons bottlenecked at the entrance to the Niemen bridges. Laden with provisions and bogged down on roads little better than mud tracks, these carts could not keep pace with the troops, pushed forward by forced marches for a battle which forever remained on the horizon. As de Ségur observed, 'The soldiers were so much engaged by so many cares, that they considered themselves less employed in making war than a fatiguing journey; but if the war and the enemy were to fall back always thus, how much further should they have to go in search of them?'

*

IT WAS the largest column, that of the centre, which suffered most. It followed the road which the Russians had ruined and of which the French advanced guard had just completed the devastation. The columns which proceeded by side roads found supplies but were not sufficiently careful in collecting and economizing them.

The responsibility for the calamities which this rapid march caused ought not, therefore, to be laid entirely on Napoleon; for order and discipline were maintained in Davout's corps and it suffered less from privation. It was nearly the same with that of Eugène. When pillage was resorted to in these two corps it was always with method and nothing but necessary damage was inflicted. Their soldiers were made to carry several days' rations and prevented from wasting them. The same precautions might have been taken elsewhere; but whether it was due to the habit of campaigning in rich countries or to incessant zeal, many of the other chiefs thought less of management than of fighting.

Napoleon was, therefore, frequently compelled to close his eyes to a system of plunder which he vainly prohibited: too well aware of the appeal which that mode of living had for the soldier; that it made him love war because it enriched him; that it gratified him by the authority which it frequently gave him over classes superior to his own; that in his eyes it had all the attraction of a war of the poor against the rich; finally, that the pleasure of feeling and proving himself the strongest was, under such circumstances, constantly repeated and brought home to him.

Napoleon, however, grew indignant at the news of these excesses. He issued a threatening proclamation and directed flying columns of French and Lithuanians to see to its execution.[3] We who were irritated at the sight of pillagers were eager to pursue them: but when we had stripped them of their bread or the cattle which they had been stealing; when we saw them slowly retreating (sometimes eyeing us with a look of concentrated despair, sometimes bursting into tears); when we heard them murmuring that, not content with giving them nothing, we took everything from them and that we must, therefore, mean to let them perish of hunger; we then, in our turn, accused ourselves of barbarity to our own people and restored them their prey. Indeed, it was necessity which drove them to plunder. The officers themselves only lived on the share which the soldiers allowed them.

A situation of so much excess engendered fresh excesses. These rough men, when assailed by so many monstrous sufferings, could not remain reasonable. When they arrived near any dwellings they were famished. At first they asked: but either for want of being understood or from the refusal (or impossibility) of the inhabitants to satisfy their demands, quarrels generally arose. Then, as they became more and more exasperated with hunger, they became furious; and after tumbling either cottage or palace upside-down without finding the food they were in search of, they, in the violence of their despair, accused the inhabitants of being their enemies and revenged themselves upon them by destroying their property.

There were some who actually destroyed themselves rather than proceed to such extremities: others, after having done so. These were the youngest. They placed their foreheads on their muskets and blew out their brains in the middle of the highroad. But many became hardened: one excess led them on to another, as people often get angry with the blows they inflict. Among the latter, some vagabonds took vengeance for their distress upon civilians. In the midst of so unfavourable an aspect of nature, they became denaturalized. Left to themselves at so great a distance from home, they imagined that everything was allowed them and that their own sufferings authorized them to make others suffer.

In an army so numerous and composed of so many nations, it was natural to find more sinners than in smaller ones. The causes of so many evils induced fresh ones:

already weakened by hunger, it was necessary to make forced marches in order to escape from it and to reach the enemy. At night, when they halted, the soldiers swarmed into the houses: there, worn out with fatigue and want, they threw themselves upon the first dirty straw they met with.

The most robust had barely spirits left to knead the flour which they found and to light the ovens with which all those wooden houses were provided. Others had scarcely strength to go a few paces in order to make the fires necessary to cook some food. Their officers, exhausted like themselves, feebly gave orders to take more care and neglected to see that their orders were obeyed. A piece of burnt wood, at such times escaping from the ovens or a spark from the fire of the bivouacs, was sufficient to set fire to a castle or a whole village and to cause the deaths of many unfortunate soldiers who had taken refuge in them.

The Emperor was not ignorant of these details but he was already committed. Even at Vilna, all these disorders had taken place. Marshal Mortier, among others, informed him of them: he had seen, from the Niemen to the Vilia, nothing but ruined homes and baggage wagons abandoned! They were found dispersed on the highways and in the fields: overturned, broke open and their contents scattered here and there; pillaged, as if they had been taken by the enemy. He should have imagined himself following a defeated army! Ten thousand horses had been killed by the cold rains of the great storm and by the unripe rye, which had become their new and only food: their carcasses were lying encumbering the road; they sent forth a stench impossible to breathe.[4] But the last was much more terrible: several soldiers of the Young Guard had already perished of hunger.

Up to that point, Napoleon listened with calmness but here he abruptly interrupted the speaker. Wishing to escape his distress by incredulity, he exclaimed, 'It is impossible! Where are their twenty-days' rations? Soldiers well commanded never die of hunger!'

A general, the author of this last report, was present. Napoleon turned towards him and pressed him with questions; and that general, either from weakness or uncertainty, replied that the individuals referred to had not died of hunger but from intoxication.

The Emperor then remained convinced that the misery of the soldiers had been exaggerated to him. As to the rest, he exclaimed that the loss of the horses must be borne with, of some carriages and even houses: it was a torrent that rolled away; the worst side of the picture of war; an evil exchanged for a good; and to Misery her share must be given. His treasures, his benefits, would repair the loss. One great result would make amends for all! He required a single victory. If sufficient means remained for accomplishing that, he should be satisfied.

Mortier remarked that a victory might be gained by a more methodical march, followed by the magazines, but he was not listened to. Those to whom this marshal (who had just returned from Spain) complained, told him that, in fact, the Emperor grew angry at the account of evils which he considered incurable, his policy imposing on him the necessity of a prompt and decisive victory.

They added that they saw too clearly that the health of their leader was impaired and that being compelled, meanwhile, to cast himself into positions more and more critical, he could not see without ill-humour, the difficulties which he passed by and suffered to accumulate behind him. Difficulties which he then affected to treat with contempt, in order to disguise their importance and preserve the energy of mind which he himself needed to surmount them. This was the reason that, being already disturbed by the new and difficult situation into which he had thrown himself – and impatient to escape from it – he kept marching on, always pushing his army forward, in order to bring matters quickly to a conclusion.

Thus it was that Napoleon was forced to shut his eyes to facts. It is well known that the greater part of his ministers were not flatterers. Both facts and men spoke sufficiently. But what could they teach him? Of what was he ignorant? Had not all his preparations been dictated by the most clear-sighted strategy? What could be said to him which he had not himself said and written a hundred times? It was after having anticipated the minutest details, having prepared for every inconvenience, having provided everything for a slow and methodical war, that he rid himself of all these precautions; that he abandoned all these preparations and suffered himself to be hurried away by habit, by the necessity of short wars, rapid victories and sudden treaties of peace.

It was in the midst of these grave circumstances that Balashov, a minister of the Russian Emperor, presented himself with a flag of truce at the French outposts. He was received and the army (now become less spirited) indulged in hopes of peace.[5]

He brought this message from Alexander to Napoleon: that it was not yet too late to negotiate. A war which the soil, the climate and the character of Russia made everlasting was begun; but a compromise had not become impossible and from one bank of the Niemen to the other they might yet come to an understanding. He added that his master declared in the face of Europe, that he was not the aggressor; that his ambassador at Paris, in demanding his passports, did not consider himself as having broken the peace: thus the French had entered Russia without a declaration of war. There were, however, no fresh overtures, either verbal or written, proposed by Balashov.

The choice of this flag of truce had been remarked. He was the minister of the Russian police: that office required an observant spirit and it was thought that he was sent to exercise it among us. What made us more suspicious of the character of the go-between was that the negotiation appeared to have no point: unless it were that of great moderation which, under the circumstances, was taken for weakness.

Napoleon did not hesitate. He had not been able to stop

at Paris, should he then retreat at Vilna? What would Europe think of him? What result could he offer to the French and Allied armies as a motive for so many fatigues, such vast movements, such enormous individual and national expenditure? It would be at once confessing himself beaten. Besides, his language before so many princes since his departure from Paris had pledged him as much as his actions so that, in fact, he found himself as much compromised before his allies as he did before his enemies. Even then, it is said, the heat of conversation with Balashov carried him to still greater lengths. What had brought him to Vilna? What did the Emperor of Russia want with him? Did he pretend to resist him? He was only a parade ground general! As to himself, his head was his counsellor, from that everything proceeded.

But as to Alexander, who was there to counsel him? He had only three generals: Kutusov, whom he did not like because he was a Russian; Bennigsen, pensioned off six years ago and now in his second childhood; and Barclay. The last could certainly manoeuvre; he was brave; he understood war; but he was a general only good for a retreat. And he added, 'You all fancy you understand the art of war because you have read Jomini;[6] but if his book could have taught it you, do you think that I would have allowed him to publish it?' In this conversation, of which the above is the Russian version, it is certain he added that, however, the Emperor Alexander had friends even in the imperial headquarters. Then, pointing out Caulaincourt, the grand equerry, to the Russian minister: 'There,' said he, 'is a knight of your Emperor! He is a Russian in the French camp!'

Probably Caulaincourt did not sufficiently grasp that by this expression Napoleon only wished to prepare for himself a negotiator who was agreeable to Alexander; for as soon as Balashov was gone he advanced towards the Emperor and in an angry tone asked him why he had insulted him, exclaiming that he was a Frenchman. A true Frenchman! That he had proved it already and would prove it again by repeating that this war was impolitic and dangerous; that it would destroy his army, France and himself. That, moreover, as he had just insulted him, he should quit him; that all he asked was a division in Spain, where nobody wished to serve and the furthest possible from his presence! The Emperor attempted to appease him; but not being able to obtain a hearing, he withdrew with Caulaincourt still pursuing him with his reproaches. Berthier, who was present at this scene, interposed without effect. Bessières, more in the background, had vainly tried to keep back Caulaincourt, holding him by the coat.[7]

The next day, Napoleon was unable to bring his grand equerry into his presence without formal and repeated orders. At length he soothed him with soft words and by the expression of an esteem and attachment which Caulaincourt well deserved. But he dismissed Balashov with verbal (and impossible) proposals.[8]

Alexander made no reply to them. The full importance of the step he had just taken was not at the time properly understood: he could no longer either address himself to Napoleon or even return him any answer. It was the last word prior to an irreparable breach and that circumstance rendered it remarkable.

Meantime, Murat pursued the flying steps of that victory which was so much coveted. He commanded the cavalry of the advanced guard and at last reached the enemy on the road to Sventziany and drove him in the direction of Druïa. Every morning the Russian rearguard appeared to have escaped him; every evening he overtook it again and attacked it but always in a strong position, after a long march, too late and before his men had taken any refreshment. There was, consequently, every day fresh combats producing no important results.[9]

3 'Here I Stop!'

> Vitebsk is a large town. There I met my old comrades and officers. We remained there waiting for supplies. The excessive heat, added to all our other privations, brought on dysentery, from which our army suffered considerable loss.
>
> Captain Coignet[1]

Napoleon remained at Vilna for two weeks, in order to reorganize Lithuania. A provisional government was set up, the main function of which was to oversee the exaction of men, horses and provisions for the Grand Army. Local peasants, therefore, suffered the double indignation of having their possessions both plundered and requisitioned by their so-called liberators. Meanwhile, deputations of enthusiastic Poles, eager for the restoration of their country, were turned away empty-handed.[2]

In Napoleon's temporary absence, the Grand Army pushed on in pursuit of the Russians, moving eastwards over difficult terrain and through atrocious weather. Murat, Ney and Oudinot trailed after Barclay; while Jérôme and his Westphalian army, hampered by flooded rivers and wretched roads, plodded after Bagration.

As already stated, Napoleon's strategy called for an early coup: his campaign was simply not designed to last longer than a few weeks. Having failed, however, to bring Barclay to battle, his attention now fixed on Bagration, commander of the Second Army of the West. Napoleon correctly guessed that the Russian prince was in the vicinity of Minsk and requested Jérôme to make haste in his advance on that place. He despatched Davout to the scene and Bagration looked set to be caught in the jaws of a giant pincer: Jérôme closing from the west and Davout from the north. What followed was a fiasco which probably cost Napoleon the campaign.

On 3 July Napoleon received a despatch from Jérôme: but instead of announcing Bagration's destruction, Jérôme simply informed his imperial brother that he had halted operations in order to dismiss General Vandamme, commander of VIII Corps, who stood accused of embezzlement. Although Jérôme's motives were laudable, his timing was lamentable: Bagration evaded the trap and slipped out of reach. Napoleon went into a rage. He blamed Jérôme for ruining his plans and losing him the war.[3] *He even went so far as to authorize Davout to take command of Jérôme's men; but in a blunder of breathtaking tactlessness, neglected to inform his wayward brother.*

Thus, when an authoritative Davout met a mystified Jérôme, another delay ensued while the latter, in a fit of pique, dashed off a bitter despatch to imperial headquarters, assembled the soldiers of his bodyguard and quit the army. Fed up with being bossed about, Jérôme Bonaparte simply packed up and went home. Although Davout captured Minsk on 8 July, his troops took time out to ransack the place and Bagration, a mere sixty miles distant, escaped once more. Now the two Russian armies were free to join forces: the initiative was slipping from Napoleon's fingers.

Meanwhile, Barclay continued his orderly and methodical retreat. Accompanied by Alexander, he reached Drissa on 11 July. At the sight of von Pfuel's much boasted fort, Alexander reputedly shed tears of disillusionment, for it was obvious that if the Russians remained, they would be annihilated. The historian Edward Foord summed it up nicely when he wrote: 'In a sentence, Drissa was absolutely useless.' Three days later, the Russians were on the march again.

By 18 July, they had reached Polotsk and Barclay, who as minister of war was supposedly running the campaign, was suddenly faced with a new crisis: Alexander, feeling that his honour was at stake, had decided to lead the army in person against Napoleon. Painfully aware of Alexander's military shortcomings, his ministers tried to dissuade him but he remained adamant. Eventually, it was put to him that, as he had received his crown from God – unlike Bonaparte, who had merely received his from the people – he was, in effect, Napoleon's social superior and was free, therefore (according to the code of honour), to leave the army without fear of losing face. This he did, arriving at Moscow on the 24th.

Barclay resumed his retreat until, on 23 July, he arrived at Vitebsk, some 200 miles east of Vilna. There, he determined to make his stand, provided Bagration could arrive in time to support him. Two days later, Murat's advanced guard collided with Barclay's outposts ten miles west of Vitebsk, at Ostrovno. Sharp fighting ensued and in the words of A.H. Atteridge, Murat's biographer, 'Murat's cavalry, first into action, bore the brunt of the fighting and he himself led more than one charge. Once, to rescue a hard-pressed regiment, he dashed at the Russian horsemen with his staff and personal escort, some sixty sabres at most. It was one of the few occasions when he drew his diamond-hilted sword at the head of a charge. His life was saved by one of his equerries killing a Russian who was on the point of cutting him down.' The Russian rearguard retired and on 27 July, according to de Ségur, 'The Emperor appeared at the advanced posts before sunrise; its first rays exhibited to him at last the Russian army encamped on an elevated plain, which commanded all the avenues of Vitebsk.'

NAPOLEON ANNOUNCED a battle for the following day. His parting words to Murat were these: 'Tomorrow at five o'clock, the sun of Austerlitz!'[4] These words afford an explanation of the suspension of hostilities in the midst of a success which filled the troops with fire. They were astonished at this inactivity at the moment of overtaking an army, the pursuit of which had completely exhausted them. Murat, who had been daily deluded by a similar expectation, remarked to the Emperor that Barclay only made a demonstration of boldness at that hour, in order to more readily effect his retreat during the night. Finding himself unable to convince his chief, he rashly proceeded to pitch his tent on the banks of the Luczissa, almost in the midst of the enemy. It was a position which gratified his desire of hearing the first signs of their retreat, his hope of disturbing it and his adventurous character.

Murat was deceived and yet he appeared to have been most clear-sighted: Napoleon was in the right and yet the event placed him in the wrong. Such are the freaks of fortune! The Emperor of the French had correctly appreciated the designs of Barclay. The Russian general, believing Bagration to be still near Orsha, had resolved upon fighting in order to give him time to rejoin him. It was the news which he received that very evening, of the retreat of Bagration towards Smolensk, which suddenly changed his determination.

In fact, by daybreak on the 28th, Murat sent word to the Emperor that he was about to pursue the Russians, who had already disappeared. Napoleon still persisted in his opinion, obstinately pronouncing that the whole Russian army was in front of him and that it was necessary to advance with care. This caused a considerable delay. At length he mounted his horse: every step he took destroyed his illusion and he soon found himself in the midst of the camp which Barclay had just abandoned.

Everything about it displayed the scientific knowledge of war: its advantageous site; the arrangement of all its parts; the exact use to which each of them had been assigned; the order and harmony which thence resulted. Finally, nothing had been left behind – not one weapon, nor a single valuable – which could demonstrate, beyond the bounds of the camp, the route which the Russians had taken. There appeared more order in their defeat than in our victory! Though conquered, their flight left us lessons by which conquerors never profit: that good fortune is contemptuous or that it waits for misfortune to correct it.

A Russian soldier, who was found asleep under a bush, was the solitary result of that day, which was expected to be so decisive. We entered Vitebsk, which was found equally deserted as the camp of the Russians. Some Jews and Jesuits were all that remained. They were interrogated but without effect. All the roads were abortively reconnoitred. Were the Russians gone to Smolensk? Had they reascended the Düna? At length, a band of Cossacks attracted us in the latter direction, while Ney explored the former. We marched six leagues over deep sand, through thick dust and a suffocating heat. Night halted our march in the neighbourhood of Agaponovitzy.

While parched, fevered and exhausted by fatigue and hunger, the army met with nothing there but muddy water. Napoleon, Murat, Eugène and Berthier held a council in the imperial tents, which were pitched in the courtyard of a castle, situated upon a hill to the left of the main road.

That victory which was so fervently desired, so rapidly pursued and rendered more necessary by the lapse of every succeeding day had, it seemed, just escaped from our grasp, as it had at Vilna. True, we had come up with the Russian rearguard but was it that of their army? Was it not more likely that Barclay had fled towards Smolensk by way of Rudnia? How far, then, must we pursue the Russians in order to make them fight? Did not the necessity of organizing reconquered Lithuania, of establishing magazines and hospitals, of fixing a new centre of repose, defence and departure, decidedly prove the necessity of halting on the borders of Old Russia?[5]

A skirmish had just happened, not far from there, respecting which Murat remained silent. Our vanguard had been repulsed: some of the cavalry had been obliged to dismount in order to make their retreat; others had been unable to bring off their beaten horses other than by dragging them by the bridle. The Emperor having questioned Belliard on the subject, that general frankly declared that the regiments were already very much weakened; that they were harassed to death and stood in absolute need of rest; that if they continued to march for six days longer there would be no cavalry remaining and that it was high time to halt.[6] To these motives were added the effects of a blistering sun reflected from burning sands. Exhausted as he was, the Emperor now decided: the course of the Düna and of the Dnieper would mark out the French line.

As soon as the Emperor had come to a decision, he returned to Vitebsk with his Guard. There, on 28 July, on entering the imperial headquarters, he detached his sword and throwing it carelessly on his maps, with which the tables were covered, exclaimed, 'Here I stop! Here I must look round me; rally, refresh my army and organize Poland. The campaign of 1812 is finished; that of 1813 will do the rest.'

With the conquest of Lithuania the object of the war was attained and yet the war appeared scarcely to have begun, for places only had been vanquished and not men: the Russian army was unbroken, its two wings – which had been separated by the speed of our first strike – had once more united. It was in this situation that Napoleon believed himself irrevocably decided to halt on the banks of the Dnieper and the Düna. At that time he could much more easily deceive others as to his intentions (as he actually deceived himself).

His line of defence was already traced upon his maps: the siege equipment was proceeding towards Riga (the left of the army would rest on that strong place); from there, proceeding to Dünaborg and Polotsk, it would maintain a menacing defensive; Vitebsk, so easy to fortify with its wooded heights, would serve as an entrenched camp for the centre; thence, towards the south, the Berezina and its marshes, covered by the Drieper, provide no other passage but a few defiles (a very few troops would be sufficient to guard them); further on, Bobruisk marked out the right of this great line and orders were given to obtain possession of that fortress. In addition, an uprising of the populous provinces of the south was calculated on: they would assist Schwarzenberg in ejecting Tormassov[7] and the army would be increased by their numerous Cossacks.

In this position nothing would be wanting: Courland would support MacDonald; Samogitia, Oudinot; the fertile plain of Klubokoë, the Emperor; the southern provinces would supply the rest. In addition, the grand magazine of the army was at Danzig, its intermediate ones at Vilna and Minsk. In this manner the army would be connected with the country which it had just set free and all things relating to that country – its rivers, marshes, produce, and inhabitants – would be united with us. All things would be agreed for the purposes of defence.

Such was Napoleon's plan. He was at that time seen exploring Vitebsk and its environs, as if to reconnoitre places where he was likely to make a long residence. Establishments of all kinds were formed there. Thirty-six ovens, capable of baking at once 29,000 pounds of bread, were constructed. Neither was utility alone attended to, embellishment was also considered. Some stone houses spoiled the appearance of the square of the palace: the Emperor ordered his Guard to pull them down and to clear away the rubbish. Indeed, he was already anticipating the pleasures of winter: Parisian actors must come to Vitebsk and as that city was abandoned, spectators of the fair sex must be attracted from Warsaw and Vilna.

His star at that time enlightened his path (happy had it been for him, if he had not afterwards mistaken the movements of his impatience for the inspirations of genius). But whatever may be said, it was by himself alone that he suffered himself to be hurried on; for in him everything proceeded from himself.

But Murat was the individual whose arguments were most frequent and animated. Weary of rest and insatiable for glory, that monarch, who considered the enemy to be within his grasp, was unable to repress his emotions. He quitted the advanced guard, went to Vitebsk, and in a private interview with the Emperor gave way to his recklessness. He accused the Russian army of cowardice: according to him, it had failed in the rendezvous before Vitebsk, as if it had been an affair of a duel; it was a panic-stricken army, which his light cavalry alone was sufficient to put to flight! This excitement extorted a smile from Napoleon; but in order to moderate his fervour, he said to him, 'Murat, the first campaign in Russia is finished: let us here plant our eagles. Two great rivers mark out our position; let us raise block-houses on that line; let our fires cross each other on all sides; let us form in battalion square, cannon at the angles and the exterior, and let the interior contain our quarters and our magazines. 1813 will see us at Moscow, 1814 at Petersburg. The Russian war is a war of three years.'

But the moderation of the first speeches of Napoleon had not deceived the members of his household. They recollected that, at the first sight of the deserted camp of Barclay and of Vitebsk abandoned, when he heard them congratulating each other on this conquest, he turned sharply round to them and shouted, 'Do you think, then, that I have come so far to conquer these huts?' They also knew perfectly that when he had a great object in view, he never devised any other than a vague plan, preferring to take counsel of opportunity: a system more consistent with the production of his genius.

In other respects, the whole army was loaded with the favours of its commander. If he happened to meet with convoys of wounded, he stopped them, informed himself of their condition, of their sufferings, of the actions in which they had been wounded, and never quitted them without consoling them by his words or making them partakers of his bounty.

He bestowed particular attention on his Guard. He daily reviewed some part of them, lavished commendation and sometimes blame: but the latter seldom fell on any but the administrators, which pleased the soldiers and diverted their complaints.

Every day he went and visited the ovens, tasted the bread, and satisfied himself of the regularity of all the distributions. He frequently sent wine from his table to the sentry who was nearest to him. One day he assembled the elite of his Guard for the purpose of giving them a new leader.[8] He made them a speech and with his own hand and sword introduced him to them. Afterwards he embraced him in their presence. So many attentions were ascribed by some to his gratitude for the past; by others, to his expectations for the future.

The latter saw clearly that Napoleon had at first flattered himself with the hope of receiving fresh overtures of peace from Alexander and that the misery and debility of his army had occupied his attention. It was necessary to allow the long train of stragglers and sick sufficient time: the one for joining their corps and the latter for reaching the hospitals. Finally, to establish these hospitals, to collect provisions, replenish the horses and wait for the hospital wagons, the artillery and the pontoons, which were still laboriously dragging after us across the Lithuanian sands. His correspondence with Europe must also have occupied his attention. To conclude, a destructive environment stopped his progress! Such, in fact, is that climate. The weather is always in the extreme, always in excess: it either parches or floods, burns up or freezes the soil and its inhabitants, for whose protection it appears expressly framed.

The Emperor was not less sensible of its effects than others but when he found himself somewhat refreshed by repose, when no envoy from Alexander made his appearance and his first dispositions were completed, he was seized with impatience. He was observed to grow restless. Perhaps it was that inactivity annoyed him – as it does all men of active habits – and that he preferred danger to the weariness of expectation; or that he was agitated by that desire of acquisition which, with the majority mankind, has greater influence than the pleasure of preserving or the fear of losing.[9]

It was then especially that the image of captive Moscow besieged him: it was the boundary of his fears, the object of his hopes; possessed of that, he would possess everything. From that time it was foreseen that an eager and restless genius like his – and accustomed to shortcuts – would not wait eight months when he felt his object within reach and when twenty days were sufficient to attain it.

We must not, however, be too hasty in condemning this extraordinary man for weaknesses common to all men. We shall presently hear from himself; we shall see how much his political position tended to complicate his military position. At a later period, we shall be less tempted to blame the resolution he was now about to take, when it is seen that the fate of Russia depended upon only one more day's health, which failed Napoleon, even on the very field of the Moskva.

In the first instance he appeared hardly bold enough to confess to himself a project of such great audacity. But by degrees he assumed courage to look it in the face. He then began to deliberate and the state of great irresolution which tormented his mind affected his whole frame. He was seen to pace his apartments as if pursued by some dangerous temptation. Nothing could fix his attention. Every moment he began, quitted, and resumed his occupation. He walked about without any purpose, enquired the hour and remarked the weather. Completely absorbed, he stopped, then hummed a tune with an absent air and again began pacing.

In the midst of his perplexity he occasionally addressed the people he met with such half-sentences as, 'Well! What shall we do? Shall we stay where we are, or advance? How is it possible to stop short in the midst of so glorious a career?' He did not wait for their reply but still kept wandering about, as if he was looking for something or someone to end his indecision.

At length, quite sinking under the weight of such important considerations and in a way overwhelmed with this great uncertainty, he would throw himself on one of the beds which he had caused to be laid on the floor of his apartments. His body, exhausted by the heat and the struggles of his mind, could only bear a light garment. In this manner did he pass a portion of his day at Vitebsk.

But when his body was at rest, his spirit was only the more active. How many motives urged him towards Moscow! How to support at Vitebsk the weariness of seven winter months? He, who till then had always been the aggressor, was about to be reduced to a defensive role, a part unworthy of him, of which he had no experience and undeserving of his genius.

Moreover, at Vitebsk, nothing had been decided and yet, at what a distance was he already from France! Europe, then, would at length see him stopped: him, whom nothing had been able to stop! Would not the duration of the enterprise increase its danger? Ought he allow Russia time to arm herself completely? How long could he protract this uncertain condition without breaking the spell of his infallibility (which the resistance in Spain had already weakened) and without engendering dangerous hopes in Europe? What would be thought if it were known that a third of his army, dispersed or sick, were no longer in the ranks? It was indispensable, therefore, to dazzle the world quickly with the brilliance of a great victory and hide so many sacrifices under a heap of laurels.

If he remained at Vitebsk, he considered that he should have the displeasure, the whole expense and all the inconveniences and anxieties of a defensive position to bear; while at Moscow there would be peace, abundance, a reimbursement of the expenses of the war and immortal glory. He persuaded himself that boldness was the only prudential course; that it is the same with all hazardous undertakings, in which there is always risk at the beginning but frequently gain at the finish; that it was indispensable, therefore, to terminate this operation; to push it to the utmost, astonish the universe, beat down Alexander by daring and carry off a prize which might compensate so many losses.

Thus it was, that the same danger which perhaps ought to have recalled him to the Niemen or kept him stationary on the Düna urged him towards Moscow! Such is the nature of false positions: everything in them is perilous. There is only a choice of errors. There is no hope but in those of the enemy and in chance.

Having at last decided, he hastily arose – as if not to allow time for his own reflections to renew so painful a state of uncertainty – and already quite full of the plan which was to secure his conquest, he hastened to his maps. They presented to his view the cities of Smolensk and Moscow. The great Moscow! The holy city! Names which he repeated with self-satisfaction and which served to add new fuel to his ambitious flame.

His resolution once taken, he was anxious that it should satisfy his counsellors. He conceived that by persuading them, they would be motivated by greater zeal than by commanding their obedience. It was, moreover, by their sentiments that he was enabled to judge those of the rest of his army: in short, like all other men, the silent discontent of his household disturbed him. Surrounded by disapproving looks and opinions contrary to his own, he felt uncomfortable. And besides, to obtain their assent to his plan was in some degree to make them share the responsibility of it, which possibly weighed upon his mind.

But all the officers about his person opposed his plan, each in the way that marked his particular character: Berthier with a sorrowful face, lamentations and even with tears; Lobau and Caulaincourt with a frankness which, in the first was stamped by a cold and haughty bluntness (excusable in such a brave warrior), and which in the second was persevering even to obstinacy. The Emperor rejected their observations with some ill humour. Addressing himself more especially to his aide-de-camp, as well as to

Berthier, he exclaimed that he had enriched his generals too much; that all they now aspired to was to follow the pleasures of the chase and to display their brilliant carriages in the capital; and that, doubtless, they had become disgusted with war. When their honour was thus attacked, there was no longer any reply to be made: they merely bowed and remained silent. During one of his impatient fits, he told one of the generals of his Guard, 'You were born in a bivouac and in a bivouac you will die!'

As to Duroc, he first displayed his disfavour by a chilling silence and afterwards by short answers, reference to accurate reports and by brief remarks. To him, the Emperor admitted that he saw clearly enough that the Russians wanted to draw him on but that nevertheless, he must proceed as far as Smolensk; that there he would establish his headquarters and in the spring of 1813, if Russia did not previously make peace, she would be ruined; that Smolensk was the key of the two roads to St Petersburg and Moscow; that he must get possession of it; and that he would then be able to march on both those capitals at once, in order to destroy everything in the one and preserve everything in the other.

Here Duroc observed to him that he was not more likely to make peace at Smolensk or even at Moscow than he was at Vitebsk; and that, in removing to such a distance from France, the Prussians constituted an intermediate body, on whom little reliance could be placed. But the Emperor replied that on that supposition, as the Russian war no longer offered him any advantageous result, he ought to renounce it; and if so, he must turn his arms against Prussia and compel her to pay the expenses of the war.

It was now Daru's turn. This minister is straightforward even to stiffness and possesses immovable firmness. The grand question of the march upon Moscow produced a discussion with him which lasted for eight successive hours and at which only Berthier was present: 'It is not a national war,' concluded Daru, 'the introduction of some English merchandise into Russia and even the restoration of the Kingdom of Poland are not sufficient reasons for engaging in so distant a war; neither your troops nor ourselves understand its necessity or its objects and to say the least, all things recommend the policy of stopping where we now are.'

The Emperor rejoined: did they take him for a madman? Did they imagine he made war from inclination? Had they not heard him say that the wars of Spain and Russia were two ulcers which ate into the vitals of France and that she could not bear them both at once? He was anxious for peace but in order to treat for it, two persons were necessary and he was only one.

Had a single letter from Alexander yet reached him? What, then, should he wait for at Vitebsk? Rivers, it was true, traced out the line of our position but during the winter there were no longer any rivers in this country. It was, therefore, a visionary line which they traced out; it was rather a line of demarcation than of separation. It was necessary, therefore, to build an artificial line; to construct towns and fortresses capable of defying the elements and every species of scourge; that if he returned to Vilna he might, indeed, more easily find supplies but that he should not be in a better condition to defend himself; that in that case it would be necessary for him to fall back to the Vistula and to lose Lithuania. Whereas at Smolensk, he would be sure to gain either a decisive battle or at least a fortress and a position on the Dnieper; that he perceived clearly that their thoughts were dwelling on Charles XII[10] but that if the expedition to Moscow lacked a fortunate precedent, it was because it had lacked a man capable of undertaking it; that in war, fortune went for one-half in everything; that if people always waited for a complete assemblage of favourable circumstances, nothing would ever be undertaken; that we must begin in order to finish; that there was no enterprise in which everything concurred and that, in all human projects, chance had its share; that, in short, it was not the rule which created the success but the success the rule; and that, if he succeeded by new means, that success would create new principles.

'Blood has not yet been spilled,' said he, 'and Russia is too powerful to yield without fighting. Alexander can only negotiate after a great battle. If it is necessary, I will even proceed to the holy city in search of that battle. And I will gain it. Peace waits for me at the gates of Moscow!'

4 The Phantom of Victory

> . . . there was a kind of inexplicable stillness. The weather was also calm, the sky was cloudless, the sunset was gorgeous. No sooner, however, had twilight disappeared than the sky was reddened by the reflection of vast columns of flame, rising upwards as if the whole city of Smolensk was on fire.
>
> L.A.H. Leroy-Dupré[1]

Alexander, inept as a general, proved to a be a first-rate recruiting sergeant. By tapping into the religious fervour of his people, he swiftly mobilized their support and on 29 July (the day after Napoleon entered Vitebsk) the first intake of the Moscow militia was sworn in. According to Caulaincourt, 'We learned that he had convoked the nobility and the townsfolk; that he had not concealed the true condition of the state and had asked the various governments for aid. Moscow had offered 80,000 men and the others in proportion. Little Russia had given him 18,000 Cossacks; and private individuals had supplied battalions, squadrons and companies all fully equipped. To give this armament a national and religious character, Archbishop Platov had offered the Tsar the miracle-working icon of St Sergius, which His Majesty in turn had given to the Moscow militia. In short, a crusade was being preached against the French.'

On 31 July Barclay reached Smolensk. A Livonian of Scottish ancestry, the fifty-one-year-old Mikhail Barclay de Tolly had risen through the ranks to become both a general and Alexander's minister of war. A loyal and patriotic soldier, his policy of retreat before Bonaparte's legions had undoubtedly saved Russia. Nevertheless, his strategy was unpopular and as a 'foreigner', he became a victim of the growing xenophobia within the army and the country as a whole. A solitary figure, over-burdened with work and plagued by insubordination, it is true to say that he was forced to fight a war on two fronts: one against Napoleon, the other against his Russian colleagues. As a contemporary put it, 'People resented General Barclay. Secret meetings were held and plots hatched . . . The operations of the Commander-in-Chief were criticized openly.'[2]

Barclay's bitterest critic was none other than Prince Bagration, the man with whom he was obliged to co-operate in order to stem Napoleon's advance. The two were, in fact, complete opposites: Barclay, the self-made man, was cool and methodical but largely mistrusted by the army; while the aristocratic Bagration was a fire-eating hothead, worshipped by his troops as a true Russian hero. From the very start of the campaign, Bagration had criticized Barclay's decision to retreat, firing a barrage of letters at Alexander's advisers. According to him, Barclay was not saving the Fatherland but 'most amiably leading a guest to the capital'.[3] *To make matters worse, Bagration actually outranked Barclay but had been placed under his orders by Alexander who had thus, unwittingly, merely added to the Prince's grievances against the man he condescendingly referred to as 'the Minister'.*

On 2 August Bagration joined Barclay at Smolensk and immediately indulged in a flurry of fault-finding: no opportunity was missed to undermine 'the Minister'. Barclay, meanwhile, was coming under increasing pressure to take the initiative and launch a counter-offensive against Napoleon at Vitebsk (which, incidentally, would have suited Napoleon fine!). On 6 August, having buckled under pressure from Alexander, he held a council of war and a sortie from Smolensk was duly ordered, consisting of some 120,000 troops from the combined Russian armies. Bagration, however, refused to co-operate, keeping his men idle while Barclay pushed on alone. By 13 August, unsupported and fearing a

Napoleonic masterstroke, Barclay lost his nerve and called off the advance. As de Ségur notes, 'It is possible that Barclay, having to cope with a colossal foe, felt authorized to expect from him gigantic manoeuvres.' The fact remains, however, that the cohesion of the Russian forces was crippled by the bickering and back-biting of the top brass.

Meanwhile Napoleon, seven weeks into the campaign and 400 miles inside Russian territory, was desperate for a showdown and launched an advance on Smolensk. Changing his line of operations in order to fool the Russians, he at first headed south, passing onto the southern bank of the Dnieper before striking east for Smolensk. On 14 August Ney's III Corps bloodied Barclay's rearguard at Krasnoi, thirty miles west of their objective. Although a defeat for the Russians, Napoleon's advance was held up long enough for Barclay to be apprised of the coming storm and scamper back to Smolensk, in order to bolster the garrison.

The following day, however, happened to be Napoleon's forty-third birthday and instead of ramming home his attack, he passed the hours reviewing his troops. Marshal Ney, catching the sense of occasion, ordered a 100-gun salute in the Emperor's honour: Napoleon saw fit to reprimand Ney for wasting ammunition, while he proceeded to waste time – that most precious of commodities – on needless pomp and ceremony. The chance to take Smolensk by surprise was thus squandered.

Straddling the Dnieper, Smolensk was divided in two: on the northern bank lay the New Town or St Petersburg suburb, while to the south stood the Old City, surrounded by a medieval wall three miles long, twenty-five feet high and ten feet thick. This formidable barrier was further strengthened by some thirty-two towers, packed with artillery pieces. Huddled around these defences were more suburbs, forming a maze of timber-built houses. Early on the morning of 16 August, Murat's cavalry made the approaches to the city, driving in the Russian outposts. Ney followed with 16,000 infantry and immediately launched a reckless – and abortive – attempt to take the place solo. According to the celebrated memoirist, Baron de Marbot, 'He advanced towards the gate with a feeble escort of hussars, when suddenly a regiment of Cossacks, masked by a fold in the ground, dashed upon our troopers, drove them back and surrounded Marshal Ney, who was so close pressed that a pistol-bullet fired almost point-blank tore his coat collar.'

Napoleon arrived before the fortress at 1.00 p.m. on the 16th, clapping his hands and exclaiming, 'At last I have them!' before rashly pitching his tent within range of the Russian guns. After a brief inspection of the enemy positions, he opened the proceedings with a probing attack against the southern suburbs, which continued fitfully till dusk without a decision. Thus repelled by the defenders, Napoleon's troops contented themselves with forming a cordon around the outskirts of the Old City, while Barclay's men filed in from the west and Bagration concentrated around the New Town. For the time being, Smolensk seemed safe.

According to de Ségur, 'On the 17th, by daybreak, the hope of seeing the Russian army drawn up before him awoke Napoleon; but the field which he had prepared for it remained empty.' The fact was that Barclay, having saved Smolensk, now feared to preserve it: expecting Napoleon to outflank him and cut his line of retreat, he saw the fortress more as a snare than a sanctuary. He therefore ordered Bagration out of the city, so he could cover the river crossing at Dorogobuzh, fifty miles to the east: his departure not going unnoticed by General Belliard, Murat's chief of staff, posted on the riverbank above the city.

Meanwhile Napoleon, having been convinced by Ney and Davout that Smolensk would be an easy prize, gave up any idea of encirclement in favour of an all-out assault. Denied the showdown for which he had so ardently wished, he decided to blast his way in. It was with some incredulity, therefore, that he received the news from Belliard that the Russians were, apparently, preparing to quit.

FROM THAT moment he seemed to consider Smolensk as a mere place of passage, of which it was absolutely necessary to gain possession by force and without loss of time. But Murat, prudent when not heated by the presence of the enemy and who with his cavalry had nothing to do in an assault, disapproved of the resolution. To him so violent an effort seemed useless when the Russians were retiring of their own accord; and as to the plan of overtaking them, he observed that since they would not fight, we had followed them far enough and it was high time to stop.

The Emperor replied but the rest of their conversation was not overheard. As, however, Murat afterwards declared that he had thrown himself at the feet of his brother and begged him to stop but that Napoleon saw nothing but Moscow – that honour, glory, rest, everything for him was there – it was obvious what had been the cause of their disagreement.

So much is certain, that when Murat quitted his brother-in-law, his face wore an expression of deep indignity, his movements were abrupt, a gloomy and concentrated passion agitated him and the name of Moscow several times escaped his lips.

Not far off, on the left bank of the Dnieper, a formidable battery had been placed at the spot where Belliard had perceived the retreat of the enemy. The Russians had opposed to us two still more formidable: every moment our guns were shattered and our ammunition wagons blown up. It was into the midst of this volcano that Murat urged his horse. There he stopped, alighted and remained motionless. Belliard warned him that he was sacrificing his life to no purpose and without glory. Murat answered only by pushing on still farther. Those around him no longer doubted that despairing of the outcome of the war and foreseeing future disasters, he was seeking death in order to escape them. Belliard insisted and observed to him that his recklessness would be the destruction of those about him: 'Well then,' replied Murat, 'retire and leave me here by myself.' All refused to leave him when the King, angrily turning about, tore himself from this scene of carnage like a man in torment.

Meanwhile a general assault had been ordered. Ney had

to attack the citadel, Davout and Lobau the suburbs which cover the walls of the city. Poniatowski, already on the banks of the Dnieper with sixty pieces of cannon, was again to descend that river to the suburb which borders it, destroy the enemy's bridges and intercept the retreat of the garrison. Napoleon gave orders that at the same time the artillery of the Guard should batter the great wall with its twelve-pounders (which were ineffective against so thick a mass: it disobeyed and directed its fire into the covered way, which it cleared).

Every manoeuvre succeeded at once except Ney's attack: the only one which ought to have been decisive but which was abandoned.[4] The enemy was driven back headlong within his walls: all who had not time to regain them perished. But in mounting the assault our attacking columns left a broad track of blood, wounded and dead.

It was noticed that one battalion, which presented itself in flank to the Russian batteries, lost a whole rank of one of its platoons by a single ball: twenty-two men were felled by the same blow.

Meanwhile the army, from an amphitheatre of heights, contemplated with silent anxiety the conduct of its brave comrades; but when it saw them darting through a shower of balls and grapeshot and persisting with a passion and a regularity quite admirable, then it was that the soldiers, warmed with enthusiasm, began clapping their hands. The noise of this glorious applause was such even to reach the attacking columns. It rewarded the devotion of those warriors and although in Dalton's single brigade and in the artillery of Reindre five chiefs of battalion, 1,500 men and the general himself fell, the survivors still say that the homage which they excited was sufficient compensation for all their sufferings.

On reaching the walls of the place, they screened themselves from its fire by means of the outworks and buildings, of which they had gained possession. The fire of musketry continued and from the report – redoubled by the echo of the walls – it seemed to become more and more brisk. Thus the same blunder which Ney had made a battalion commit the preceding day was again repeated by the whole army: the one had cost 300 or 400 men; the other 5,000 or 6,000. The Emperor grew tired of this and would have withdrawn his troops but Davout persuaded him to persevere in his attack.

Night came on. Napoleon retired to his tent (which had been placed in a more secure situation than the day before) and Count Lobau, who had made himself master of the ditch but could no longer maintain his ground there, ordered shells to be thrown into the city to dislodge the enemy. Thick black columns of smoke were presently seen rising from several points; these were soon lighted at intervals by flickering flashes, then by sparks and at last long spires of flame burst from all parts. It was like a great number of distinct fires. It was not long before they united and formed but one vast blaze which, whirling as it rose, covered Smolensk and entirely consumed it with a dismal roaring.

Count Lobau was dismayed by so great a disaster, which he believed to be his own work. The Emperor, seated in front of his tent, contemplated in silence this awful spectacle.[5] It was as yet impossible to ascertain either the cause or the result and the night passed under arms.

About three in the morning, one of Davout's subalterns ventured to the foot of the wall, which he scaled without a noise. Emboldened by the silence which reigned around him, he penetrated into the city. All at once several voices were heard and the Frenchman, surprised and surrounded, thought that he had nothing to do but sell his life dearly or surrender. The first rays of dawn however, showed him in those he mistook for enemies some of Poniatowski's Poles. They had been the first to enter the city, which Barclay had just evacuated.[6]

After Smolensk had been reconnoitred and its approaches cleared, the army entered within the walls. It crossed the reeking and blood stained ruins with its accustomed order, pomp and martial music; triumphing over the deserted wreck and having no other witness of its glory but itself: a show without spectators, an almost fruitless victory, a sanguinary glory.

When the Emperor knew that Smolensk was occupied and its fires extinguished; and when daylight and the different reports had sufficiently instructed him; when, in short, he saw that there, as at the Niemen, Vilna and Vitebsk, the phantom of victory which drew him forward – and which he always imagined himself to be on the point of seizing – had once more slipped his grasp, he proceeded slowly towards his barren conquest. He inspected the field of battle (according to his custom) in order to appreciate the value of the attack, the merit of the resistance and the loss on both sides.[7]

He found it strewed with a great number of Russian dead and very few of ours. Most of them, especially the French, had been stripped (they might be known by the whiteness of their skin and their forms, less bony and muscular than those of the Russians). A melancholy review of the dead and dying! A dismal account to make up and deliver! The pain felt by the Emperor might be judged by the contraction of his features and his irritation; but in him policy was a second nature, which soon imposed silence on the first.

Continuing his reconnaissance, he came to one of the gates of the citadel, near the Dnieper, facing the suburbs on the right bank, which was still occupied by the Russians. There, surrounded by Marshals Ney, Davout, Mortier, Duroc, Count Lobau and another general, he sat down on some mats before a hut: not so much to observe the enemy, as to relieve his heart from the load which oppressed it.

He talked long and without interruption: what a disgrace for Barclay, to have given up without fighting, the key of Old Russia! And yet, what a field of honour he had offered to him! How advantageous it was for him! A fortified town to support and take part in his efforts! The same town and a river to receive and cover the wreck of his army, if defeated! Barclay had lacked nothing but resolution. It was, therefore, all over with Russia. She had no army but to witness the fall of her cities and not to defend them. For, in fact, on what more favourable ground could Barclay make a stand? What position would he determine to dispute? He, who had forsaken that Smolensk which, as it had been given out, was to prove the grave of the French!

While the Emperor was thus talking, the balls of the Russian riflemen were whizzing about his ears but he was worked up by his subject. He launched out against the enemy's general and his army, as if he would have destroyed them by his reasoning. No one answered him. It was evident that he was not asking for advice; that he had been talking to himself; that he was fighting against his own feelings and that, by this torrent of speculations, he was attempting to make others participate in the same illusions.

Indeed, he did not give anyone time to interrupt him. As to the weakness and disorganization of the Russian army, nobody believed it: but what could be urged in reply? After an hour's conversation, the Emperor, looking at the heights on the right bank, which were almost abandoned by the enemy, concluded by exclaiming that the Russians were women and that they acknowledged themselves vanquished!

Meanwhile, the Russians still defended the suburb on the right bank of the Dnieper. On our side, the 18th and the night of the 19th were employed in rebuilding the bridges. On 19 August, before daybreak, Ney crossed the river by the light of the suburb which was on fire. At first he saw no enemies but the flames and he began to climb the long and rugged slope on which it stands. His troops proceeded slowly and with caution, making a thousand circuits to avoid the fire. The Russians had managed it with skill: it met at every point and obstructed the principal avenues.

Ney and the foremost of his soldiers advanced silently into this labyrinth of flames with anxious eye and attentive ear, not knowing if the Russians might be waiting on the summit to pour suddenly upon them, to overthrow and drive them back into the flames and the river. But they breathed more freely, relieved from the weight of apprehension, when they saw on the crest of the ravine, at the branching-off of the roads to St Petersburg and Moscow, nothing but a band of Cossacks, who immediately fled by those two roads. Having neither prisoners, peasants, nor spies, the ground was – as at Vitebsk – the only thing they could interrogate. But the enemy had left as many traces in one direction as in the other, so that the Marshal paused in uncertainty between the two until midday.

During this interval, a passage had been effected across the Dnieper at several points: the roads to the two hostile capitals were reconnoitred to the distance of a league and the Russian infantry was discovered in that leading to Moscow. Ney would soon have overtaken it but as the road skirted the Dnieper, he had to cross the streams which fall into it. Each of them, having dug its own bed, marked the bottom of a valley, the opposite side of which was a position where the enemy posted himself and which it was necessary to carry. The first, that of the Stubna, did not detain him long; but the hill of Valutina, at the foot of which runs the Kolodnia, became the scene of an obstinate conflict.

We have seen that the Moscow road, on leaving Smolensk, skirted the Dnieper and that the fire of the French artillery on the other bank traversed it. Barclay dared not take this road at night for fear of risking his artillery and baggage: the rolling of which would have betrayed his retreat.

The St Petersburg road quitted the river more abruptly. Two marshy crossroads branched off from it to the right, one at the distance of two leagues from Smolensk, the other at four: they ran through the woods and rejoined the highroad to Moscow after a long circuit, the one at Bredichino, two leagues beyond Valutina, the other farther off at Slobneva.

Into these defiles Barclay was bold enough to commit himself with his numerous horses and vehicles; so that this long, heavy column had thus to cross two large arcs of a circle, of which the highroad from Smolensk to Moscow, which Ney soon attacked, was the chord. Every moment, as always happens in such cases, the overturning of a carriage, the sticking fast of a wheel or a single horse in the mud stopped the whole. The sound of the French cannon, meanwhile, drew nearer and seemed to have already got before the Russian column and to be on the point of reaching and shutting up the passage which it was striving to gain.

At length, after an arduous march, the head of the enemy's convoy came in sight of the highroad at the moment when the French had only to force the height of Valutina and the passage of the Kolodnia, in order to reach that outlet. Ney had furiously carried that of the Stubna; but Korv,[8] being furiously driven back upon Valutina, had summoned to his aid the column which preceded him. It is asserted that the latter, being in disorder and badly officered, hesitated to comply but that Voronzov,[9] aware of the importance of that position, prevailed upon its commander to turn back.

The Russians defended themselves to save everything: cannon, wounded, baggage; the French attacked in order to take everything. Napoleon had halted a league and a half in the rear of Ney. Thinking that it was but an affair between his advanced guard and the rear of the enemy, he sent Gudin[10] to the assistance of the Marshal, rallied the other divisions and returned to Smolensk. But this fight became a regular battle: 30,000 men were successively engaged in it on both sides; soldiers, officers, generals encountered each other; the action was long, the struggle terrible. Even night did not suspend it. At length, in possession of the plateau, exhausted by loss of strength and blood, Ney, finding himself surrounded only by dead, dying and darkness, became fatigued. He ordered his troops to cease firing, to keep silence and present bayonets. The Russians, hearing nothing more, were silent also and availed themselves of the gloom to effect their retreat.

There was almost as much glory in their defeat as in our victory. The two chiefs carried their point: the one in conquering; the other in not being conquered till he had saved the Russian artillery, baggage and wounded. One of the enemy's generals (the only one left unhurt on this field of carnage) endeavoured to escape from among our soldiers by repeating the French word of command: he was recognized by the flashes of their firearms and secured. Other Russian generals had perished but the Grand Army sustained a greater loss.

At the passage of the bridge over the Kolodnia, which had been badly repaired, General Gudin had alighted from his horse to cross the stream when, at that moment, a cannon ball skimming the surface of the ground broke both his legs. When the news of this misfortune reached the Emperor it put a stop to everything, discussion and action. Everyone was thunderstruck. The victory of Valutina seemed no longer to be a success.

Gudin was carried to Smolensk and there received the unavailing attentions of the Emperor; but he soon expired. His remains were interred in the citadel of the city,[11] to which they do honour: a worthy tomb for a soldier who was a good citizen, a good husband, a good father, an intrepid general, a man of both principle and talent. A rare assemblage of qualities in an age when virtuous men are too frequently devoid of abilities and men of abilities without virtue. It was a fortunate chance that he was worthily replaced: Gérard, the oldest general of brigade in the division, took command of it and the enemy, who knew nothing of our loss, gained nothing by the dreadful blow he had just dealt us.

The Russians, astonished at having been attacked only in front, conceived that all the military actions of Murat were confined to following them: they therefore called him in mockery, 'the General of the highroads'. In fact, while Ney was attacking, Murat scoured his flanks with the cavalry without being able to bring it into action: woods on the left and bogs on the right obstructed his movements. But while they were fighting in front, they were both anticipating the effect of a flanking march of the Westphalians, commanded by Junot.[12]

From Stubna the highroad, in order to avoid the marshes formed by the various tributary streams of the Dnieper, turned off to the left, ascended the heights and went farther from the basin of the river, to which it afterwards returned in a more favourable situation. It had been noticed that a byroad, bolder and shorter, ran straight across these low marshy grounds between the Dnieper and the highroad, which it rejoined behind the plateau of Valutina.

It was this crossroad which Junot pursued after crossing the river at Prudiszy. It soon led him into the rear of the Russians, upon the flank of the columns which were returning to the assistance of their rearguard. His attack was all that was wanted to render the victory decisive. Those who were engaged in front with Marshal Ney would have been daunted at hearing an attack in their rear; while the disorder into which, in the midst of an action, it would have thrown the multitude of men, horses and carriages (crowded together in one road) would have been incurable: but Junot, though personally brave, was irresolute as a general. His responsibility frightened him.

Meanwhile Murat, judging that he must have come up, was astonished at not hearing his attack. The firmness of the Russians opposed to Ney led him to suspect the truth. He left his cavalry and, crossing the woods and marshes almost alone, he hastened to Junot and upbraided him with his inaction. Junot alleged in excuse that he had no orders to attack; his Würtemberg cavalry was fearful, its efforts feigned and it would never be brought to charge the enemy's battalions.

These words Murat answered with actions. He rushed on at the head of that cavalry which, with a different leader, were quite different troops. He urged them on, launched them against the Russians, overthrew their *tirailleurs*, returned to Junot and said to him, 'Now finish the business, your glory and your marshal's *bâton* are still before you!' He then left to rejoin his own troops and Junot, confounded, remained motionless. Too long around Napoleon, whose active genius directed everything, both the plan and the detail, he had learned only to obey. Besides, fatigue and wounds had made him an old man before his time.[13]

That such a general should have been selected for so important a movement was not at all surprising. It is well known that the Emperor was attached to him both from habit (for he was his oldest aide-de-camp) and from a secret weakness: for, as the presence of that officer was associated with all the recollections of his victories and glory, he disliked to part from him. It is also reasonable to suppose that it flattered his vanity to see men who had been his pupils commanding armies; and it was, moreover, natural that he should have a firmer reliance on their attachment than on that of any others.

When, however, on the following day he inspected the places themselves, at the sight of the bridge where Gudin fell, he made the remark that it was not there he ought to have debouched; when afterwards, gazing with an angry look on the position Junot had occupied, he exclaimed, 'It was there, no doubt, that the Westphalians should have attacked! All the battle was there! What was Junot about?' His anger became so violent that nothing could at first allay it. He called Rapp and told him to take command from Junot; he would dismiss him from the army; he had lost his marshal's *bâton* for ever; this blunder would probably block the road to Moscow against us; that to him, Rapp, he gave the command of the Westphalians; that he could speak to them in their own language and would know how to make them fight. But Rapp refused the place of his old companion-in-arms. He appeased the Emperor, whose anger always subsided quickly, as soon as it had vented itself in words.

Ney's troops and those of Gudin's division (deprived of their general) had drawn up on the corpses of their companions and of the Russians, amidst the stumps of broken trees, on ground trampled by the feet of the combatants, furrowed with balls, strewed with the fragments of weapons, tattered uniforms, overturned carriages and scattered limbs. For such are the trophies of war! Such are the beauties of a field of victory!

Gudin's battalions appeared to be melted down to platoons. The more they were reduced, the prouder they seemed to be. Close to them one still breathed the smell of burnt cartridges and gunpowder, with which their clothes were covered and their faces quite begrimed. The Emperor could not pass along their front without having to avoid, pass over or tread upon carcasses and bayonets twisted by the violence of the shock. But over all these horrors he threw a veil of glory. His gratitude transformed this field of death into a field of triumph where, for some hours, satiated honour and ambition held exclusive sway.

He was aware that it was high time to encourage his soldiers by commendations and rewards. Never, therefore, were his looks more kind and as to his language: this battle was the most glorious achievement in our military history! The soldiers who heard him were men with whom one might conquer the world! The slain, warriors who had died an immortal death! He spoke thus, well aware that it is more especially amid such destruction that men think of immortality.

He was profuse in his rewards: on the 12th, 21st, 127th of the Line, and the 7th Light, he conferred eighty-seven decorations and promotions. These were Gudin's regiments. The 127th had previously marched without an eagle, for at that time it was necessary for a regiment to earn its colours in a field of battle to prove that in the future it would know how to preserve them there.

The Emperor delivered the eagle to it with his own hands. He also satisfied Ney's corps. His favours were as great in themselves as they were in their form. The value of the gift was enhanced by the manner in which he gave it. He was successively surrounded by each regiment as by a family. There he addressed himself in a loud voice to the officers, subalterns and privates: inquiring who were the bravest of all those brave men – or the most successful – and recompensing them on the spot. The officers named, the soldiers confirmed, the Emperor approved. Thus, as he himself observed, the elections were made instantaneously, in a circle in his presence and confirmed with acclamations by the troops.

These fatherly manners, which made the private soldier the comrade of the ruler of Europe, these forms, which revived the still regretted usages of the Republic, delighted the troops. He was a monarch – but the monarch of the Revolution – and they could not but love a fortunate sovereign who led them on to fortune. In him there was everything to excite and nothing to reproach them.

Never did a field of victory exhibit a spectacle more capable of exalting: the presentation of that richly merited eagle, the pomp of the promotions, the shouts of joy; the glory of those warriors, rewarded on the very spot where it had just been acquired, their valour proclaimed by that great captain, whose bulletins would carry their names over the whole world; and more especially among their countrymen and into the bosoms of their families, which they would at once cheer and make proud. How many favours at once! They were absolutely intoxicated with them. He himself seemed at first to share their emotions.

But when he was out of sight of his troops, the attitude of Ney and Murat and the words of Poniatowski (who was as frank and judicious in council as he was intrepid in the field) cooled him; and when the close heat of the day began to overpower him and he learned from the reports that his men had proceeded eight leagues without overtaking the enemy, the spell was entirely dissolved. On his return to Smolensk, the jolting of his carriage over the relics of the fight; the stoppages on the road by the long files of wounded, who were crawling or being carried back; and in Smolensk itself, by the carts of amputated limbs about to be thrown away at a distance – in a word, all that is horrible out of fields of battle – completely disarmed him. Smolensk was one vast hospital[14] and the loud groans which issued from it drowned the shout of glory which had just been raised on the field of Valutina.

The reports of the surgeons were frightful. In that country a spirit distilled from grain is used instead of wine and brandy made from grapes; narcotic plants are mixed with it. Our young soldiers, exhausted with hunger and fatigue, decided that this liquor would cheer them; but its treacherous fire caused them to throw out at once all the life that was yet left in them, after which they sank and became victims of disease. Others, less sober or more debilitated, were seized with dizziness, stupefaction and torpor: they squatted into the ditches and on the roads. Their half-open, watery and lacklustre eyes seemed to watch with insensibility death gradually seizing their whole frame. They expired sullenly and without a groan.

At Vilna it had not been possible to establish hospitals for more than 6,000 sick: convents, churches, synagogues and barns served to receive the suffering multitude. In these dismal places the sick were frequently without food, beds, covering, even straw and medicines. The surgeons were, from their small number, unequal to the duty; so that everything, even to the very hospitals, contributed to create disease, and nothing to health.

At Vitebsk, 400 wounded Russians were left on the field of battle; 300 more were abandoned in the town by their army and, as the inhabitants had fled, these unfortunate wretches remained three days before they were discovered huddled together pell-mell, dead and dying, amidst the horrible filth and infection. They were at length collected and mixed with our own wounded who, like those of the Russians, amounted to 700. Our surgeons tore up their own shirts to dress them, for there already began to be a scarcity of linen.

When at length the wounds of these unfortunate men were healed and they required nothing but wholesome food to complete their cure, they perished for want of sustenance. Few, either of the French or Russians, escaped. Those who were prevented from going in search of food by the loss of a limb or debility, were the first to sink. These disasters occurred wherever the Emperor was not in person: his presence bringing – and his departure carrying – everything along with it and his orders, in fact, not being scrupulously obeyed but within the circle of his own observation.

At Smolensk there was no want of hospitals: fifteen spacious brick buildings were rescued from the flames. There were even found some wine, brandy and a few medical stores; and our reserve wagons for the wounded at length rejoined us. But everything ran short. The surgeons were at work night and day but the very second night all the materials for dressing the wounded were exhausted: there was no more linen and they were forced to use paper, found in the archives, in its place. Parchment served for splinters and coarse cloth for compresses and they had no other substitute for lint except tow and birch cotton.

Our surgeons were overwhelmed with dismay. For three days a hospital of 100 wounded had been forgotten: an accident led to its discovery. Rapp penetrated into that abode of despair. I will spare my reader the horror of a description of it. Wherefore communicate those terrible impressions which harrow up the soul? Rapp did not spare them to Napoleon, who instantly caused his own wine and a sum of money to be distributed among such of those unfortunate men as a tenacious life still animated or whom a disgusting food had supported.

But to the passionate emotions which these reports excited in the bosom of the Emperor was added an alarming consideration: the conflagration of Smolensk was no longer, he saw, the effect of a fatal and unforeseen accident of war, nor even the result of an act of despair, it was the result of cool determination. The Russians had studied the time and means and taken as great pains to destroy as are usually taken to preserve.

5 Under the Storm of Iron and Lead

The sight of the dead and wounded was frightful. A description of it would be futile, since it would be too feeble. The sun would not set today.

Baron Uxkull[1]

Both sides claimed the victory at Smolensk. The Russians even went so far as to hold services of thanksgiving and a Te Deum was sung at St Petersburg: 'They lie to God as well as to men,' commented Napoleon dryly.

At first, Napoleon planned to halt at Smolensk but changed his mind for the following reasons: a speedy victory was essential if Alexander was to be crushed before British aid took effect and before Russia's immense reserves of manpower were mobilized; his own army, caught in the grip of a logistical nightmare, badly needed food and supplies which, lacking at Smolensk, should be found in plenty at Moscow; public opinion – both in Paris and the empire as a whole – demanded a swift and successful conclusion to the campaign; finally, the Russian army appeared to be on the brink of collapse and he calculated that one almighty blow would finish it off. 'Once again,' lamented Caulaincourt in his memoirs, 'we set off in pursuit of the glory, or rather the fatality, which relentlessly prevented the Emperor from holding to his good intentions.' Napoleon, however, was fixated on his goal: 'We have gone too far to turn back. Peace is in front of us; we are but ten days' march from it; so near the goal, there is nothing more to consider. Let us march on Moscow!'[2]

Meanwhile, Alexander had been forced to react to the growing clamour for Barclay's removal and on 20 August he appointed General Mikhail Kutusov as commander-in-chief. He did so reluctantly ('People wanted his appointment. I named him. As for me, I wash my hands of it.'[3]), for at sixty-seven years old, Kutusov was no longer the energetic hero of yesteryear but an overweight bon viveur; a one-eyed womanizer, who was almost certainly less able than Barclay. He was, however, a 'true' Russian, born in St Petersburg and, as a disciple of the legendary Suvarov,[4] he had the popular vote. Clausewitz, speaking for the average Russian, wrote: 'All were agreed that a true Russian was better than a foreigner and much wanted at the moment.' Barclay remained as commander of the First Army of the West.

Napoleon was also delighted at Kutusov's appointment for, as he so accurately observed, 'The new general cannot continue this plan of retreat, which is condemned by national opinion. He has been summoned to command the army on condition that he fights.'[5] Napoleon must have been further heartened by the recollection that the elderly Kutusov – known as 'the Dowager' by his enemies – had commanded at Austerlitz, the Emperor's greatest victory.

On 25 August the Grand Army – sickness, starvation, casualties and garrison duties having reduced it to 124,000 foot soldiers, 32,000 cavalrymen and 587 guns – resumed its pursuit of the Russians in the blistering heat of high summer. It was a gruelling march: the soldiers choked on thick clouds of dust, kicked up from the dirt tracks by thousands of tramping feet; food was scarce, rations non-existent; and at every village they were greeted by flames, bequeathed them by the Cossacks of the Russian rearguard. As Baron Lejeune states, 'The further we advanced, the more desolate became the country. Every village had been burnt and there was no longer even the thatch from the cottages for the horses to eat; everything that could be destroyed was reduced to ashes.' Napoleon was both alarmed and appalled by such waste. At first, he refused to believe that the Russians were burning their own property and determined to learn the truth of the matter. On hearing that Cossacks were indeed destroying whole villages rather than yield to him the least thing of value, he affected to make light of it, joking about the folly of a people who would wreck their own homes rather than let a French soldier sleep in them for a night: but in truth he was shocked by this new kind of warfare, already successfully pioneered by the British and their allies in the Iberian Peninsula.

By 29 August, the Grand Army had marched almost 100 miles deeper into the Russian heartland, reaching the small town of Viasma. De Ségur describes the scene: 'The army, thirsty from the march, the heat and the dust, was in want of water; the troops disputed the possession of a few muddy pools and fought near the springs . . . During the night the enemy destroyed the bridges over the Viasma, plundered that town and set it on fire. Murat and Davout quickly advanced to extinguish the flames.' When Napoleon entered the smoking ruins he found a ghost town, its population of 15,000 having fled. The local priest had, he was told, died of shock at the news of his approach: Napoleon ordered the troops to bury the unfortunate cleric with full military honours.

Meanwhile, Kutusov had arrived at the front to take over from Barclay. Although the latter had undoubtedly preserved the Russian army by his policy of steady retreat, Kutusov had orders to fight. No longer an active man (too obese to ride a horse, he was wheeled around in a carriage; while at staff meetings, he frequently dozed off), Kutusov at least had the power to inspire and motivate his peasant army. By playing on their patriotism, their religious fervour and their superstitious fear of Napoleon (some believed him to be the Antichrist, others that he possessed supernatural powers), he galvanized an almost fanatical resistance. Clausewitz again expresses the popular view: 'It was believed in the army that the indecision of Barclay, which prevented him from coming to a regular action and the mistrust against him as a stranger in the army, had at last decided the Emperor to place at the head of the army the man among the true Russians who had the most reputation . . . In the army there was great joy on his arrival.'

On 1 September, having advanced another forty miles or so, Napoleon entered the town of Gzhatsk, his soldiers fighting flames in place of enemies. Kutusov, meanwhile, pulled back to a strong position astride the Smolensk-Moscow road. Here, at the tiny village of Borodino, a mere seventy-five miles west of Moscow, he would make his stand. The Grand Army caught up on 4 September, driving in the Russian outposts. Napoleon, scenting battle, hurried up his artillery, announcing that he would have any carriage – even his own – burned if it blocked the passage of the guns. The Russians, having been reinforced by the 10,000 men of the Moscow militia, were, according to de Ségur, 'determined to root themselves to the soil and defend it: in short, there to conquer or die'. Napoleon's long-awaited battle of decision had at last arrived.

Next day began a fierce struggle for the outlying Russian positions. The Shevardino Redoubt was taken by the troops of Napoleon's right wing at a cost of 4,000 killed and wounded: 'This attack was carried out with such vigour that we were masters of the forts in less than an hour,' wrote Caulaincourt. The Russians counter-attacked but were repelled and forced to retire to their main position just over a mile away at Borodino. 'That very night,' says de Ségur, 'a cold mizzling rain began to fall and the autumn set in with a violent wind . . . During that night how many different agitations! The soldiers and the officers had to prepare their arms, repair their clothing and combat cold and hunger.' Next morning Napoleon inspected the scene, wishing to reward the men who had taken Shevardino. According to Baron Lejeune, he asked the colonel of the 61st Regiment, 'But where is your 3rd Battalion?' 'Sire,' came the forlorn reply, 'it is in the redoubt!'

There followed, on 6 September, a day of calm before the coming storm: 'Nothing was so calm as the day preceding that great battle,' wrote de Ségur. Meanwhile, Napoleon received from Paris a portrait of his son, the infant King of Rome, which he proudly displayed to officers and private soldiers alike, before exclaiming, 'Take him away! He is too young to look upon a field of battle!'[6] *Less pleasing was the news of a French defeat at the Spanish city of Salamanca on 22 July: the war on two fronts looked set to rumble on indefinitely.*

Meanwhile, a mere mile across the way in the Russian camp,

Kutusov had priests parade holy icons before his kneeling troops, while the French were denounced as infidels. 'All, even to the meanest soldier,' observed de Ségur, 'fancied themselves devoted by God himself to the defence of Heaven and their sacred soil!' As night fell, de Ségur describes how Napoleon – in a state of high anxiety lest the Russians slip away once more – was unable to sleep: 'What is war?' he mused. 'A trade of barbarians, the whole art of which consists in being the strongest on a given point!' And then, turning to General Rapp, his aide-de-camp, he asked if he should be victorious in the coming battle: 'No doubt,' came the reply, 'but it will be bloody.' These words proved to be prophetic: for next to Leipzig in 1813, Borodino was the bloodiest battle of the period and Rapp, though lucky enough to survive, was destined to receive four wounds within the space of an hour and a half.

Kutusov had no plan other than to block the road to Moscow. His position was well chosen: protected by the River Kalatsha, the Russian army – consisting of 120,000 men and 640 guns – was drawn up on a series of hills which dominated the surrounding countryside. Moving from north to south, their dispositions were as follows: the right wing followed the line of the Kalatsha; the centre was fixed on Borodino which, as already stated, straddled the new Smolensk-Moscow road; a mile below Borodino, the left centre was fixed on the village of Semenovska; and a mile and a half below that, the extreme left was fixed on Utitsa, a village on the old Smolensk road. Kutusov bolstered this formidable position with several hastily constructed bulwarks: the so-called Great Redoubt, packed with heavy guns and dominating the centre of the battlefield, was sited 500 yards below Borodino; while three V-shaped earthworks, known as the Bagration Flèches (literally, 'arrows'), lay roughly halfway between Semenovska and Utitsa. Kutusov set up his headquarters a mile to the rear of Borodino at Gorki.

Napoleon's strategy was also simple: a frontal assault against Kutusov's centre and left wing. Davout, however, begged for permission to attempt an outflanking manoeuvre against the Russian left but the Emperor refused. Commentators ever since have blamed him for dismissing Davout's suggestion and have cited jealousy, lethargy, illness or declining intellectual powers for his decision to overrule a bold manoeuvre in favour of an unimaginative onslaught against a fortified line. Napoleon, however, had a clutch of perfectly valid reasons: firstly, Davout's manoeuvre would take time and he was terrified lest the Russians withdraw, as they had done so many times before; secondly, the rough terrain and execrable roads did not favour swift strokes and circuitous marches; thirdly, the Grand Army was in poor shape and Napoleon favoured a plan with no complications. He also underestimated the Russian troops (understandably as, so far, he had only ever seen their backs) and did not expect the heroically stubborn resistance which, in the event, Kutusov managed to extort from them.

The battle began at dawn on the 7th, when 100 French guns opened up on the Russian centre. Within the hour, Ney was sent against the Bagration Flèches on the Russian left (Napoleon's right) and Murat's cavalry was moved up to the front. At 8.00 a.m. Eugène stormed Borodino, evicting the Russians at bayonet-point. Carried away by their success, his troops swept over the Kalatsha bridge and on towards Gorki, before being thrown back into Borodino, which they held for the rest of the day. Meanwhile Davout, Murat and Ney became embroiled in the see-saw fight for the Flèches, which raged for most of the morning (Davout's horse was killed under him and the Marshal was wounded). At around 10.00 a.m. Poniatowski's Poles took Utitsa; while the Great Redoubt was momentarily overrun by an unsupported infantry brigade under General Morand: it was ejected by overwhelming forces and suffered heavy losses. By midday, the Bagration Flèches had finally fallen into French hands and as if to symbolize this Russian catastrophe, Bagration himself was mortally wounded while attempting to lead a counter-attack. Meanwhile, Semenovska was successfully stormed and Napoleon moved his artillery up to pour a barrage into the crumbling Russian left flank. At this point, the marshals requested the Guard in order to finish the job: but Napoleon, convinced that he would have another battle to fight before he reached Moscow, refused to commit his precious reserve.

By now, the Russian line had contracted and Kutusov's troops were packed into a dense mass: an ideal target for the Grand Army's guns. The Great Redoubt, however, still 'belched out a veritable hell'[7] *on Napoleon's centre and – as the key to Kutusov's position – would have to be taken before a general advance could be made. Eugène was detailed for the task and at 3.00 p.m. his attack went in: the redoubt was stormed by three columns of infantry, while a furious cavalry charge bypassed the bulwark before smashing into it from the rear. At last the guns of the Great Redoubt fell silent, though at the cost of the lives of both General Morand and the cavalry hero Auguste de Caulaincourt, brother of Armand, Napoleon's grand equerry. By 4.00 p.m. Napoleon was master of the field and his troops had taken Kutusov's original positions. More appeals for the Guard were made and refused. Meanwhile, the Russians withdrew half a mile to new positions, from which they obstinately refused to budge. Napoleon wheeled up his artillery, saying to Sorbier, his chief gunner, 'Since they want it, let them have it!' By 5.00 p.m. the fighting had largely died down due to sheer exhaustion on both sides. As dusk fell, Kutusov had just enough time to draft a despatch to Alexander, announcing another 'great victory' before pulling out under cover of darkness. The Grand Army, prostrate, was unable to pursue. Napoleon, ill and suffering from chronic fatigue, was observed by his valet compulsively clasping his hands and whispering, 'Moscow! Moscow!'*

The Battle of Borodino lacked the finesse of earlier Napoleonic masterpieces such as Austerlitz or Jena: the very nature of the ground dictated the pace and pattern of the action and the combat quickly degenerated into a bloody slugging match. Napoleon, who was unwell and therefore not on his best form (according to the accumulated literature he appeared to be suffering from a bewildering list of complaints: cystits, dysuria, fever, flu, a head cold, to name a few), moped about in the rear, seeing little of the front-line action. Kutusov, as was his wont, refused to let what he later described as 'the most bloody battle of modern times' disturb his sangfroid and also remained at headquarters throughout the battle. Thus both commanders were content to let their generals try to harness the maelstrom, many fighting and dying like common soldiers as a consequence. With 250,000 men and over 1,000 guns packed into an area of less than eight square miles, losses were, unsurprisingly, immense: the Grand Army suffered some 6,600 killed and 21,400 wounded; the Russians probably lost (no one really knows) around 40,000 killed and wounded. As to the result, both sides – predictably – claimed the victory, though most commentators have since declared it a draw. In fact, both sides lost: Kutusov failed to prevent Napoleon from taking Moscow; and Napoleon failed to crush the Russian field army, which lived to fight another day. Baron Lejeune's summing up is particularly apt: 'The terrible struggle, so hotly contested, had won no results at all commensurate with the great losses sustained on both sides.'

As to the niggling question of whether or not Napoleon should have committed the Guard, it remains one of history's tantalizing 'what ifs?' and informed opinion is still divided. Napoleon, anticipating further fighting, wanted to keep his elite corps intact; his own top brass, however, were convinced that the Guard should have been deployed when the Russian left wing began to crack around midday and it is at this point that de Ségur takes up the story.

ABOUT MIDDAY the whole of the French right wing (Ney, Davout and Murat) after annihilating Bagration and half of the Russian line, presented itself on the half-opened flank of the remainder of the hostile army: of which they could see the whole interior, the reserves, the abandoned rear and even the start of a retreat.

But as they felt too weak to throw themselves into that gap, behind a line still formidable, they called aloud for the Guard: the Young Guard! Only let it follow them at a distance! Let it show itself and take its place upon the heights! They themselves will then be sufficient to finish!

General Belliard was sent by them to the Emperor. He declared that from their position, the eye could penetrate without difficulty as far as the road to Mojaisk, in the rear of the Russian army; that they could see a confused crowd of fleeing soldiers and carriages retreating; that it was true there was still a ravine and a thin copse between them but that the Russian generals were so confounded that they had no thought of turning these to any advantage; that in short, only a single effort was required to arrive in the middle of that disorder, seal the enemy's doom and finish the war!

The Emperor, however, still hesitated and ordered that the general go and look again, return and bring him word. Belliard, surprised, went and returned with all speed: he reported that the enemy began to think better of it; that the copse was already lined with his *tirailleurs*; that the opportunity was about to escape; that there was not a moment to be lost, otherwise it would require a second battle to finish the first!

But Bessières, who had just returned from the heights (to which Napoleon had sent him to examine the position of the Russians), asserted that far from being in disorder, they had retreated to a second position where they seemed to be preparing for a fresh attack. The Emperor then said to Belliard that nothing was yet sufficiently plain; that to make him commit his reserves he wanted to see more clearly upon his chessboard (this was his expression, which he repeated several times), at the same time pointing on one side to the old Moscow road, of which Poniatowski had not yet made himself master; on the other, to an attack of the enemy's cavalry in the rear of our left wing; and finally to the Great Redoubt, against which the efforts of Eugène had yet been in vain.

Belliard, in consternation, returned to Murat and informed him of the impossibility of obtaining the Reserve from the Emperor. He said he had found him still seated in the same place with a dejected air, his features sunk and dull-looking; giving orders weakly, in the midst of these dreadful warlike noises, to which he seemed a complete stranger! At this account, which was communicated to Ney, the latter – furious and hurried away by his passionate and impetuous nature – exclaimed, 'Are we then come so far to be satisfied with a field of battle? What business has the Emperor in the rear of the army? There, he is only within reach of reverses and not of victory. Since he will no longer make war himself, since he is no longer the general, as he wishes to be Emperor everywhere, let him return to the Tuileries and leave us to be generals for him!'

Murat was more calm. He recalled having seen the Emperor the day before, as he was riding along observing part of the enemy's line, halt several times, dismount and with his head resting upon a cannon, remain there some time in an attitude of suffering. He knew what a restless night he had passed and that a violent and incessant cough cut short his breathing. Murat guessed that fatigue had shaken his weakened frame and that at that critical moment, the action of his genius was in a sense chained down by his body; which had sunk under the triple load of fatigue, fever and a malady which, probably more than any other, drains the moral and physical strength of its victims.[8]

Shortly after Belliard, Daru, urged by Dumas and particularly by Berthier, said in a low voice to the Emperor that from all sides came the cry that the moment for sending the Guard was now come. To which Napoleon replied, 'And if there should be another battle tomorrow with what is my army to fight?' The minister urged no more, surprised to see for the first time the Emperor putting off till the morrow and postponing his victory.

Barclay, meanwhile, with his right, kept up a most obstinate struggle with Prince Eugène. The latter, immediately after the capture of Borodino, passed the Kolocha in the face of the enemy's Great Redoubt. There, particularly, the Russians had calculated upon the steep heights surrounded by deep and muddy ravines, upon our exhaustion, upon their entrenchments defended by heavy artillery: in short, upon eighty pieces of cannon planted on the borders of these heights, bristling with iron and flames! But these elements – art and nature – all failed them at once: assailed by a first burst of that *French fury*, which has been so celebrated, they saw Morand's soldiers appear suddenly in the midst of them and fled in disorder. Eighteen hundred men of the 30th Regiment, with General Bonnamy at their head, had just made this great effort.

It was there that Fabvier, the aide-de-camp of Marmont, who had arrived but the day before from the heart of Spain, made himself conspicuous: he had thrown himself as a volunteer (and on foot) at the head of the most advanced light troops – as if he had come there to represent the Army of Spain in the midst of the Grand Army – and inspired with that rivalry of glory which makes heroes, wished to be the first in every danger.

He fell wounded in that too famous redoubt, for the triumph was short-lived: the attack wanted co-ordination, either from audacity in the first assailants or caution in those who followed. There was a ravine to pass, the depth of which afforded a protection from the enemy's fire. It is given that many of our troops halted there. Morand, therefore, was left alone in the face of several Russian lines. It was only ten o'clock. Friant, who was on his right, had not yet commenced the attack on Semenovska and on his left, the divisions of Gérard, Broussier and the Italian Guard were not yet in line.

This attack, besides, should not have been made so hastily: the intention had been merely to keep Barclay in check and occupied on that side, the battle having been arranged to begin on the right wing and pivot on the left. This was the Emperor's plan and we know not why he himself altered it at the moment of its execution; for it was he who, on the first discharge of artillery, sent different officers in succession to Eugène, to urge his attack.

The Russians, recovering from their first surprise, rushed forward in all directions. The 30th Regiment, alone against a whole army, ventured to attack it with the bayonet: it was enveloped, crushed and driven out of the redoubt, where it left a third of its men and its intrepid general, pierced through with twenty wounds. Encouraged by their success, the Russians were no longer satisfied with defending themselves but attacked in their turn. Then were seen, united on that single point, all the skill, strength and fury which war can bring forth. The French stood firm for four hours on the slope of that volcano, under the storm of iron and lead which it vomited forth. But to do this required all the skill and determination of Eugène and the idea – so insupportable to long-victorious soldiers – of confessing themselves vanquished.

Each division changed its general several times. The victory went from one to the other, mingling entreaties and reproaches and, above all, reminding them of their former victories. Eugène sent to warn the Emperor of his critical situation but Napoleon replied that he could not assist him; that he must conquer; that he had only to make a greater effort; that the heat of the battle was there. Eugène was rallying all his forces to make a general assault when suddenly his attention was diverted by furious cries coming from his left.

Uvarov, with two regiments of cavalry and some 1,000 Cossacks, had attacked his reserve and thrown it into disarray. He ran thither instantly and seconded by Generals Delzons and Ornano, soon drove away that troop, which was more noisy than formidable: after which he returned to put himself at the head of a decisive attack.

It was about that time that Murat, forced to remain inactive on the plain where he commanded, had sent for the fourth time to his brother-in-law to complain of the losses which his cavalry were sustaining from the Russian troops, protected by the redoubts which were opposed to Prince Eugène. He only requested the cavalry of the Guard, with whose assistance he could turn the entrenched heights and overthrow them, along with the army which defended them.

The Emperor seemed to give his consent and sent in search of Bessières, who commanded these horse guards. Unfortunately they could not find the Marshal who, by his orders, had gone to look at the battle somewhat closer. The Emperor waited nearly an hour without the least impatience or repeating his order and when the Marshal returned, he received him with a pleasant look, heard his report calmly and allowed him to advance as far as he might judge it advisable.

But it was too late. He could no longer flatter himself with the idea of making the whole Russian army prisoners or perhaps of taking entire possession of Russia: the field of battle was all he was likely to gain. He had allowed Kutusov time to reconnoitre his positions and that general had fortified all the points of approach which remained to him, while his cavalry covered the plain.

The Russians had thus, for the third time, renewed their left wing in the face of Ney and Murat. The latter summoned the cavalry of Montbrun, who had been killed.[9] General Caulaincourt[10] succeeded him; he found the aides-de-camp of the unfortunate Montbrun in tears for the loss of their commander: 'Follow me,' he said to them, 'weep not for him but come and avenge his death!'

Murat pointed out to him the enemy's fresh wing: he must break through it and push on as far as the breast of their great battery; when there, during the time that the light cavalry followed up the advantage, he, Caulaincourt, must turn suddenly on the left with his cuirassiers, in order to take in rear that terrible redoubt whose frontal fire was still mowing down the ranks of the Viceroy.

Caulaincourt's reply was, 'You shall see me there presently, alive or dead.' He immediately set off, overthrew all before him and, turning suddenly round on the left with his cuirassiers, was the first to enter the bloody redoubt, when he was struck dead by a musket ball. His conquest was his tomb.

They ran immediately to inform the Emperor of this victory and the loss it had occasioned. The Grand Equerry, brother of the unfortunate general, listened and was at first horrified; but he soon summoned courage against this misfortune and but for the tears which silently coursed down his cheeks, you might have thought that he felt nothing. The Emperor, uttering an exclamation of sorrow, said to him, 'You have heard the news, do you wish to retire?' But as at that moment we were advancing against the enemy, the Grand Equerry made no reply except to thank the Emperor and to refuse.

While this determined charge of the cavalry was executing, Eugène with his infantry was on the point of reaching the mouth of this volcano, when suddenly he saw its fires extinguished, its smoke disappear and its summit glittering with the armour of our cuirassiers. These heights, hitherto Russian, had at last become French: he hastened forward to share and conclude the victory and to strengthen himself in this position.

But the Russians had not yet abandoned it; they returned with greater obstinacy and fury to the attack: successively as they were beaten back by our troops, they were again rallied by their generals and finally the greater part perished at the foot of these works which they themselves had raised.

Fortunately, their last attacking column presented itself towards Semenovska and the Great Redoubt without its artillery, the progress of which had, no doubt, been retarded by the ravines. Belliard had barely time to collect thirty cannon against this infantry. They came almost to the mouths of our guns, which overwhelmed them so completely that they wheeled round and retreated without even being able to deploy. Murat and Belliard then said that if they could have had at that moment 10,000 infantry of the Reserve, their victory would have been decisive; but that, being reduced to their cavalry, they considered themselves

had uttered on the plains of Austerliz: 'One is not always fit for war. I shall be good for six years longer, after which I must lie by.'

Next morning the army remained motionless until noon (or rather it might be said that there was no longer an army but a single vanguard). The rest of the troops were dispersed over the field of battle to carry off the wounded, of whom there were 20,000. They were taken to the great abbey of Kolotskoi, two leagues in the rear.

Larrey, the surgeon-in-chief, had just taken assistants from all the regiments; the ambulances had rejoined but all was insufficient. He has since complained in a printed narrative that no troop had been left him to procure the most necessary articles in the surrounding villages.

The Emperor then rode over the field of battle. Never did one present so horrible an appearance. Everything concurred to make it so: a gloomy sky, a cold rain, a violent wind; houses burnt to ashes, a plain turned topsy-turvy, covered with ruins and rubbish, and in the distance the sad, sombre trees of the north; soldiers roaming about in all directions, hunting for provisions, even in the haversacks of their dead comrades; horrible wounds (for the Russian musket balls are larger than ours), silent bivouacs, no singing or storytelling.

Around the eagles were seen the remaining officers, subalterns and a few soldiers: scarcely enough to protect the colours. Their clothes had been torn in the fury of the combat, blackened with powder and spotted with blood; and yet, in the midst of their rags, their misery and disasters, they had a proud look; and at the sight of the Emperor uttered some shouts of triumph: but they were rare and forced. For in this army, capable at once of reason and enthusiasm, everyone was sensible of the position of all.

French soldiers are not easily deceived. They were astonished to find so many of the enemy killed, so great a number wounded and so few prisoners, there being not 800 of the latter. By the number of these, the extent of a victory had been formerly calculated. But the dead bodies were rather a proof of the courage of the vanquished, than the evidence of a victory. If the rest retreated in such good order, proud and so little discouraged, what signified the gain of a field of battle? In such a vast homeland, would there ever be any want of ground for the Russians to fight on?

As for us, we had already too much and a great deal more than we were able to retain: could that be called conquering it? The long and straight furrow which we had traced with so much difficulty from Kovno, across sands and ashes, would it not close behind us, like that of a vessel on an immense ocean? A few peasants, poorly armed, might easily remove all traces of it.

The Emperor could not value his victory otherwise than by the dead. The ground was strewed to such a degree with Frenchmen, stretched prostrate on the redoubts, that they appeared to belong more to them than to those who remained standing. There seemed to be more victors killed there than there were still living.

Amidst the crowd of corpses which we were obliged to march over in following Napoleon, the foot of a horse encountered a wounded man and extorted from him a last sign of life or suffering. The Emperor, hitherto equally silent with his victory and whose heart was oppressed by the sight of so many victims, gave an exclamation: he felt relieved by uttering cries of indignation and lavishing the attentions of humanity on this unfortunate creature. To pacify him, somebody remarked that it was *only* a Russian; but he replied warmly, 'After a victory there are no enemies, only men.' He then dispersed the officers of his suite in order to succour the wounded, who were heard groaning in every direction.

Great numbers were found at the bottom of the ravines, into which the greater part of our men had been thrown and where many had dragged themselves in order to be better protected from the enemy and the violence of the storm. Some groaningly pronounced the name of their country or their mother. These were the youngest. The elder ones awaited the approach of death: some with a tranquil, others with a contemptuous air, without condescending to implore for mercy or to complain. Others begged us to kill them outright: these unfortunate men were quickly passed by, having neither the useless pity to assist them nor the cruel pity to put an end to their sufferings.

One of these, the most mutilated (one arm and his trunk being all that remained to him), appeared so animated, so full of hope and even gaiety, that an attempt was made to save him. In bearing him along, it was remarked that he complained of pain in the limbs which he no longer possessed: this is a common case with mutilated persons and seems to afford additional evidence that the soul remains entire and that feeling belongs to it alone and not to the body, which can no more feel than it can think.

The Russians were seen dragging themselves along to places where dead bodies were heaped together and offered them a horrible retreat. It has been affirmed by several persons that one of these poor fellows lived for several days in the carcase of a horse, which had been gutted by a shell and the inside of which he gnawed.[13] Some were seen straightening their broken leg by tying the branch of a tree tightly against it, then supporting themselves with another branch and walking in this manner to the next village. Not one of them uttered a groan.

During this melancholy review, the Emperor in vain sought to console himself with a cheering illusion, by ordering a second count of the few prisoners who remained and collecting together some dismounted cannon: from 700–800 prisoners and twenty broken cannon were all the trophies of this imperfect victory.

6 Encircled by a Sea of Fire

> Moscow became the grave of our every hope . . .
>
> Christian Wilhelm von Faber du Faur[1]

Four days after Borodino, Kutusov's despatch reached St Petersburg and Alexander announced the 'victory' to an ecstatic populace. Celebrations, services of thanksgiving and a grand fireworks display followed: Napoleon's arrival in chains was eagerly anticipated. Meanwhile Kutusov was made a field marshal and awarded a small fortune in silver.

Within days, however, the mood changed as the seemingly endless casualty reports flooded in: another 'victory' like Borodino and the Russian army would cease to exist. St Petersburg quickly sobered up as it became clear that the war was far from over; public morale plummeted – even members of the royal family began to talk of parleying with Bonaparte – but Alexander refused to budge: 'We would rather perish under the ruins than make peace with the modern Attila.'[2]

Meanwhile, the 'modern Attila' had reached Mozhaisk, a mere fifty miles or so from Moscow. Laid low by sickness and fatigue, he had temporarily lost the use of his voice and was reduced to scribbling commands on scraps of paper: illegible jottings which only his secretaries could decipher. He was heartened, however, by Kutusov's disappearing act and correctly guessed that the Russians were running away. Perhaps there would be no battle for Moscow after all? Peace, surely, was just around the corner.

By 13 September Kutusov had reached Moscow. He did not –

as was expected – organize the city's defences or prepare for battle: instead, he held a council of war. Declaring that the struggle was for the salvation of the Fatherland and not Moscow alone, Kutusov advocated further retreat and the abandonment of the capital. His priority, he argued, was to save the army, without which Russia would never defeat Napoleon. Moscow, for the time being, must be sacrificed. Backed up by Barclay, Kutusov – who broke down in tears – got his way; and at 2.00 a.m. on the morning of 14 September, the Russian troops, 'in the deepest dejection, tramped through the streets with furled standards and silent bands, many of them, officers and men, sobbing with rage and despair'.[3] *Kutusov, in order to avoid unwanted public attention, quitted the city by back streets.*

Meanwhile, Moscow's governor, Count Feodor Rostopchin, before joining the flood of refugees heading east, issued a series of orders which would incriminate him for ever as history's greatest incendiary: the prisons were to be opened; fires started upon Napoleon's entry into the capital; and all fire-fighting equipment sent out of the city under an escort of dragoons. On leaving the doomed metropolis, he told his son to turn around and take a good look: within hours, he assured him, Moscow would be a heap of ashes.[4]

On the afternoon of 14 September, the Grand Army arrived before Moscow. Weak with hunger, sickness and fatigue, the troops climbed the Hill of Salvation, overlooking the city. According to de Ségur, 'It was two o'clock. The sun caused this great city to glisten with a thousand colours. Struck with astonishment at the sight, they paused, exclaiming "Moscow! Moscow!" Everyone quickened his pace; the troops hurried on in disorder and the whole army, clapping their hands, repeated with joy, "Moscow! Moscow!" just as sailors shout "Land! Land!" at the end of a long and wearisome voyage.' Napoleon, gazing at the longed-for prize, exclaimed, 'There, at last, is that famous city . . . it's about time!'

When Napoleon arrived before the Dorogomilov gate, he followed form and waited for the city to surrender. Murat, meanwhile, was sent ahead to reconnoitre. According to A.H. Atteridge,

'Murat, with no suspicion of what was coming, rode proudly into Moscow. He made his entry at the head of a regiment of Polish hussars . . . few witnessed his triumphal entry. The streets were empty, most of the houses deserted.' Murat's advanced guard arrived as the Russian rearguard was still trying to extricate itself. Miloradovich, the Russian commander on the spot, suggested a deal: Moscow would be surrendered intact, in return for the safe conduct of his men. Murat happily agreed a truce until 7.00 p.m. that evening and made the most of the occasion by fraternizing with the enemy. Atteridge continues, 'The Cossacks gathered round Murat, who evoked their admiration by riding along their line at a headlong gallop, acknowledging their cheers with a wave of his hand.' Resplendent in bright yellow boots, crimson breeches, sky-blue tunic and scarlet pelisse (made of velvet and trimmed with fur) and with a hat festooned with ostrich feathers, Murat – a handsome and charismatic man – made a devastating impression. Relishing the attention, he humoured his awe-struck admirers by giving away his watch: the members of his staff gladly followed suit, believing the war to be as good as over.

Napoleon, meanwhile, was still waiting outside the city. He had expected to be met by a civic deputation, tamely bearing the keys to the capital; but the only Russian to materialize was an old peasant, who sidled up and offered to show the Emperor and his glittering suite the major places of interest. Napoleon exploded with impatience and aides were sent scurrying off to discover what was causing the delay. When they returned with the news that Moscow was deserted the Emperor was incredulous. Deprived of his moment of glory, he decided to postpone his formal entry until the morrow and – with a thunderstorm brewing – put up for the night at a nearby tavern.

Meanwhile, the last Russian troops slipped away in the darkness: 'What pain, what rage to know Moscow is in the hands of Napoleon!' confided the Estonian nobleman Baron Uxkull, to his diary. 'We shall see who's going to pay for the broken china!'[5]

*

NAPOLEON DID not enter Moscow till after dark. He stopped in one of the first houses of the Dorogomilov suburb. There he appointed Marshal Mortier governor of the capital: 'Above all,' he said to him, 'no pillage! For this you shall be answerable to me with your life. Defend Moscow against all, whether friend or foe.'

That night was a gloomy one. Sinister reports followed one upon the heels of another. Some Frenchmen, resident in the country, and even a Russian police officer, came to denounce the fire. The Emperor, alarmed by these accounts, tried in vain to take some rest. He called every moment and had the fatal news repeated to him. He nevertheless entrenched himself in his disbelief till about two in the morning, when he was informed that the blaze had actually broken out. It was at the Exchange, in the centre of the city, in its richest quarter.

He instantly issued orders upon orders. As soon as it was light, he himself hastened to the spot and threatened the Young Guard and Mortier. The Marshal pointed out to him some houses covered with iron; they were closely shut up, still untouched and yet a black smoke was already issuing from them. Brooding, Napoleon entered the Kremlin.

At the sight of this half-Gothic and half-modern palace of the Ruriks and the Romanovs, of their throne still standing, of the cross of the great Ivan and of the finest part of the city, which is overlooked by the Kremlin and which the flames – as yet confined to the bazaar – seemed disposed to spare, his former hopes revived. His ambition was flattered by this conquest. 'At last, then,' he exclaimed, 'I am in Moscow, in the ancient palace of the Tsars, in the Kremlin!' He examined every part of it with pride, curiosity and gratification.

He required a statement of the resources afforded by the city and in this brief moment given to hope, he sent proposals of peace to the Emperor Alexander. A senior officer of the enemy had just been found in the great hospital: he was charged with the delivery of this letter. It was by the baleful light of the flames of the bazaar that Napoleon finished it and the Russian departed. He was to be the bearer of the news of this disaster to his sovereign, whose only answer was this conflagration.

Daylight favoured the efforts of Marshal Mortier to subdue the fire; the incendiaries kept themselves concealed: doubts were entertained of their existence. At length, strict injunctions being issued, order restored and alarm suspended, each took possession of a grand house or sumptuous palace, under the idea of finding there comforts that had been dearly bought by long and excessive privations.

Two officers had taken up their quarters in one of the buildings of the Kremlin.[6] The view hence embraced the north and west of the city. About midnight they were awakened by an extraordinary light. They looked and beheld palaces filled with flames, which at first merely illuminated but presently consumed these elegant structures. They observed that the north wind drove these flames directly towards the Kremlin and became alarmed for the safety of that fortress, in which the flower of the army and its commander rested. They were apprehensive also for the surrounding houses, where our soldiers, attendants and horses, weary and exhausted, were doubtless buried in sleep. Sparks and burning fragments were already flying over the roofs of the Kremlin, when the wind, shifting from north to west, blew them in another direction.

One of these officers, relieved from apprehension respecting his own corps, then composed himself again to sleep, exclaiming, 'Let others look to it now; 'tis no affair of ours.' For such was the unconcern produced by the multiplicity of events and misfortunes, and such the selfishness arising from excessive suffering and fatigue, that they left to each only just enough strength and feeling sufficient for his personal service and preservation.

It was not long before dazzling and brilliant lights again awoke them. They beheld other flames rising precisely in the new direction which the wind had taken towards the

Kremlin and they cursed French imprudence and want of discipline, to which they attributed the disaster. But three times did the wind thus change from north to west; and three times did these hostile fires, as if obstinately bent on the destruction of the imperial quarters, appear eager to follow this new direction.

At this sight a strong suspicion seized their minds. Could the Muscovites, aware of our rash and thoughtless negligence, have conceived the hope of burning with Moscow our soldiers, heavy with wine, fatigue and sleep; or rather, have they dared to imagine that they should involve Napoleon in this catastrophe; that the loss of such a man would be fully equivalent to that of their capital; that it was a result sufficiently important to justify the sacrifice of all Moscow to obtain it; that perhaps Heaven, in order to grant them so signal a victory, had decreed a great sacrifice; and lastly, that so immense a colossus required a not less immense funeral pile?

Whether this was their plan we cannot tell but nothing less than the Emperor's good fortune was required to prevent its being realized. In fact, not only did the Kremlin contain, unknown to us, a magazine of gunpowder but that very night the guards, asleep and carelessly posted, suffered a whole convoy of artillery to enter and draw up under the windows of Napoleon!

It was at this moment that the furious flames were driven from all quarters with the greatest violence towards the Kremlin; for the wind, attracted no doubt by this vast inferno, increased every moment in strength. The flower of the army and the Emperor would have been destroyed if but one of the brands that flew over our heads had alighted on one of the powder wagons. Thus upon each of the sparks that were for several hours floating in the air, depended the fate of the whole army.

At length the day, a gloomy day, appeared: it came to add to the horrors of the scene and to deprive it of its brilliancy. Many of the officers sought refuge in the halls of the palace. The chiefs and Mortier himself, overcome by the fire with which, for thirty-six hours, they had been contending, there dropped down from fatigue and despair.

They said nothing and we accused ourselves. Most of us imagined that want of discipline in our troops and drunkenness had begun the disaster and that the high wind had completed it. We viewed ourselves with a sort of disgust. The cry of horror which all Europe would not fail to set up terrified us. Filled with consternation by so tremendous a catastrophe, we approached each other with downcast looks. It sullied our glory. It deprived us of the fruits of it; threatened our present and our future existence: we were now an army of criminals whom Heaven and the civilized world would severely judge. From these overwhelming thoughts and outbursts of rage against the incendiaries, we were roused only by an eagerness to obtain intelligence: and all the accounts began to accuse the Russians alone of this disaster.

In fact, officers arrived from all quarters and they all agreed. The very first night, that of the 14th, a fire-balloon had settled on the palace of Prince Trubetskoi and consumed it.[7] This was a signal. Fire had been immediately set to the Exchange. Russian police officers had been seen stirring it up with tarred lances. Here howitzer shells, treacherously placed, had discharged themselves in the stoves of several houses and wounded the soldiers who crowded round them.

All had seen hideous-looking men covered with rags and women resembling furies, wandering among these flames and completing a frightful image of the infernal regions.[8] These wretches, intoxicated with wine and the success of their crimes, no longer took any pains to conceal themselves: they succeeded in triumph through the blazing streets. They were caught, armed with torches, industriously striving to spread the flames. It was necessary to strike down their hands with sabres to make them loose their hold. It was said that these *banditti* had been released from prison by the

Russian generals for the purpose of burning Moscow; and that in fact so extreme a resolution could only have been conceived by patriotism and executed by guilt.

Orders were immediately issued to shoot all the incendiaries on the spot.[9] The Old Guard, which exclusively occupied one part of the Kremlin, was under arms; the baggage and the horses ready loaded filled the courts. We were struck dumb with astonishment, fatigue and disappointment on witnessing the destruction of such excellent quarters. Though masters of Moscow, we were forced to go and bivouac without provisions outside its gates.

While our troops were yet struggling with the fire and the army was disputing their prey with the flames, Napoleon, whose sleep none had dared to disturb during the night, was woken by the twofold light of day and of the fire. His first feeling was that of irritation and he would have commanded the devouring element; but he soon paused and yielded to impossibility. Surprised that when he had struck at the heart of an empire, he should find there any other sentiment than submission and terror, he felt himself vanquished and surpassed in determination.

This conquest, for which he had sacrificed everything, was like a phantom which he had pursued and which, at the moment when he imagined he had grasped it, vanished in a mingled mass of smoke and flame. He was then seized with extreme agitation: he seemed to be consumed by the fires which surrounded him. He rose every moment, paced to and fro and again sat down abruptly. He crossed his apartments with quick steps; his sudden and excited gestures betrayed painful uneasiness; he quitted, resumed, and again quitted an urgent occupation to hasten to the windows and watch the progress of the conflagration: 'What a tremendous spectacle! It is their own work! So many palaces! What extraordinary resolution! What men! These are indeed Scythians!'

Between the fire and him there was a broad empty space, then the Moskva and its two quays, and yet the panes of the windows against which he leaned felt burning to the touch; and the constant exertions of sweepers, placed on the iron roofs of the palace, were not sufficient to keep them clear of the numerous flakes of fire which alighted upon them.

At this moment a rumour was spread that the Kremlin was mined: this was confirmed, it was said, by the Russians and by written documents. Some of his attendants were beside themselves with fear; while the army awaited unmoved for what the Emperor and fate should decree: and to this alarm the Emperor replied only with a smile of disbelief.

But he still walked convulsively. He stopped at every window and beheld the terrible, the victorious fire furiously consuming his brilliant conquest; seizing all the bridges, all the avenues to his fortress; enclosing and, as it were, besieging him in it; spreading every moment among the neighbouring houses and reducing him within narrower and narrower limits: confining him at length to the site of the Kremlin alone.

We already breathed nothing but smoke and ashes. Night approached and was about to add darkness to our dangers. The equinoxial gales, in alliance with the Russians, increased in violence. Murat and Prince Eugène hastened to the spot. In company with Berthier they made their way to the Emperor and insisted on removing him from this scene of desolation. All was in vain.

Napoleon, in possession of the palace of the Tsars, was bent on not yielding that conquest even to the flames; when all at once the shout of 'The Kremlin is on fire!' passed from mouth to mouth and roused us from the stupor with which we had been seized. The Emperor went out to ascertain the danger. Twice had the fire communicated to the building in which he was and twice had it been extinguished; but the tower of the arsenal was still burning. A soldier of the police had been found in it. He was brought in and Napoleon caused him to be interrogated in his presence. This man was the incendiary; he had executed his charge at the signal given by his chief. It was evident that everything was devoted to destruction, the ancient and sacred Kremlin itself not excepted.

The gesture of the Emperor betokened disdain and vexation: the wretch was hurried into the first court, where the enraged grenadiers despatched him with their bayonets.

This incident decided Napoleon. He hastily descended the northern staircase and desired to be conducted out of the city to the distance of a league, on the road to St Petersburg, towards the imperial palace of Petrovsky.[10]

But we were encircled by a sea of fire which blocked up all the gates of the citadel and frustrated the first attempts that were made to depart. After some searching, we discovered a postern gate leading between the rocks to the Moskva. It was by this narrow passage that Napoleon, his officers and Guard, escaped from the Kremlin. But what had they gained by this movement? They had approached nearer to the fire and could neither retreat nor remain where they were; and how were they to advance? How force a passage through the waves of this ocean of flame? Those who had crossed the city, stunned by the tempest and blinded by the ashes, could not find their way, since the streets themselves were no longer distinguishable amidst smoke and ruins.[11]

There was no time to be lost. The roaring of the flames around us became every moment more violent. A single narrow street, completely on fire, appeared to be rather the entrance than the exit to this hell. The Emperor rushed on foot without hesitation into this winding passage. He advanced amid the crackling of the flames, the crash of floors and the fall of burning timbers which tumbled around him. These ruins impeded his progress. The flames, which with a wild bellow consumed the buildings between which we were proceeding, spreading beyond the walls, were blown about by the wind and formed an arch over our heads. We walked on a ground of fire, beneath a fiery sky and between two walls of fire. The intense heat burned our eyes, which we were nevertheless obliged to keep open and fixed on the danger. A consuming atmosphere parched our throats and rendered our breathing short and dry; and we were already almost suffocated by the smoke. Our hands were burned, either in attempting to protect our faces from the heat, or in brushing off the sparks which every moment covered and penetrated our clothes.

In this inexpressible distress and when a rapid advance seemed to be our only means of safety, our guide stopped in uncertainty and agitation. Here would probably have ended our adventurous career, had not some pillagers of I Corps recognized the Emperor amidst the whirling flames: they ran up and guided him towards the smoking ruins of a quarter which had been reduced to ashes in the morning.

It was then that we met Davout. This marshal, who had been wounded at the Moskva, had desired to be carried back among the flames to rescue Napoleon or to perish with him. He threw himself into his arms with delight: the Emperor received him kindly but with that composure which in danger he never lost for a moment.

Next morning, 17 September, Napoleon cast his looks towards Moscow, hoping to see that the conflagration had subsided. He beheld it again raging with the utmost violence: the whole city appeared like a vast spout of fire rising in whirling eddies to the sky, which it deeply coloured. Absorbed by this melancholy contemplation, he preserved a long and gloomy silence, which he broke only by the exclamation, 'This forebodes great misfortunes to us!'

The effort which he had made to reach Moscow had expended all his means of warfare. Moscow had been the end of his projects, the aim of his hopes and Moscow was no more! What was now to be done? Here this decisive genius was forced to hesitate. Never had he communicated his most daring projects to the most confidential of his ministers except in the order for their execution: now he was forced to consult and put to the proof the moral and physical energies of those about him.

In doing this, however, he still preserved the same forms. He declared, therefore, that he should march on St Petersburg. This conquest was already marked out on his maps, hitherto so prophetic: orders were even issued to the different corps to hold themselves in readiness. But his decision was only a feint. It was but a better face that he strove to assume or an expedient for diverting his grief for the loss of Moscow, so that Berthier, and more especially Bessières, soon convinced him that he had neither time, provisions, roads, nor a single requisite for so extensive an expedition.

At this moment he was informed that Kutusov, after having fled eastward, had suddenly turned to the south and thrown himself between Moscow and Kaluga. This was an additional motive against the expedition to St Petersburg. It was a threefold reason for marching upon this beaten army for the purpose of extinguishing it: to secure his right flank and his line of operation; to possess himself of Kaluga and Tula, the granary and arsenal of Russia; and lastly, to open a safe, short, new and untouched retreat to Smolensk and Lithuania.

Someone proposed to return upon Prince Wittgenstein[12] and Vitebsk. Napoleon remained undecided between all these plans. That for the conquest of St Petersburg alone flattered him: the others appeared but as ways of retreat; as acknowledgements of error; and whether from pride or policy, which will not admit itself to be in the wrong, he rejected them.

Besides, where was he to halt in case of a retreat? He had so fully calculated on concluding peace at Moscow that he had no winter quarters provided in Lithuania. Kaluga had no temptations for him. Why lay waste fresh provinces? It would be wiser to threaten them and leave the Russians something to lose, in order to induce them to conclude a peace by which they might be preserved. Would it be possible to march to another battle, to fresh conquests, without exposing a line of operation covered with sick, stragglers, wounded and convoys of all sorts? Moscow was the general rallying point: how could it be changed? What other name would have any attraction?

Lastly and above all, how could he relinquish a hope to which he had made so many sacrifices, when he knew that his letter to Alexander had just passed the Russians' advanced posts; when eight days would be sufficient for receiving an answer so ardently desired; when he required that time to rally and reorganize his army, to collect the relics of Moscow (the conflagration of which had but too strongly sanctioned pillage) and to draw his soldiers from that vast infirmary!

Meanwhile, scarcely a third of his army – and of that capital – now existed. But himself and the Kremlin were still standing. His renown was still intact and he persuaded himself that those two great names, Napoleon and Moscow combined, would be sufficient to accomplish everything. He determined, therefore, to return to the Kremlin, which a battalion of his Guard had unfortunately preserved.[13]

The camps which he crossed on his way there presented an extraordinary sight. In the fields, amidst thick and cold mud, large fires were kept up with mahogany furniture, windows and gilded doors. Around these fires, on a litter of damp straw, imperfectly sheltered by a few boards, were seen the soldiers and their officers, splashed all over with mud and blackened with smoke, seated in armchairs or reclined on silken couches. At their feet were spread or heaped cashmere shawls, the rarest furs of Siberia, the gold stuffs of Persia and silver dishes, off which they had nothing to eat but a black dough baked in the ashes and half-broiled and bloody horseflesh. A singular assemblage of abundance and want, of riches and filth, of luxury and wretchedness!

Between the camp and the city were met troops of soldiers dragging along their booty or driving before them – like beasts of burden – Muscovites bending under the weight of the plunder of their capital: for the fire brought to view nearly 20,000 inhabitants, previously unobserved in that immense city. Some of these Muscovites, of both sexes, were well dressed: they were trades people. They came with the wreck of their property to seek refuge at our fires. They lived pell-mell with our soldiers, protected by some and tolerated – or rather scarcely noticed – by others.

About 10,000 of the enemy's troops were in the same predicament. For several days they wandered about among us free and some of them still armed! Our soldiers met these vanquished enemies without animosity and without thinking of making them prisoners: either because they considered the war at an end, from thoughtlessness or pity, or because when not in battle the French delight in having no enemies. They permitted them to share their fires; nay, more, they allowed them to pillage in their company! When some degree of order was restored – or rather, when the officers had organized this marauding as a regular system of forage – the great number of these Russian stragglers then attracted notice. Orders were given to secure them but 7,000–8,000 had already escaped. It was not long before we had to fight them.

On entering the city, the Emperor was struck by a sight still more extraordinary: a few houses scattered among the ruins were all that was left of the mighty Moscow. The smell issuing from this colossus – overthrown, burned, consumed – was horrible. Heaps of ashes and, at intervals, fragments of walls or half-demolished pillars were now the only vestiges that marked the site of the streets.

The suburbs were sprinkled with Russians of both sexes. They flitted like spectres among the ruins, squatted in the gardens, some of them were scratching up the earth in search of vegetables, while others were bickering with the crows for the remains of the dead animals which the army had left behind. Farther on, others again were seen plunging into the Moskva to bring out some of the corn which had been thrown into it by command of Rostopchin and which they devoured without preparation, soured and spoiled as it already was.

Meanwhile the sight of the booty, in such of the camps where everything was yet wanting, inflamed the soldiers whom their duty or stricter officers had kept with their colours. They murmured: why were they to be kept back? Why were they to perish by famine and want when everything was within their reach? Was it right to allow the enemy's fires to destroy what might be saved? Why was such respect to be paid to the flames? They added that, as the inhabitants of Moscow had not only abandoned but even endeavoured utterly to destroy it, all that they could save would be fairly gained; that the remains of that city, like the relics of the arms of the conquered, belonged by right to the victors, as the Muscovites had turned their capital into a vast machine of war, for the purpose of annihilating us.

The best principled and the best disciplined were those who argued thus and it was impossible to reply satisfactorily to them. Exaggerated scruples, however, at first preventing the issuing of orders for pillage, it was permitted, unrestrained by regulations. Then it was, that urged by the most imperious wants, all hurried to share the spoil, the soldiers of the elite and even officers. Their chiefs were obliged to shut their eyes: only such guards as were absolutely indispensable remained with the eagles.

The Emperor saw his whole army dispersed over the city. His progress was obstructed by a long line of marauders going in quest of booty or returning with it; by riotous gangs of soldiers grouped around the entrance of cellars or the doors of palaces, shops and churches, which the fire had nearly reached and which they were endeavouring to break into.

His steps were impeded by the fragments of furniture of every kind which had been thrown out of the windows to save it from the flames or by plunder which had been abandoned on a whim for some other booty: for such is the way with soldiers; they are incessantly beginning their fortune afresh, taking everything without discrimination, loading themselves beyond measure, as if they could carry all they find, then, after they have gone a few steps, forced by fatigue to throw away successively the greatest part of their burden.

The roads were obstructed with it; the open places, like the camps, were turned into markets, where everyone resorted to exchange superfluities for necessaries. There the rarest articles, the value of which was not known to their possessors, were sold at a low price; others, of false appearance, were purchased at a price far beyond their worth. Gold, from being more portable, was bought at an immense loss with silver, which the knapsacks were incapable of holding. Everywhere soldiers were seen seated on bales of merchandise, on heaps of sugar and coffee, amidst wines and the most exquisite liqueurs, which they were offering in exchange for a morsel of bread. Many, in an intoxication aggravated by starvation, had fallen near the flames, which reached them and put an end to their lives.

Most of the houses and palaces which had escaped the fire served as quarters for the officers: all of them beheld with pain this vast destruction and the pillage which was its necessary consequence. Some of our men belonging to the elite were reproached with taking too much pleasure in collecting what they were able to save from the flames; but their number was so few that they were mentioned by name. In these spirited men, war was a passion which presupposed the existence of others. It was not greed, for they did not hoard: they spent lavishly what they picked up, taking in order to give, believing that one hand washed the other and that they paid for everything with the danger.

Besides, on such an occasion, there is scarcely any distinction to be made, unless in the motive: some took with regret, others with pleasure and all from necessity. Amidst wealth which had ceased to belong to any individual, ready to be consumed or to be buried in ashes, we were placed in a quite novel situation, where right and wrong were confused and for which no rule was laid down. The most refined, either from principle or because they were richer than others, bought of the soldiers the provisions and clothes which they required; some sent agents to plunder for them; and the most needy were forced to help themselves with their own hands.[14]

It was amidst this confusion that Napoleon again entered Moscow. He had allowed this pillage, hoping that his army, scattered over the ruins, would not ransack them in vain. But when he learned that the disorder increased; that the Old Guard itself was seduced; that the Russian peasants, who at length were enticed thither with provisions (for which he caused them to be liberally paid for the purpose of inducing others to come), were robbed of the rations which they brought us by our famished soldiers; when he was informed that the different corps, destitute of everything, were ready to fight for the relics of Moscow; that finally, all the existing resources were wasted by this irregular pillage; he then issued strict orders and forbade his Guard to leave their quarters. The churches, in which our cavalry sheltered themselves, were restored to the Greek worship. The business of plunder was ordered to be taken in turn by the corps like any other duty and directions were at length given for securing the Russian stragglers.

But it was too late: these soldiers had fled; the affrighted peasants returned no more; and great quantities of provisions were spoiled. The French army have sometimes fallen into this fault but on the present occasion the fire pleads their excuse: no time was to be lost in anticipating the flames. It is, however, a remarkable fact that, at the first command, perfect order was restored.

Some writers – even French ones – have ransacked these ruins in search of outrages which might have been committed in them. There were very few. Most of our men behaved generously, considering the small number of inhabitants and the great number of enemies that they met with. But if in the first moments of pillage some excesses were committed, ought this to appear surprising in an army exasperated by such urgent needs, such severe sufferings and composed of so many different nations?

Misfortunes have since overwhelmed these warriors; reproaches have, as is always the case, been raised against them. Who can be ignorant that such disorders have always been the bad side of great wars, the inglorious part of glory; that the renown of conquerors casts its shadow like everything else in this world? Does there exist a creature ever so small, on which every side of the sun, great as it is, can shine at once? It is therefore a law of nature that great bodies have great shadows.

Moreover, people have been too much astonished at the virtues as well as the vices of that army. They were the virtues of the moment, the vices of the age and for that very reason, the former were less praiseworthy and the latter less reprehensible, inasmuch as they were, if I may so express myself, prescribed by example and circumstance.

7 Never to Recede, Never Retreat

> Matters had reached such a point that a sort of tacit armistice was in operation with the advanced guard, and the enemy profited by this to lull our suspicions.
>
> Armand de Caulaincourt

By 20 September the great fire had been extinguished: doused by autumnal rains, Moscow was left a blackened heap of hissing, smoking ruins. Enough remained, however, to provide shelter for the troops. Some, like Sergeant Bourgogne of the Guard, found themselves in a more than agreeable situation: 'We took possession of our quarters in a fine street hitherto preserved from fire, not far from the first enclosure of the Kremlin. Our company had a large café assigned to it; one of the rooms contained two billiard tables . . . We found a great quantity of wine in the cellars and some Jamaica rum, also a large cellar filled with barrels of excellent beer, packed in ice to keep it fresh during the summer.'

Meanwhile, as de Ségur notes, 'It seemed as though the war was finished for our emperor and that he was only waiting for an answer from Petersburg. He nourished his hopes with the recollections of Tilsit and Erfurt. Was it possible that at Moscow he should have less ascendancy over Alexander? Then, like men who have long been favourites of fortune, what he ardently wished he confidently expected.'

Although Napoleon has been severely criticized for lingering at Moscow, it must be stated that – generally speaking – Alexander was expected to cave in. The Tsar, however, remained resolute in his determination to resist the invader: furthermore, he had found religion. Guided by the scriptures and with a growing fascination with mysticism, Alexander was now a man with a mission: 'Let us vow redoubled courage and perseverance!' de Ségur has him saying. 'The enemy is in deserted Moscow as in a tomb, without means of domination or even of existence. He entered Russia with 300,000 men of all countries, without union or any national or religious bond; he has lost half of them by the sword, famine and desertion: he has but the wreck of his army at Moscow. He is in the heart of Russia and not a single Russian is at his feet!' Far from caving in, Alexander had become the messianic leader of all those dedicated to Napoleon's downfall.

As for Kutusov, after quitting Moscow, he marched his troops eastwards for a couple of days but then, screening his movements behind a horde of Cossacks, he swung south and then west. By 2 October, he was firmly entrenched behind the River Nara, at Tarutino, forty-five miles south-west of Moscow. It was an excellent site. Not only did he now threaten Napoleon's exposed lines of communication, he also blocked the road to Kaluga and the fertile lands thereabouts. Murat and the advanced guard stumbled upon the Russian outposts on 4 October but, finding their position too strong to attack, pulled back a couple of miles to Vinkovo. Both sides settled down to a waiting game: time, however, was on Kutusov's side.

Back in Moscow, the soldiers of the Grand Army discovered that they were not alone, the fire having flushed out a bizarre assortment of individuals: wounded Russian soldiers, criminals, prostitutes, lunatics and a great many foreign nationals who, having decided to throw in their lot with the advancing French, had been hiding from the wrath of the retreating Russians. The scene resembled a sort of macabre Mardi Gras, with all classes mingling freely in a drunken fancy dress parade through the smouldering ruins in search of plunder.

Meanwhile, Alexander's silence was becoming a source of embarrassment to Napoleon and he began to look for distractions: he would build a theatre and send for actors from France and singers from Italy! He would ransack the city for trophies to take back to Paris! He would prepare to march on St Petersburg! In the event he did very little except read novels and play cards with his stepson, Eugène. Ostensibly the most powerful man in the world, he could take no action which did not betray his weakness: everything depended upon Alexander; but Alexander was only taking orders from God.

As September gave way to October, it became clear that Alexander was not going to play ball. Napoleon's big gamble – that the fall of Moscow would either topple his errant protégé or bring him to heel – had not paid off. Sitting out winter at Moscow was not an option: the army would eventually run out of supplies while Kutusov, reinforced by new levies, would launch a massive counter-offensive. Napoleon had convinced himself that Moscow was a political prize: it was not. Moscow was merely a burnt-out city in the middle of a hostile nation itching for revenge. There was only one course of action left – retreat – but this he could not do. Not yet. Surely he was due one more throw of the dice? He decided, therefore, to contact Alexander yet again.

At first, Napoleon approached Armand de Caulaincourt, his grand equerry and ex-ambassador to St Petersburg, to be his messenger-boy. Caulaincourt refused. A critic of the campaign from the start, he astutely pointed out that by sending another missive to St Petersburg, Napoleon was simply highlighting 'the embarrassment of our situation'. Napoleon then turned to another ex-diplomat, General Jacques-Alexandre Lauriston, and on 5 October this officer duly set off for Kutusov's headquarters. According to de Ségur, Napoleon's last words to Lauriston were: 'I want peace, I must have peace, I absolutely will have peace – only save my honour!'

Later that day, Lauriston arrived at the Russian outposts. He was kept waiting until midnight for an audience with Kutusov, only to be denied a safe passage to St Petersburg. Instead, Napoleon's message would be carried by Prince Volkonsky, Alexander's aide-de-camp, and a ceasefire observed until his return with the Tsar's reply. Kutusov, aware of Napoleon's predicament, took full advantage of this delay to lull the French into a false sense of security. Lauriston and Murat (who was especially courted) were given every impression that the Russians were war-weary and on the brink of collapse: meanwhile, reinforcements poured into Tarutino and Kutusov quietly prepared his coming offensive. As for Napoleon's overture, upon reading it Alexander exclaimed, 'Peace? My campaign is just beginning!'[1] *He did not bother to pen a reply and Kutusov – despite his cunning duplicity – was reprimanded for parleying with the enemy.*

Napoleon was delighted with the result of Lauriston's mission and overjoyed when he heard of the apparent dejection and defeatism of Kutusov's officers: 'Credulous from hope, perhaps from despair,' writes de Ségur, 'he was eager to escape from the inward feeling which oppressed him.' The same could also be said of Murat, sitting with his puny advanced guard before the whole Russian army, in a dangerous and isolated spot forty miles from Moscow. According to Baron Lejeune: 'Our one hope was that the enemy would sue for peace. The Russians took pains to encourage this hope and the leaders of the advanced guard, ready to believe what they so ardently wished, were far too easily deceived.'

THIS ARMISTICE was a singular one. If either party wished to break it, three hours' notice was to be sufficient. It was confined to the fronts of the two camps but did not extend to their flanks. Such at least was the interpretation put upon it by the Russians. We could not bring up a convoy or send out a foraging party without fighting; so that the war continued everywhere, except where it could be favourable to us.

In the first of the subsequent days, Murat took it into his head to show himself at the enemy's advanced posts. There he was gratified by the notice which his fine person, his reputation for bravery and his rank brought him. The Russian officers took good care not to displease him: they were profuse of all the marks of respect calculated to strengthen his illusion. He could give his orders to their *vedettes*, just as he did to the French. If he took a fancy to any part of the ground which they occupied, they cheerfully gave it up to him.

Some Cossack chiefs even went so far as to affect devotion and to tell him that they had ceased to acknowledge any other emperor but him who reigned at Moscow. Murat believed for a moment that they would no longer fight against him. He went even farther: Napoleon was heard to exclaim while reading his letters, 'Murat, King of the Cossacks! What madness!' The most extravagant ideas were conceived by men on whom fortune had lavished all sorts of favours.

As for the Emperor, who was not so easily deceived, he had but a few moments of joy. He soon complained that an annoying warfare of partisans hovered around him; that notwithstanding all these peaceful demonstrations, he was aware that troops of Cossacks were prowling on his flanks and in his rear. Had not 150 dragoons of his Old Guard been surprised and routed by a number of these barbarians? And this two days after the armistice, on the road to Mozhaisk, that by which the army communicated with its magazines, its reinforcements, its depots and himself with Europe!

In fact, two convoys had just fallen into the enemy's hands on that road: one through the negligence of its commander, who put an end to his life in despair; and the other through the cowardice of an officer, who was about to be punished when the retreat commenced (to the destruction of the army he owed his own escape).

Our soldiers – and especially our cavalry – were obliged every morning to go a great distance in search of provisions for the evening and the next day; and as the environs of Moscow and Vinkovo became gradually more and more drained, they were daily required to extend their excursions. Both men and horses returned worn out with fatigue: that is to say, such of them as returned at all, for we had to fight for every bushel of rye and every truss of forage. It was a series of incessant surprises and skirmishes and of continual losses. The peasantry took a part in it. They punished with death such of their number as the prospect of gain had brought to our camp with provisions. Others set fire to their own villages to drive our foragers out of them and to give them up to the Cossacks, whom they had previously summoned and who kept us there in a state of siege.

It was the peasantry also who took Vereia, a town in the neighbourhood of Moscow. One of their priests is said to have planned and executed this *coup-de-main*. He armed the inhabitants, obtained some troops from Kutusov, then on 10 October before daybreak, he caused the signal of a false attack to be given in one quarter, while in another he himself made an attack upon our palisades, destroyed them, penetrated into the town, and put the whole garrison to the sword.[2]

Thus the war was everywhere: in our front, on our flanks and in our rear. Our army was weakening and the enemy becoming daily more enterprising. This conquest was destined to fare like many others, which are won in the mass and lost in detail.

Murat himself at length grew uneasy. In these daily skirmishes he had seen half his cavalry melt away. At the advanced posts, the Russian officers on meeting with ours – either from vanity or military frankness carried to indiscretion – exaggerated the disasters which threatened us. They were particularly astonished at our confidence on the approach of their mighty winter, which was their natural and most formidable ally and which they expected every moment. They pitied us and urged us to fly: 'In a fortnight,' they said, 'your nails will drop off and your weapons will fall from your benumbed and half-dead fingers.'

The language of some of the Cossack chiefs was also remarkable. They asked our officers if they had not, in their own country, corn enough, air enough, graves enough: in short, room enough to live and die? Why then did they come so far from home to throw away their lives and fatten a foreign soil with their blood?

The Emperor was not ignorant of these warnings but he would not suffer his resolution to be shaken by them. The uneasiness which had again seized him betrayed itself in angry orders. It was then that he caused the churches of the Kremlin to be stripped of everything that could serve for a trophy to the Grand Army. These objects, devoted to destruction by the Russians themselves, belonged, he said, to the conquerors by the double right conferred by victory and the fire.

It required long efforts to remove the gigantic cross from the steeple of Ivan the Great, to the possession of which the Russians attached the salvation of their empire. The Emperor determined that it should adorn the dome of the Invalides at Paris. During the work it was noticed that a great number of ravens kept flying round this cross and that Napoleon, weary of their hoarse croaking, exclaimed that it seemed as if these flocks of ill-omened birds meant to defend it. We cannot pretend to tell all that he thought but it is well known that he was susceptible to every kind of presentiment.

His daily excursions, always illumined by a brilliant sun, in which he strove to see – and to make others recognize – his star, did not amuse him. To the sullen silence of inanimate Moscow was added that of the surrounding deserts and the still more menacing silence of Alexander. It was not the faint footsteps of our soldiers, wandering in this vast sepulchre, that could rouse our emperor from his reverie and snatch him from his painful recollections and still more painful anticipations.

His nights in particular became irksome to him. He passed part of them with Count Daru. It was only then that he admitted the danger of his situation: from Vilna to Moscow what submission, what point of support, rest or retreat, marked his power? It was a vast, bare and forsaken field of battle, in which his diminished army was imperceptible, insulated, and, as it were, cast adrift in the horrors of an immeasurable void. In this country of foreign manners and religion, he had not conquered a single individual: he was, in fact, master only of the ground on which he stood. That which he had just quitted and left behind him was no more his than that which he had not yet reached. Insufficient for these great deserts, he was lost in their immense space.

He then reviewed the different resolutions of which he still had the choice. People imagined, he said, that he had nothing to do but march, without considering that it would take a month to refit his army and evacuate his hospitals; that if he relinquished his wounded, the Cossacks would celebrate daily triumphs over his sick and stragglers. He would appear to fly. All Europe would resound with the report! Europe, which envied him, which was seeking a rival under whom to rally, would imagine that it had found one in Alexander.

Then appreciating all the power which he derived from the notion of his infallibility, he trembled at the idea of giving it the first blow. What a frightful succession of dangerous wars should date from his first retrograde step! Let not then his inactivity be censured! 'As if I did not know,' added he, 'that from a military point of view Moscow is of no value! But Moscow is not a military position, it is a political position. People look upon me as a general here, when in fact I am merely Emperor!' He then exclaimed that in political measures we ought never to recede, never retreat, never admit ourselves to be wrong, as it lessened our prestige; that even when in error, we ought to persist in order to have the appearance of being in the right.

His distress meanwhile increased. He knew that he must not depend upon the Prussian army. An intimation from too authentic a source, addressed to Berthier, extinguished his confidence in the support of the Austrians.[3] He was aware that Kutusov was only trifling with him but he had so far committed himself that he could neither advance nor stay where he was; nor retreat, nor fight with honour and success. Thus alternately encouraged and held back by all that can decide and dissuade, he remained upon those ashes, almost ceasing to hope but continuing to desire.

The letter of which Lauriston was the bearer had been despatched on 6 October; the answer to it could scarcely arrive before the 20th; and yet in spite of so many threatening demonstrations, the pride, policy and perhaps the health of Napoleon induced him to pursue the worst of all courses: that of waiting for an answer and of trusting to time, which was destroying him. But in this critical military position, which by its complication with a political position became the most delicate which ever existed, it was hardly to be expected that a character which had hitherto been so great from its unshaken constancy would make a speedy renunciation of the object which he had proposed to himself ever since he left Vitebsk.

Napoleon, however, was completely aware of his situation. To him everything seemed lost if he retreated in the face of astonished Europe and everything saved if he could yet overcome Alexander in determination. He appreciated but too well the means that were left him to shake the constancy of his rival; he knew that the number of effective troops, his situation, the season – in short, everything – would become daily more and more unfavourable to him; but he reckoned upon that force of illusion which his renown gave to him. Hitherto, that had borrowed for him a real and never-failing strength. He endeavoured, therefore, to keep up by plausible arguments the confidence of his people and perhaps also the faint hope that was yet left to himself.

Moscow, empty of inhabitants, no longer furnished him with anything to lay hold of. 'It is no doubt a misfortune,' said he, 'but this misfortune is not without advantage. They have left us nothing but ruins, but at least we are quiet among them. Millions have no doubt slipped through our hands but how many thousand millions is Russia losing! Her commerce is ruined for a century to come. The nation is thrown back fifty years: this, of itself, is an important result. When the first moment of enthusiasm is passed, this reflection will fill them with consternation.' The conclusion which he drew was that so violent a shock would convulse the throne of Alexander and force that prince to sue for peace.

Murat, nevertheless, transmitted to him tidings of the distressed state of his advanced guard. They terrified Berthier but Napoleon sent for the officer who brought them, pressed him with his own questions, overawed him with his looks and browbeat him with his disbelief: the statements of Murat's envoy lost much of their assurance. Napoleon took advantage of his hesitation to keep up the hopes of Berthier and to persuade him that matters were not yet so very urgent; and he sent back the officer to Murat's camp with the opinion (which he would no doubt propagate) that the Emperor was immovable; that he doubtless had his reasons for thus persisting; and that they must all redouble their exertions. And really, for several more days, the pride of an unshaken face was the only means by which he could keep up the prospect of negotiation.

Meanwhile, the attitude of his army seconded his wishes. Most of the officers persevered in their confidence. The common soldiers who, seeing their whole lives in the present moment and expecting but little from the future, concerned themselves but little about it, and retained their thoughtlessness: the most valuable of their qualities. The rewards, however, which the Emperor bestowed profusely upon them in the daily reviews, were received with a muted joy, mingled with some degree of dejection. The vacant places that were about to be filled up were yet dyed with blood.

On the other hand, ever since they had left Vilna, many of them had thrown away their winter garments that they might load themselves with provisions. Their shoes were worn out by the length of the march and the rest of their clothes by the actions in which they had been engaged; but in spite of all, their attitude was still proud. They carefully concealed their wretched plight from the notice of the Emperor and appeared before him with their weapons bright and in the best order. In this first court of the palace of the Tsars, 800 leagues from their resources and after so many battles and bivouacs, they were anxious to appear still clean, ready and smart: for herein consists the pride of the soldier; here they piqued themselves upon it the more on account of the difficulty, in order to surprise and because man prides himself on everything that requires extraordinary effort.

The Emperor passively affected to know no better, catching at everything to keep up his hopes, when all at once the first snows fell. With them fell all the illusions with which he had endeavoured to surround himself. From that moment he thought of nothing but retreat: without, however, pronouncing the word and no positive order for it could be obtained from him. He merely said that in twenty days the army must be in winter quarters and he urged the departure of the wounded. On this, as on other occasions, he would not consent to the voluntary concession of anything, however trifling. There was a deficiency of horses for his artillery – now too numerous for an army so reduced – but he flew into a passion at the proposal to leave part of it in Moscow: 'No, the enemy would make a trophy of it!' and he insisted that everything should go along with him.

In this barren country, he gave orders for the purchase of 20,000 horses; and he expected forage for two months to be provided on a tract where the most distant excursions were not sufficient for the supply of the passing day. Some of his officers were astonished to hear orders which it was impossible to execute; but we have already seen that he sometimes issued such orders to deceive his enemies and most frequently to indicate to his own troops the extent of his necessities and the exertions which they ought to make for the purpose of supplying them.

His distress manifested itself only in some outbursts of ill humour. It was in the morning at his *levée*. There, amid the assembled chiefs, in whose anxious looks he imagined he could read disapproval, he seemed desirous to awe them by the severity of his attitude, by his sharp tongue and his abrupt language. From the paleness of his face, it was evident that Truth, whose best time for obtaining a hearing is in the darkness of night, had oppressed him grievously by her presence and tired him with her unwelcome light. Sometimes, on these occasions, his bursting heart would overflow and pour forth his sorrows around him by moments of impatience; but so far from lightening his afflictions, he aggravated them by those acts of injustice for which he reproached himself and which he was afterwards anxious to repair.

It was to Count Daru alone that he unburdened himself frankly. He said he should march upon Kutusov, crush or drive him back and then turn suddenly towards Smolensk. Daru, who had before approved this course, replied that it was now too late; that the Russian army was reinforced, his own weakened, his victory forgotten; that the moment his troops should turn their faces towards France, they would slip away from him by degrees; that each soldier, laden with booty, would try to get the start of the army for the purpose of selling it in France. 'What, then, is to be done?' exclaimed the Emperor. 'Remain here,' replied Daru, 'make one vast entrenched camp of Moscow and pass the winter in it. Here we might stay till the return of spring, when our reinforcements and all Lithuania in arms should come to relieve us and complete the conquest.'

After listening to this proposal the Emperor was for some time silent and thoughtful; he then replied, 'This is a lion's counsel! But what would Paris say? What would they do there? What have they been doing for the last three weeks that they have not heard from me? Who knows what would be the effect of a suspension of communications for six months? No: France would not accustom itself to my absence and Prussia and Austria would take advantage of it.'

Still Napoleon could not make up his mind either to stay or to depart. Overcome in this struggle of obstinacy, he deferred from day to day the declaration of his defeat. Amid the dreadful storm of men and elements which was gathering round him, his ministers and his aides saw him pass whole days in discussing the merits of some new verses which he had received or the regulations for the Comédie Française at Paris, which he took three evenings to finish. As they were acquainted with his deep anxiety, they admired the strength of his mind and the facility with which he could take off or fix the whole force of his attention on whatever he pleased.

It was merely remarked that he prolonged his meals, which had hitherto been simple and short. He would then pass whole hours, half reclined, as if lifeless, and awaiting with a novel in his hand the catastrophe of his terrible history. On beholding this obstinate and inflexible character, struggling with impossibility, his officers would then observe to one another that, having arrived at the summit of his glory, he no doubt foresaw that from his first retrograde step would date its decline; that for this reason he continued immovable, clinging to and lingering a few moments longer on this peak.

Kutusov, meanwhile, was gaining the time which we were losing. His letters to Alexander described his army as being in the midst of plenty; his recruits arriving from all quarters and being trained; his wounded recovering in the bosom of their families; the whole of the peasantry on the march. His partisans were every day bringing in some hundreds of prisoners. Everything concurred to destroy the enemy's army and to strengthen his own; to serve him and to betray us: in a word, the campaign – which was over for us – was but just about to begin for them.

Kutusov neglected no advantage. He made his camp ring with the news of the victory of Salamanca: 'The French,' said he, 'are expelled from Madrid. The hand of the Most High presses heavily upon Napoleon. Moscow will be his prison, his grave and that of his army. We shall soon take France in Russia!' It was in such language that the Russian general addressed his troops and his emperor; but nevertheless, he still kept up appearances with Murat. At once bold and crafty, he contrived slowly to prepare a sudden and impetuous warfare and to cover his plans for our destruction with demonstrations of kindness and honeyed words.

At length, after several days of illusion, the charm was dispelled. A Cossack completely dissolved it. This barbarian shot at Murat, at the moment when that prince came as usual to show himself at the advanced posts. Highly exasperated, Murat immediately declared to Miloradovich[4] that an armistice which was incessantly violated was at an end and that thenceforward each must look to himself.

At the same time he informed the Emperor that the wooded country on his left might favour the enemy's attempts to turn his flank and rear; that his first line, being backed against a ravine, might be driven into it; that, in short, the position which he occupied in advance of a defile was dangerous and made a retrograde movement absolutely necessary. But Napoleon would not consent to this step, though he had first pointed out Voronovo as a more secure position. In this war, still in his view more political than military, he dreaded above all the appearance of retreating. He preferred risking everything.

However, on 13 October, he sent back Lauriston to Murat, to examine the position of the vanguard. As to the Emperor, either from a tenacious adherence to his first hope, or that any movement which might be construed as a preparation for retreat equally shocked his pride and policy, a singular negligence was remarked in his arrangements for departure. He nevertheless thought of it, for that very day he traced his plan of retreat by Voloklamsk, Zubzov, and Bieloi, on Vitebsk. A moment afterwards he dictated another on Smolensk. Junot received orders to burn, on the 21st, at Kolotskoi, all the muskets of the wounded and to blow up the ammunition wagons. D'Hilliers was to occupy Elnia and to form magazines at that place. It was not until the 17th, at Moscow, that Berthier thought of causing leather to be distributed for the first time among the troops.[5]

Napoleon, meanwhile, rallied his *corps d'armée*: the reviews which he held in the Kremlin were more frequent; he formed all the dismounted cavalry into battalions and lavishly distributed rewards; the division of Claparède, the trophies and all the wounded that could be removed, set out for Mozhaisk, the rest were collected in the great Foundling Hospital. The French surgeons were placed there and the Russian wounded, intermixed with ours, were intended to serve them for a safeguard.

But it was too late. Amid these preparations and at the moment when Napoleon was reviewing Ney's divisions in the first court of the Kremlin, a report was all at once circulated around him that the sound of cannon was heard towards Vinkovo. It was some time before anyone dare inform him of the circumstance: some from disbelief or uncertainty (and dreading the first move of his impatience), others from weakness, hesitating to provoke a terrible alarm or apprehensive of being sent to verify this assertion and of exposing themselves to a fatiguing journey.

Duroc, at length, took courage to tell him. The Emperor was at first agitated but, quickly recovering himself, he continued the review. An aide-de-camp, young Beranger, arrived shortly after with the news that Murat's first line had been surprised and overthrown, his left turned by favour of the woods, his flank attacked, his retreat cut off; that twelve pieces of cannon, twenty ammunition wagons and thirty wagons belonging to the train were taken, two generals killed, 3,000–4,000 men lost as well as the baggage; and lastly, that Murat was wounded. He had not been able to rescue the survivors of his advanced guard from the enemy except by repeatedly charging their numerous troops, which already occupied the high road in his rear, his only retreat.[6]

Our honour, however, was saved. The attack in front,

directed by Kutusov, was feeble; Poniatowski, at some leagues' distance on the right, made a glorious resistance; Murat and his *carabinières*, by supernatural exertions, checked Bagavout, who was ready to penetrate our left flank, and restored the fortune of the day. Claparède and Latour-Maubourg cleared the defile of Spaskaplia, two leagues in the rear of our line, which was already occupied by Platov. Two Russian generals were killed and others wounded: the loss of the enemy was considerable but the advantage of the attack, our cannon, our position – the victory, in short – were theirs.[7]

As for Murat, he no longer had an advanced guard. The armistice had destroyed half the remnant of his cavalry: this engagement finished it. The survivors, emaciated with hunger, were so few as scarcely to furnish a charge. Thus had the war recommenced. It was now 18 October.

At these tidings Napoleon recovered the fire of his youth. A thousand orders, general and particular, all differing, yet all in unison and all necessary, burst at once from his impetuous genius. Night had not yet arrived and the whole army was already in motion for Voronovo: Broussier was sent in the direction of Fominskoië and Poniatowski towards Medyn. The Emperor himself quitted Moscow before daylight on 19 October: 'Let us march on Kaluga,' said he, 'and woe be to those whom I meet with by the way!'

8 An Impetuous Attack

> After several days' march, our troops, which, since Murat had rejoined them, amounted still to over 100,000 men, found themselves in presence of the Russian army, occupying the little town of Maloyaroslavets . . .
>
> Baron de Marbot

Leaving behind a reluctant Marshal Mortier with 183,000 pounds of gunpowder and instructions to blow up the Kremlin,[1] *Napoleon quit Moscow on 19 October. His army, although to some extent rested by its sojourn, was a mere shadow of its former self: 'In this column of 140,000 men and 50,000 horses of all kinds,' wrote de Ségur, '100,000 combatants marching at the head with their knapsacks, their arms, upwards of 550 pieces of cannon and 2,000 artillery wagons, still exhibited a formidable appearance, worthy of soldiers who had conquered the world. But the rest, in an alarming proportion, resembled a horde of Tartars after a successful invasion.' Clothed in rags, their ranks swollen by civilian hangers-on, de Ségur describes the column as 'a caravan, a wandering nation or rather one of those armies of antiquity returning loaded with slaves and spoil after a great devastation'. Napoleon himself had difficulty making his way through the throng, consisting of a 'multitude of men of all nations', pulling, pushing or dragging an assortment of vehicles loaded with booty and 'swearing in every language'. Thus, in the words of Edward Foord, 'Ill-clothed, ill-supplied, deficient in transport but laden with useless plunder, encumbered with sick, wounded and helpless non-combatants and with demoralisation latent everywhere, the Grande Armée set out from Napoleon's Farthest to fight its way home.'*

Despite the tough talk, Napoleon was not seeking another encounter with Kutusov. His aim was to reach the richly provisioned town of Kaluga – some 100 miles to the south – in order to refit his army and march it back to Poland through fertile country untouched by the hand of war. Although he set off down the old Kaluga road, in the direction of Kutusov's camp at Tarutino, Napoleon quit this route at Troitskoië on 20 October and, cutting across country, joined the new Kaluga road at Fominskoië on the 22nd: Kutusov was to be quietly bypassed; left dozing at Tarutino, waiting for an attack which would never come. Napoleon's star, however, was on the wane and before he could outflank his enemy, the heavens burst, turning roads into mires, and instead of slipping southwards unnoticed, the Grand Army sank in the slough. There would be no quick getaway.

Twenty miles to the south-east, Kutusov – as yet unaware of Napoleon's movements – began to receive reports from Cossack patrols of a French column near Fominskoië. Believing it to be a stray foraging party, Kutusov despatched General Dmitri Docturov[2] *with 15,000 men to investigate. That night, however, he was awoken with the eagerly awaited news of Napoleon's departure from the capital.*[3] *The old campaigner thanked the icon of Christ hanging on his wall for Moscow's deliverance: unaware of Napoleon's attempts to outflank him, he braced himself for a second Battle of Vinkovo.*

The following afternoon, Docturov was approaching Fominskoië when his scouts reported a heavy French column on the move. The General halted. More reports followed, indicating strong enemy formations. Docturov decided to lie low. Then, towards evening, a French prisoner was brought in and betrayed the momentous news: Napoleon had left Moscow and was marching south down the new Kaluga road. Docturov had almost walked straight into the Grand Army's left flank. Keeping his head – his presence having gone undetected by the French – Docturov sent word flying back to Kutusov, before making a dash for the crucial river crossing of Maloyaroslavets, some fifteen miles to the south.

This small, timber-built town was perched high above the River Luzha. A bridge stood at its northern end, then, continuing southwards, came a steep bank, followed by a church, a cemetery, and the bulk of the town, which was overlooked by a plateau on its southern approaches. If only Docturov could destroy the bridge before the Grand Army appeared, Napoleon's advance would be held up, giving Kutusov time to mobilize his army and bring it to the battlefront. With this end in mind, Docturov marched his weary men through the night, at first shadowing and then overtaking the Grand Army in the darkness. He arrived at Maloyaroslavets before dawn, only to find it occupied by a French advance party.

The command of Napoleon's advanced guard had passed to Eugène and this conscientious soldier had sent General Delzons ahead to secure the all-important bridge at Maloyaroslavets. Delzons arrived at 6.00 p.m. on 23 October and, finding the place undefended, saw fit to post a mere two battalions of infantry inside the town, bivouacking the remainder of his force – about 12,000 men – on the northern bank of the Luzha. He sent word back that his objective had been secured: that night Napoleon (at Borovsk, twenty miles to the north) rested in the belief that Maloyaroslavets was his.

Docturov attacked at dawn and, although he quickly evicted Delzons's troops from the town, they clung obstinately to the church and bridge: the fateful and bloody Battle of Maloyaroslavets had begun. Both sides fought with fierce desperation, realizing that reinforcements from the rival armies were hastening to the scene. Eugène's men battled to preserve the bridge at all costs; Docturov's to destroy it. A see-saw struggle of attack and counter-attack soon developed with the place changing hands seven times during the course of the fighting. The town – a wooden tinder-box – went up in flames and its terrified inhabitants[4] fled in panic and terror amid the carnage and savage street fighting: 'The conflict was horrible beyond description,' commented Edward Foord, 'the opposing soldiery fought to the death amid conflagration and ruin . . .'

Meanwhile Napoleon, unaware that the fate of the campaign – and indeed his empire – was hanging in the balance at Maloyaroslavets, left Borovsk late that morning. Blithely setting off down the Kaluga road around 10.00 a.m., he had just dictated a letter to the Empress Marie-Louise, informing her of how well his affairs were going, when the sound of distant gunfire stopped him in his tracks.

THE EMPEROR was still listening. The noise increased. 'Is it then a battle?' he exclaimed. Every explosion agitated him, for the chief point with him was no longer to conquer but to preserve; and he urged on Davout, who accompanied him: but he and that marshal did not reach the field of battle till dark,[5] when the firing was subsiding and the whole was over.

The Emperor saw the end of the battle but without being able to assist the Viceroy. A band of Cossacks nearly captured one of his officers, who was only a short distance from him.

It was not till then that an officer, sent by Prince Eugène, came to him to explain the whole affair. The troops had, he said, been obliged to cross the Luzha at the foot of Maloyaroslavets, at the bottom of an elbow which the river makes in its course and then to climb a steep hill: it is on this headlong slope, broken by pointed crags, that the town is built. Beyond is a high plain surrounded with woods, from which run three roads: one in front coming from Kaluga and two on the left from Lectazovo, the seat of the entrenched camp of Kutusov.

On the preceding day Delzons found no enemy there; but he did not think it prudent to place his whole division in the upper town, beyond a river and a defile and on the edge of a precipice, down which it might have been thrown by a surprise night attack. He remained, therefore, on the low bank of the Luzha, sending only two battalions to occupy the town and to watch the elevated plain.

The night was drawing to a close; it was four o'clock and all were asleep in Delzons' bivouacs except a few guards, when Docturov's Russians suddenly rushed out of the woods with tremendous shouts. Our sentries were driven back on their posts, the posts on their battalions, the battalions on the division: and yet it was not a *coup-de-main*, for the Russians had not brought up cannon. At the very commencement of the attack, its volleys carried the news of a serious affair to the Viceroy, who was three leagues distant.

The report added that Eugène had immediately hastened up with some officers and that his divisions and his guard had swiftly followed him. As he approached, a vast amphitheatre where all was bustle opened before him: the Luzha marked the foot of it and a multitude of Russian light troops already disputed its banks.

Behind them, from the summit of the slopes on which the town was situated, their advanced guard poured their fire on Delzons. Beyond that, on the elevated plain, the whole army of Kutusov was rapidly advancing in two long black columns by the two roads from Lectazovo.[6] They were seen stretching out and entrenching themselves on this bare slope, upon a line of about half a league, where they commanded and embraced everything by their number and position. They were already placing themselves across the old road to Kaluga, which was open the preceding day – which we might have occupied and travelled if we had pleased – but of which Kutusov would now have it in his power to defend every inch.

The enemy's artillery had at the same time taken advantage of the heights which bordered the river on their side: their fire traversed the low ground in the bend of the river, where Delzons and his troops were. The position was untenable and hesitation would have been fatal. It was necessary to get out of it either by a prompt retreat or by an impetuous attack; but it was before us that our retreat lay and Eugène gave orders for the attack.

After crossing the Luzha by a narrow bridge, the high-road from Kaluga runs along the bottom of a ravine which ascends to the town and then enters Maloyaroslavets. The Russians in mass occupied this hollow way. Delzons and his Frenchmen[7] rushed upon them pell-mell: the Russians were broken and overthrown; they gave way and presently our bayonets glistened on the heights.

Delzons, thinking himself sure of the victory, announced it as won. He had nothing but a pile of buildings to storm but his soldiers hesitated. He himself advanced and was encouraging them by his words when a ball struck him in the forehead and laid him on the ground. His brother threw himself upon him, covered him with his body, clasped him in his arms and would have carried him off out of the fire and fray but a second ball hit him also and both died together.

This loss left a great gap which needed to be filled. Guilleminot[8] succeeded Delzons and the first thing he did was to throw 100 grenadiers into a church and churchyard, in the walls of which they made loopholes. This church stood on the left of the highroad, which it commanded, and to the possession of this building we owed the victory. Five times during the day this post was passed by the Russian columns (which were pursuing ours) and five times did its fire, seasonably poured upon their flank and rear, harass them and hinder their progress. Afterwards, when we resumed the offensive, this position placed them between two fires and ensured the success of our attacks.

Scarcely had that general made this disposition when he was assailed by hosts of Russians: he was driven back towards the bridge where the Viceroy had stationed himself, in order to judge how to act and prepare his reserves. At first the reinforcements which he sent came up but slowly, one after another, and (as is almost always the case) each of them being inadequate to any great effort was successively destroyed without result.

At length, the whole of the 14th Division was engaged. The combat was then carried for the third time to the heights. But when the French had passed the houses and reached the plain where they were exposed, they could advance no farther. Overwhelmed by the fire of a whole army, they were scared and shaken. Fresh Russians incessantly came up; our thinned ranks gave way and were broken; the obstacles of the ground increased their confusion: they again descended swiftly and abandoned everything.

Meanwhile, the shells having set fire to the wooden town behind them, in their retreat they were stopped by the blaze: one fire drove them back upon another. The Russian recruits, wound up to a pitch of fanatic fury, closely pursued them. Our soldiers became enraged: they fought man to man. Some were seen seizing each other by one hand and striking with the other until both victors and vanquished rolled down the rocks into the flames without quitting their hold. There the wounded expired, either suffocated by the smoke or consumed by the fire. Their burned and blackened skeletons soon presented a hideous sight.

The 15th Division was still left. The Viceroy summoned it. As it advanced, it threw a brigade into the suburb on the left and another into the town on the right. It consisted of Italians: recruits who had never before been in action. They ascended, shouting enthusiastically, ignorant of the danger – or despising it – from that singular outlook which renders life less dear in its flower than in its decline (either because while young we fear death, less from the feeling of its distance or because at that age, rich in years and reckless of everything, we are reckless of life, as the wealthy are of their fortune).

The shock was terrible. Everything was reconquered for the fourth time and lost in like manner. More eager to begin than their seniors, these young troops were sooner disheartened and returned flying to the old battalions, which were obliged to lead them back to the danger.

The Russians, emboldened by their increasing number and success, then descended by their right to gain possession of the bridge and to cut off our retreat. Prince Eugène had nothing left but his last reserve: he and his guard now took part in the combat. At this sight and in obedience to his call, the remains of the 13th, 14th and 15th Divisions mustered their courage: they made a last and powerful effort and for the fifth time the combat was transferred to the heights.

At the same time Colonel Peraldi and the Italian *chasseurs* overthrew with their bayonets the Russians who were already approaching the left of the bridge. Intoxicated by the smoke and the fire through which they had passed, by the havoc which they made and by their victory, they pushed forward without stopping and endeavoured to make themselves masters of the enemy's cannon; but one of those deep clefts, with which the soil of Russia is intersected, stopped them in the midst of a destructive fire: their ranks opened, the enemy's cavalry attacked them and they were driven back to the very gardens of the suburbs. There they paused and rallied. All, both French and Italians, obstinately defended the upper avenues of the town and the Russians, being at length repulsed, drew back and concentrated themselves on the road to Kaluga, between the woods and Maloyaroslavets.

In this manner did 18,000 Italians and French crowded together at the bottom of a ravine defeat 50,000 Russians[9] posted over their heads and seconded by all the obstacles that a town built on a steep slope is capable of presenting.

The army, however, surveyed with sorrow this field of battle, where seven generals and 4,000 Italians had been killed or wounded. The sight of the enemy's loss afforded no consolation: it was not twice the amount of ours and their wounded would be saved; but what caused the greatest pain was the reflection that so bloody a conflict might have been spared.

In fact, the fires which were discovered on our left, in the night between the 23rd and 24th, had informed us of the movement of the Russians towards Maloyaroslavets; and yet the French army had marched there lethargically. A single division had been thrown the distance of three leagues from all support and carelessly risked. The different corps had remained out of reach of each other. Where now the rapid movements of Marengo, Ulm and Eckmühl? Why so slow and drawling a march on such a critical occasion? Was it our artillery and baggage that had caused this tardiness? Such was at least the most plausible supposition.[10]

When the Emperor received the report of this combat he was a few paces to the right of the highroad, at the bottom of a ravine close to the stream and the village of Gorodnia, in the house of a weaver (an old, shaky, filthy hut). Here he was half a league from Maloyaroslavets. It was in this worm-eaten dwelling, in a dark, dirty room, parted off into two by a cloth, that the fate of the army and of Europe was about to be decided.

The first hours of the night were spent in receiving reports. All agreed that the enemy was making preparations for a battle on the following day, which all were disposed to decline. About eleven o'clock Bessières entered. This marshal owed his elevation to honourable services and above all to the affection of the Emperor, who had become attached to him as to a creation of his own. It is true, a man could not be a favourite with Napoleon as with any other monarch: it was necessary at least to have followed and been of some service to him, for he sacrificed little to the graces. In short, it was essential that he should have been more than a witness of so many victories and the Emperor, when fatigued, accustomed himself to see with eyes which he believed to be of his own making.

He had sent this marshal to examine the situation of the enemy and in obedience to his orders Bessières had carefully explored the front of the Russian position: 'It is,' said he, 'unassailable!' 'Oh, heavens!' exclaimed the Emperor clasping his hands. 'Are you sure you are right? Are you not mistaken? Will you answer for that?' Bessières repeated his assertion. He affirmed that 'Three hundred grenadiers would there be sufficient to keep in check a whole army.'[11] Napoleon then crossed his arms with a look of consternation, hung his head and remained as if overwhelmed with the deepest dejection. His army was victorious and himself conquered! His route was intercepted, his manoeuvre thwarted! Kutusov, an old grey-headed Scythian, had been a step ahead of him![12] And he could not accuse his star. Did not the sun of France seem to have followed him to Russia? Was not the road to Maloyaroslavets open but to the preceding day? It was not his fortune then, that had failed him but he who had been wanting to his fortune.

Absorbed in this abyss of painful reflections, he fell into so profound a stupor that none of those about him could draw from him a single word. At length he tried to take some rest but a feverish anxiety prevented him from closing his eyes. During the rest of that cruel night he kept rising, lying down again and calling incessantly: but not a word escaped him to betray his distress. It was only from the agitation of his body that the anguish of his mind was to be inferred.

About four in the morning one of his orderly officers, Prince d'Aremberg, came to inform him that under cover of the night, of the woods and some inequalities of ground, the Cossacks were slipping in between him and his advanced posts. The Emperor had just sent off Poniatowski on his right to Kremenskoië; so little did he expect the enemy from that side, that he had neglected to order out any scouts on his right flank. He therefore neglected the report of his orderly officer.

No sooner did the sun appear above the horizon on the 25th than he mounted his horse and advanced on the Kaluga road, which to him was now nothing more than the road to Maloyaroslavets. To reach the bridge of that town he had to cross the plain, about a league in length and breadth, embraced by the bend of the Luzha. A few officers only attended him. The four squadrons of his usual escort, not having been previously informed, hastened to rejoin but had not yet overtaken him. The road was covered with hospital wagons, artillery and vehicles of luxury: it was the interior of the army and everyone was marching on without mistrust.

In the distance, towards the right, a few small groups of men were at first seen running and then large black lines advancing. Cries were presently heard; some women and attendants were met running back, too much frightened and out of breath either to listen to anything or to answer any question. At the same time the file of vehicles stopped in uncertainty; disorder arose in it; some endeavoured to proceed, others to turn back; they crossed, jostled and upset one another and the whole was soon a scene of complete uproar and confusion.

The Emperor looked on and smiled, still advancing and believing it to be a groundless panic. His aides-de-camp suspected that it was the Cossacks they saw; but they marched in such regular platoons that they still had doubts on the subject; and if those wretches had not howled at the moment of attack (as they all do to stifle the sense of danger), it is probable that Napoleon would not have escaped them. A circumstance which increased the peril was that their cries were at first mistaken for acclamations and their hurrahs for shouts of *'Vive l'Empereur!'*

It was Platov and 6,000 Cossacks[13] who, in the rear of our victorious advanced guard, had ventured to cross the river, the low plain and the highroad, driving all before them; and it was at the very moment when the Emperor – perfectly tranquil in the midst of his army – was advancing, refusing belief to so audacious a plan, that they put it into execution.

When they had once started, they approached with such speed that Rapp had but just time to say to the Emperor, 'It is the Cossacks! Turn back!' The Emperor, whose eyes deceived him or who disliked running away, stood firm and was on the point of being surrounded, when Rapp seized the bridle of his horse and turned him round, crying, 'Indeed you must!' And really it was high time to fly, although Napoleon's pride would not allow him to do so. He drew his sword, Berthier and Caulaincourt did the same; then placing themselves on the left side of the road, they waited the approach of the horde, from which they were scarcely forty paces distant.

Rapp had barely time to turn himself round to face these barbarians, when the foremost of them thrust his lance into the chest of his horse with such force as to throw him down. The other aides-de-camp and a few troopers belonging to the Guard saved the General. This action, the bravery of Le Coulteux,[14] the efforts of a score of officers and *chasseurs* and, above all, the thirst of these barbarians for plunder, saved the Emperor. And yet they needed only to have stretched out their hands and seized him, for at the same moment the horde, in crossing the highroad, overthrew everything before them: horses, men and carriages, wounding and killing some and dragging them into the woods for the purpose of plundering them; then, loosing the horses harnessed to the guns, they took them along with them across country.

But they only had a momentary victory, a triumph of surprise. The cavalry of the Guard galloped up; at this sight they let go their prey and fled and this torrent subsided: leaving indeed melancholy traces but abandoning all that it was hurrying away in its course.

Some of these barbarians, however, carried their audacity even to insolence. They were seen retiring at a foot-pace across the interval between our squadrons and coolly reloading their arms. They reckoned upon the heaviness of our cavalry and the swiftness of their own horses, which they urge with a whip. Their flight was effected without disorder: they faced round several times but without waiting till within reach of fire, so that they left scarcely any wounded and not one prisoner. At length they enticed us on to ravines covered with bushes, where we were stopped by their artillery. All this furnished subject for reflection: our army was worn down and the war had begun again with new and undiminished spirit.

The Emperor, struck with astonishment that the enemy had dared to attack him, halted until the plain was cleared: after which he returned to Maloyaroslavets, where Eugène pointed out to him the obstacles which had been conquered the preceding day.

The ground itself spoke sufficiently. Never was a field of battle more terribly eloquent: its marked features; its ruins covered with blood; the streets, the line of which could no longer be recognized but by the long train of the dead, whose heads were crushed by the wheels of the cannon; the wounded, who were still seen issuing from the rubbish and crawling along with their clothes, hair and limbs half consumed by the fire and uttering lamentable cries; finally, the doleful sound of the last melancholy honours which the grenadiers were paying to the remains of their colonels and generals who had been slain. All attested the extreme obstinacy of the conflict. In this scene the Emperor, it was said, beheld nothing but glory. He exclaimed that, 'The honour of so proud a day belonged exclusively to Prince Eugène.'

Can you forget, comrades, the fatal field which put a stop to the conquest of the world, where the victories of twenty years were blasted, where the great edifice of our fortune began to totter to its foundation? Do you not still picture to yourselves the bloodstained ruins of that town, those deep ravines and the woods which surround that high plain and convert it, as it were, into a tented field? On one side were the French, quitting the north, which they shunned; on the other, at the entrance to the wood, were the Russians, guarding the south and striving to drive us back upon their mighty winter. In the midst of this plain, between the two armies, was Napoleon; his steps and his eyes wandering from south to west, along the roads to Kaluga and Medyn. Both were closed against him. On that to Kaluga were Kutusov and 120,000 men, ready to dispute with him twenty leagues of defiles; towards Medyn he beheld a numerous cavalry: it was Platov and those same hordes which had just penetrated into the flank of the army, pierced it through and through and burst forth, laden with booty, to form again on his right wing, where reinforcements and artillery were waiting for them. It was on that side that the eyes of the Emperor were fixed longest. It was there that he received the reports of his officers and consulted his maps. Then, oppressed with regret and gloomy forebodings, he slowly returned to his headquarters.

Murat, Prince Eugène, Berthier, Davout and Bessières followed him. This mean habitation of a humble workman contained within it an emperor, two kings and three generals. Here they were about to decide the fate of Europe and of the army which had conquered it. Smolensk was the goal. Should they march thither by Kaluga, Medyn or Mozhaisk? Napoleon was seated at a table, his head supported by his hands, which concealed his features, as well as the anguish which they no doubt expressed.

A silence fraught with such imminent destinies continued to be respected until Murat, whose actions were always the result of impetuous emotions, wearied of this hesitation. Rising, he exclaimed that he might possibly be again accused of imprudence but that in war circumstances decided and gave to everything its name; that where there is no other course than to attack, prudence becomes audacity and audacity prudence; that to stop was impossible, to fly dangerous; consequently, they ought to pursue. What signified the menacing attitude of the Russians? For his part he cared not for them. Give him but the remnant of his cavalry and that of the Guard and he would force his way into their forests and their battalions, overthrow all before him and open anew the road to Kaluga.

Here Napoleon, raising his head, extinguished all this fire by saying that we had exhibited audacity enough already; that we had done too much for glory and it was high time to give up thinking of anything but how to save the rest of the army.

Bessières – either because his pride revolted at the idea of being put under the command of the King of Naples or from a desire to preserve uninjured the cavalry of the Guard, which he had formed and which he exclusively commanded – finding himself supported, then ventured to add that neither the army nor even the Guard had sufficient spirit left for such efforts. It was already said in both that as the means of transportation were inadequate, henceforth the victor, if overtaken, would fall a prey to the vanquished; that consequently every wound would be fatal. Murat would therefore be but feebly seconded. And in what a position! Its strength had just been but too well demonstrated. Against what enemies! Had they not noticed the field of the preceding day's battle and with what fury the Russian recruits, only just armed and clothed, had there fought and fell? The Marshal concluded by voting in favour of retreat, which the Emperor approved by his silence.

Davout immediately observed that as a retreat was decided upon, he proposed that it should be via Medyn and Smolensk. But Murat interrupted him and, whether from enmity or that discouragement which usually succeeds the rejection of a rash measure, he declared his astonishment that anyone would dare to propose so imprudent a step to the Emperor. Had Davout sworn the destruction of the army? Would he have so long and so heavy a column trail along without guides and in uncertainty, on an unknown track, within reach of Kutusov, presenting its flank to all the attacks of the enemy? Would he, Davout, defend it? Why – when in our rear, Borovsk and Vereia would lead us without danger to Mozhaisk – reject that safe route? There, provisions must have been collected, there everything was known to us and we could not be misled by any traitor.

At these words Davout, burning with a rage which he had great difficulty in repressing, replied that he proposed a retreat through a fertile country, by an untouched, plentiful and well-supplied route, villages still standing and by the shortest road, that the enemy might not avail himself of it, to cut us off from the route from Mozhaisk to Smolensk, recommended by Murat. And what a route! A desert of sand and ashes, where convoys of wounded would increase our embarrassment, where we should meet nothing but ruins, traces of blood, skeletons and famine!

Moreover, though he deemed it his duty to give his opinion when asked, he was ready to obey orders contrary to it with the same zeal as if they were consistent with his suggestions; but that the Emperor alone had a right to impose silence on him and not Murat, who was not his sovereign and never should be!

The quarrel growing warm, Bessières and Berthier interposed. As for the Emperor, still absorbed in the same attitude, he appeared insensible to what was passing. At length he broke up this council with the words: 'Well, gentlemen, I will decide.'

He decided on retreat and by that road which would carry him most speedily to a distance from the enemy; but it required another desperate effort before he could bring himself to give an order of march so new to him. So painful was this effort, that in the inward struggle which it occasioned, he lost the use of his senses. Those who attended him have asserted that the report of another warm encounter with the Cossacks, towards Borovsk, a few leagues in the rear of the army, was the last shock which induced him finally to adopt this fatal resolution.

It is a remarkable fact that he issued orders for this retreat northward at the very moment that Kutusov and his Russians, dismayed by the defeat of Maloyaroslavets, were retiring southward.

9 The Fatal and All-Devouring Highroad

> Wherever we passed, every refuge still left standing was crowded with wounded . . . and as we rode away we turned aside our heads that we might not see their despairing gestures, whilst our hearts were torn by their terrible cries, to which we tried in vain to shut our ears.
>
> Baron Lejeune

'So far as a single event can be fixed upon as the decisive point of Napoleon's career,' wrote the historian Edward Foord, 'that event is undoubtedly the Battle of Maloyaroslavets.' The fact is that Napoleon, by breaking off the battle in an attempt to preserve his army, actually lost his last chance to save it: for, during the small hours of 25 October, Kutusov, beset by doubts as to his army's ability to resist an attack prosecuted by Napoleon in person, decided to throw in the towel and retreat on Kaluga. Thus, on 26 October – by a bizarre twist of fate – both commanders were actually marching their armies away from each other! Believing his route south to be blocked, Napoleon ordered his troops north and thus, in the words of Baron de Marbot, 'The army left a fertile region to follow a route which they had devastated and traversed in September amid blazing villages and heaps of corpses.'

The balance of power had now decisively shifted in Alexander's favour: from now on, Napoleon was in full retreat. In a sense, the Emperor took his first step towards St Helena at Maloyaroslavets.

On 27 October, yet another Te Deum was sung at St

Petersburg, this time with good cause: Moscow had been delivered. On the following day, Kutusov learned of Napoleon's about-face and realized that what he had taken for a tactical setback at Maloyaroslavets, was in fact a strategic triumph. His course now became clear: he need only shadow Napoleon in order to block any attempt he might make to break into the fertile southern territories. In this way, the Grand Army would simply be shepherded out of Russia: 'General Winter' would do the rest.[1] *It was a simple and logical plan but in the event was not enough for the vengeful Alexander and the younger breed of vainglorious army hotheads, baying for French blood. Sir Robert Wilson,*[2] *an English liaison officer serving with the Russians, was particularly appalled, declaring the plan cowardly and Kutusov a poltroon. The aged warrior, however – like his predecessor, Barclay de Tolly – was destined to save Russia by manoeuvring rather than fighting.*

Meanwhile, for the soldiers of the Grand Army, the bitter prospect of a harrowing hike home beckoned. According to de Ségur, they marched 'with downcast eyes, as if ashamed and humbled'. They had good cause, for defeat was staring them in the face; and unused to the experience, the Grand Army soon began to disintegrate. With winter just around the corner and nothing to look forward to but the desolation of the Smolensk highroad, all hopes were pinned on the anticipated sanctuary of that ravaged city, some 180 miles to the west.

Napoleon continued to wear the mask of optimism which he had adopted at Moscow: even now, at this late stage, maintaining that Alexander was on the point of surrender. The Emperor has since been accused by historians of losing his grip on reality; but as the army's leader and moral foundation, what else could he have done? Doubtless he believed that if he was seen to lose his nerve, then all really would be lost. Faith and stoicism are the last resources of a gambler on a losing streak and Napoleon, having chanced everything on a mistaken belief in Alexander's timidity, was left with nothing but a brave face. Only much later, while languishing in exile, could he afford to be truthful: 'We are all liable to make mistakes. Mine was in staying too long in Moscow.'[3] *And more darkly: 'Had I died at Moscow I should have left behind me a reputation as a conqueror without parallel in history. A ball ought to have put an end to me there.'*[4]

On 29 October the Grand Army approached the great battlefield of 7 September: called 'the Moskva' by the French and 'Borodino' by the world. Captain Coignet of the Imperial Guard informs us that the Emperor 'sighed when he saw the dead still unburied'. The description of Sergeant Bourgogne – also of the Guard – is somewhat more graphic: 'Most of the bodies were Russian as ours had been buried – as far as possible – but as everything had been very hastily done, the heavy rain had uncovered many of them. It was a sad spectacle, the dead bodies hardly retaining a human appearance.'

AFTER PASSING the River Kologa we marched on, absorbed in thought, when some of us, raising our eyes, uttered an exclamation of horror. Each instantly looked around him and beheld a plain bare and devastated, all the trees cut down within a few feet from the surface; and farther off craggy hills, the highest of which appeared to be the most misshapen. It had all the appearance of an extinguished volcano. The ground was covered all round with fragments of helmets and *cuirasses*, broken drums, gunstocks, tatters of uniforms and standards stained with blood.

On this desolate spot lay 30,000 half-devoured corpses.[5] A number of skeletons, left on the summit of one of the hills overlooked the whole. It seemed as if here Death had fixed his empire. It was that terrible redoubt, the conquest and the grave of Caulaincourt. Presently the cry, 'It is the field of the great battle!' formed a long and doleful murmur. The Emperor passed quickly. Nobody stopped. Cold, hunger and the enemy urged us on. We merely turned our faces as we proceeded to take a last melancholy look at the vast grave of so many companions-in-arms, uselessly sacrificed and whom we were obliged to leave behind.

It was here that we had inscribed with the sword and blood one of the most memorable pages of our history. A few relics yet recorded it and they would soon be swept away. Some day the traveller will pass with indifference over this plain, undistinguished from any other. But when he shall learn that it was the theatre of the great battle, he will turn back, long survey it with inquisitive looks, impress its minutest features on his greedy memory and doubtless exclaim, 'What men! What a leader! What a destiny! These were the soldiers who thirteen years before, in the south, attempted a passage to the east through Egypt and were dashed against its gates.[6] They afterwards conquered Europe and here they came by the north to present themselves again before that same Asia, to be broken again. What then urged them into this roving and adventurous life? They were not barbarians seeking a warmer climate, more comfortable quarters, greater wealth; on the contrary, they possessed all these advantages and yet they forsook them to live without shelter and food, to fall daily, either slain or mutilated. What necessity drove them to this? Why, what but confidence in a leader hitherto infallible! The ambition to complete a great work gloriously begun! The intoxication of victory and, above all, that insatiable thirst for fame which drives man to seek death in order to obtain immortality.'[7]

While the army was passing this fatal field in grave and silent reflection, one of the victims of that bloody day was seen, it is said, still living and piercing the air with his groans. It was found by those who ran up to him that he was a French soldier. Both his legs had been broken in the battle and he had fallen among the dead where he remained unnoticed. The body of a horse, gutted by a shell, was his first refuge. For fifty days, the muddy water of a ravine and the putrefied flesh of the dead had served as dressing for his wounds and food for the support of his weakening existence. Those who say that they discovered this man affirm that they saved him.[8]

Farther on we beheld the great abbey or hospital of Kolotskoi, a sight still more hideous than that of the battle-field. At Borodino all was death but it was not without its tranquillity: there, at least, the battle was over. At Kolotskoi it was still raging. Death here seemed to be pursuing his victims, who had escaped from the engagement, with the utmost venom: he penetrated into them by all their senses at once. They were destitute of every means for repelling his attacks except orders, which it was impossible to execute in these deserts.

Still, in spite of famine, cold and the most complete destitution, the devotedness of a few surgeons – and a scrap of hope – still supported a number of wounded in this treacherous place. But when they saw the army repass and that they were about to be left behind, the least infirm crawled to the door, lined the way and extended towards us their outstretched hands.

The Emperor had just given orders that each carriage, of whatever kind it might be, should take up one of these unfortunate creatures; that the weakest should be left, as at Moscow, under the protection of the wounded and captive Russian officers as had recovered by our attentions.[9] He halted to see this order carried into execution and it was at a fire kindled with his forsaken wagons that he and his staff warmed themselves. Ever since the morning a multitude of explosions proclaimed the numerous sacrifices of this kind which it had already been found necessary to make.

During this halt an atrocious action was witnessed. Several of the wounded had just been placed in the suttlers' carts. These wretches, whose vehicles were overloaded with the plunder of Moscow, complained at the new burden imposed upon them; but being forced to accept it, they held their peace. No sooner, however, had the army recommenced its march than they slackened their pace, dropped behind the columns and, taking advantage of a lonely situation, threw all the unfortunate men committed to their care into the ditches. One only lived long enough to be picked up by the next carriage that passed: he was a general and through him this atrocious procedure became known. A shudder of horror spread throughout the column.

In the evening of this long day, as the imperial column was approaching Gzhatsk, it was surprised to find Russians quite recently killed on the way. It was noticed that each of them had his head shattered in the same manner and that his bloody brains were scattered near him. It was known that 2,000 Russian prisoners were marching on before and that their guard consisted of Spaniards, Portuguese and Poles. On this discovery each according to his disposition was indignant, approved or remained indifferent. Around the Emperor these various feelings were mute. Caulaincourt broke out into the exclamation that it was an atrocious cruelty. Here was a pretty specimen of the civilization which we were introducing into Russia! What would be the effect of this barbarity on the enemy? Were we not leaving our wounded and a multitude of prisoners at his mercy? Did he lack the means of wreaking the most horrible retaliation?

Napoleon preserved a gloomy silence but on the following days these murders ceased. These unfortunate men were then merely left to die of hunger in the enclosures where, at night, they were confined like cattle. This was no doubt a barbarity too; but what could we do? Exchange them? The enemy rejected the proposal. Release them? They would have gone and reported the general distress and, soon joined by others, they would have returned to pursue us. In this deadly warfare, to give them their lives would have meant sacrificing our own. We were cruel from necessity. The mischief arose from our having involved ourselves in so dreadful an alternative. Besides, in the interior of Russia our soldiers, who had been made prisoners, were not more humanely treated and there, certainly, imperious necessity was not an excuse.[10]

At length the troops arrived with the night at Gzhatsk. But this first day of winter had been cruelly occupied: the sight of the field of Borodino and of two forsaken hospitals; the multitude of wagons consigned to the flames; the Russians with their brains blown out; the excessive length of the march; the first severities of winter; all concurred to render it horrible. The retreat became a flight and Napoleon forced to yield and run away was a spectacle perfectly novel.

Several of our allies enjoyed it with that inward satisfaction which is felt by inferiors when they see their chiefs at last thwarted and obliged in their turn to give way. They indulged the miserable envy that is excited by extraordinary success, which rarely occurs without being abused and which shocks that equality which is the first feeling of man. But this malicious joy was soon extinguished and lost in the universal distress.

From Gzhatsk the Emperor proceeded in two marches to Viasma. There he halted to wait for Eugène and Davout and to reconnoitre the road to Medyn and Yukhnov, which runs at that place into the highroad to Smolensk. It was this crossroad which might bring the Russian army from Maloyaroslavets onto his route. But on 1 November, after waiting thirty-six hours, Napoleon had not seen any sign of that army. He set out, therefore, wavering between the hope that Kutusov had fallen asleep and the fear lest the Russians had left Viasma on his right and proceeded two marches farther towards Dorogobuzh to cut off his retreat. At any rate, he left Ney at Viasma to collect the I and IV Corps and to relieve Davout as the rearguard, whom he judged to be fatigued.

He complained of the slowness of the latter. He wrote to reproach him with being still five marches behind him, when he ought to have been no more than three. He considered the mind of that marshal to be too methodical to direct in a suitable manner so irregular a march.

On 3 November Eugène was proceeding towards Viasma, preceded by his equipages and his artillery, when the first light of day showed him at once his retreat threatened by an army on his left; behind him his rearguard cut off; and on his left the plain covered with stragglers and scattered vehicles, fleeing before the lances of the enemy. At the same time, towards Viasma, he heard Marshal Ney, who should have assisted him, fighting for his own preservation.

It was only an advanced guard but they were alarmed at the noise of this fight in the rear of their own, threatening their retreat. The action had lasted ever since seven in the morning; night was approaching; the baggage must by this time have got away: the French generals therefore began to retire.

This retrograde movement increased the enthusiasm of the enemy and, but for a memorable effort by the 25th, 57th and 85th Regiments and the protection of a ravine, Davout's corps would have been broken, turned by its right and destroyed. Prince Eugène, who was not so briskly attacked, was able to effect his retreat more rapidly through Viasma; but the Russians followed him and had penetrated into the town when Davout, pursued by 20,000 men and overwhelmed by eighty pieces of cannon, attempted to pass in his turn.

Morand's division first entered the town. It was marching on with confidence, under the idea that the action was over, when the Russians, who were concealed by the windings of the streets, suddenly fell upon it. The surprise was complete and the confusion great. Morand, nevertheless, rallied and encouraged his men, retrieved matters and fought his way through.

It was Compans who put an end to the whole. He closed the march with his division. Finding himself too closely pressed by the bravest troops of Miloradovich, he turned about, dashed in person at the most eager, overthrew them and, having thus made them fear him, he finished his retreat without further molestation. This conflict was glorious to each and its results disastrous to all. It was without order and unity. There would have been troops enough to conquer, had there not been too many commanders. It was not till near two o'clock that the latter met to agree their manoeuvres and even then they were executed without harmony.

When at length the river, the town of Viasma, night,

mutual fatigue, and Marshal Ney had separated them from the enemy – the danger being adjourned and the bivouacs established – the numbers were counted. Several pieces of cannon which had been broken, the baggage and 4,000 killed or wounded, were missing. Their honour was saved but there were immense gaps in the ranks. It was necessary to close them up, to form what remained into a more compact whole. Each regiment scarcely composed a battalion, each battalion a platoon. The soldiers had no longer their accustomed places, comrades or officers.

This sad reorganization took place by the light of the blaze of Viasma and during the successive volleys of the cannon of Ney and Miloradovich. Several times the survivors of these brave troops, thinking that they were attacked, crawled to their arms. Next morning, when they again fell into their ranks, they were astonished at the smallness of their numbers.

The spirits of the troops were still supported by the example of their leaders, by the hopes of finding all their wants supplied at Smolensk and still more by the aspect of a yet brilliant sun – that universal source of hope and life – which seemed to contradict and deny the spectacles of despair and death that already surrounded us.

But on 6 November the heavens declared against us. Their azure disappeared. The army marched enveloped in fogs. These fogs became thicker and presently an immense cloud descended upon it in large flakes of snow. It seemed as if the very sky was falling and joining the earth and our enemies to complete our destruction. All objects changed their appearance and became confused, not to be recognized again. We proceeded without knowing where we were, without perceiving the point to which we were bound. Everything was transformed into an obstacle. While the soldiers were struggling with the tempest of wind and snow, the flakes, driven by the storm, lodged and accumulated in every hollow: their surfaces concealed unknown abysses, which treacherously opened beneath our feet. There men were engulfed and the weakest, resigning themselves to their fate, found a grave in these snow-pits.

Those who followed turned aside but the storm drove into their faces both the snow that was falling from the sky and that which it raised from the ground. It seemed bent on opposing their progress. The Russian winter, under this new form, attacked them on all sides: it penetrated their light garments and their torn shoes and boots; their wet clothes froze upon their bodies; an icy envelope encased them and stiffened their limbs; a keen and violent wind broke their breathing.

The unfortunate creatures still crawled on, shivering, till the snow, gathering like balls under their feet or the fragment of some broken article – a branch of a tree or the bodies of one of their comrades – caused them to stumble and fall. There they groaned in vain. The snow soon covered them. Small heaps marked the spot where they lay: such was their only grave! The road was studded with these mounds, like a cemetery. The most intrepid and the most indifferent were affected: they passed on quickly with averted looks. But before them, around them, there was nothing but snow. This immense and dreary uniformity extended farther than the eye could reach. The imagination was astounded! It was like a vast winding-sheet which Nature had thrown over the army. The only objects not enveloped by it were some gloomy pines – trees of the tomb with their funereal colours and dismal look – which completed the doleful appearance of a general mourning and of an army dying, amidst a nature already dead.

Everything, even to their weapons, turned against them: these seemed to their frozen limbs insupportably heavy. The fingers of many were frozen to the muskets which they still held, which deprived them of the motion necessary for keeping up some degree of warmth and life.

We soon met with numbers of men belonging to all the corps, sometimes singly, others in troops. They had not deserted their colours: it was cold and starvation which had separated them from their columns. In this general and individual struggle they had parted from one another and there they were, disarmed, vanquished, defenceless, without leaders, obeying nothing but the urgent instinct of self-preservation.

Most of them, attracted by the sight of side roads, dispersed themselves over the country in the hope of finding bread and shelter for the coming night. But on their first passage all had been laid waste to the extent of seven or eight leagues. They met with nothing but Cossacks and an armed population which surrounded, wounded and stripped them naked: then left them – with ferocious bursts of laughter – to die in the snow. These people, who had risen at the call of Alexander and Kutusov and who had not then learned, as they since have, to avenge nobly a country which they were unable to defend, hovered on both flanks of the army under cover of the woods. Those whom they did not despatch with their pikes and hatchets, they brought back to the fatal and all-devouring highroad.

Night then came on. A night of sixteen hours! But in that snow, which covered everything, they knew not where to halt, where to sit, where to lie down, where to find some root or other to eat or dry wood to kindle a fire. They tried to establish themselves but the tempest, still active, scattered the first preparations for bivouacs: the pines, laden with frost, obstinately resisted the flames. When at length the blaze gained the ascendancy, the officers and soldiers around them prepared their wretched repast: it consisted of bloody pieces of flesh torn from the horses that were exhausted and a few spoonfuls of rye flour mixed with melted snow. Next morning circular ranges of soldiers, lying lifeless, marked the bivouacs and the ground about them was strewed with the bodies of several thousand horses.

From that day we began to place less reliance on one another. In that lively army, susceptible of all impressions and taught to reason by an advanced civilization, despondency and neglect of discipline spread rapidly: the imagination knowing no bounds in evil as in good. Henceforward, at every bivouac, at every difficult passage, at every moment, some portion separated from the yet organized troops and fell into disorder. There were some, however, who were proof against this widespread disease of despondency. These were extraordinary men. They encouraged one another by repeating the name of Smolensk, which they knew they were approaching and where they had been promised that all their wants should be supplied.

It was in this manner that, after this deluge of snow and the increase of cold which it predicted, each, whether officer or soldier, preserved or lost his fortitude according to his disposition, his age and his constitution. One of our leaders who had hitherto been the strictest in enforcing discipline, now paid little attention to it. Thrown out of all his fixed ideas of regularity, order and method, he was seized with despair at the sight of such universal disorder and, conceiving before the others that all was lost, he felt himself ready to abandon all.[11]

From Gzhatsk to Mikhailevska, a village between Dorogobuzh and Smolensk, nothing remarkable occurred in the imperial column, unless that it was found necessary to throw the spoils of Moscow into the lake of Semlevo: cannon, Gothic armour, the ornaments of the Kremlin and the cross of Ivan the Great were buried in its waters. Trophies, glory – all those acquisitions to which we had sacrificed everything – became a burden to us. Our object was no longer to enrich, to adorn life, but to preserve it. In this vast wreck, the army, like a great ship tossed by the most tremendous of tempests, threw without hesitation into that sea of ice and snow everything that could slacken or impede its progress.

10 An Empty Name

> When overwhelmed with disasters we cursed the Emperor; we blamed him for our sufferings: if he appeared, his prestige, the kind of halo that surrounds great men, dazzled us and everyone regained confidence and obeyed his slightest wish.
>
> B.J. Duverger[1]

And so 'General Winter' had arrived: heralded by gales, snowstorms and sub-zero temperatures. The effect on the Grand Army, snaking along the devastated road to Smolensk, was catastrophic. Still wearing their tattered, rotting, summer uniforms, the troops were reduced to stripping the dead for extra clothing; or wrapping themselves in the feminine cloaks, furs and pelisses which they had plundered in Moscow (and which they had hoped to sell for a fortune back home). Laden with looted luxuries, the army lacked the basic essentials to combat cold and hunger. No one was spared the cruelty of the season: officers, unable to ride in the blizzard, trudged alongside the men, leading their mounts by the bridle; while Napoleon, in an attempt to combat frostbite, forsook his carriage and pressed forward on foot, arm in arm with Berthier and Caulaincourt. It was the horses, however, which were in a particularly pitiful state: weakened by lack of adequate forage, they were suffered to slip and fall on the icy road for want of winter shoes. Over 5,000 perished within a matter of days: those which survived were, for the most part, destined for the pot.

It was on the same day, at Mikhailevska, some forty miles from

Smolensk, that according to de Ségur, 'an express, the first that had been able to reach us for ten days, brought news of that strange conspiracy, which had been hatched in Paris itself and in the depths of a prison by an obscure general.' The 'strange conspiracy' was a madcap attempt to overthrow the Napoleonic régime by announcing the Emperor's death; the 'obscure general' one Claude François de Malet, a veteran of both the old Royalist and Revolutionary armies. A dedicated Napoleon-hater, Malet had been imprisoned in 1807 as a political agitator but was later transferred to a Paris mental institution where, it was hoped, he would sit out his term quietly. On 22 October 1812, however, he had made good his escape and with the aid of forged papers took command of a unit of National Guardsmen. What followed was a hare-brained attempt to seize power and restore the Republic. Proclaiming to a stunned capital that Napoleon had died in Russia, Malet proceeded to arrest the minister of police, shoot the city's governor[2] *and spring his Republican cronies from gaol. For ten hours Paris was in turmoil until, recognized as a lunatic, Malet was seized and confined. Hastily tried and sentenced to death, along with his hapless associates, the deranged general met his end bravely and with perfect poise: coolly commanding his own firing squad.*[3] *'In short,' wrote Bourrienne, Napoleon's ex-schoolmate and biographer, when reminiscing on* l'affaire *Malet, 'his enterprise was quite that of a madman.'*

On hearing the news, Napoleon affected to make light of the débâcle ('The French are like women, one must not stay away from them too long.'[4]*) but was secretly shocked: not so much at Malet's audacity as the fact that no one had rallied round the Bonaparte dynasty in the person of his infant son. 'How was it no one thought of speaking of the King of Rome?' he mused. 'It would have been so natural, so proper a thing!'*[5] *Evidently, the Bonaparte name minus his own presence counted for nothing, even at the heart of his empire. 'Misfortune never comes alone,' he observed to Rapp, his faithful aide-de-camp. 'This is an appropriate finish to what is passing here. I cannot be everywhere but I must go back to Paris, my presence there is indispensable to reanimate* *public opinion. I must have men and money; great successes and great victories will repair all.'*[6]

Each new day, however, brought fresh disasters: on 7 November, Vitebsk was taken by troops from Prince Wittgenstein's Army of Finland; on the 9th, a column of 2,000 reinforcements under General Augereau[7] *was captured by partisans; while Eugène's IV Corps was caught crossing the freezing waters of the River Vop by Platov's Cossacks and forced to bolt for the safety of Smolensk, leaving behind its guns and baggage.*[8] *As the weather worsened, the Grand Army shivered and splintered into two groups: a small core consisting of those capable of keeping their ranks, followed by a sea of starving, demoralized stragglers. Meanwhile, a net began to close around Napoleon, as various Russian commanders converged upon his line of retreat: Prince Wittgenstein from the north; Chichagov from the south-west; Miloradovich from the east; and Kutusov from the south.*

On 9 November Napoleon arrived at Smolensk. The city was still a scene of desolation and destruction, following the assault of the previous August; the ruins now shrouded in a thick layer of snow. The city's governor, General Charpentier, had received little warning of Napoleon's approach. Although he had gathered up as many provisions as possible and set up field kitchens, he had no idea of the appalling state of the army and was totally unprepared for the avalanche of human suffering which swept into town between 8 and 14 November. 'As corps after corps reached the town in their misery,' wrote Edward Foord, 'the hospitals were choked with sick and wounded, who were literally heaped into these dens of horror without provision of any kind. The cold was worse than it had yet been and the men were frost-bitten by hundreds.'

Napoleon, anxious to preserve the elite soldiers of the Guard for the hard fighting which surely lay ahead, ordered that they should be issued with fifteen days' rations, while the ordinary troops were to make do with a mere six. The Guard, however, ransacked the stores upon their arrival, gorged themselves at their comrades' expense and – adding insult to injury – proceeded to set up a bazaar in order to sell their loot and leftovers to the famished troops of the line. By the time Ney's III Corps arrived, having heroically covered the retreat as rearguard, there was nothing left. Scenes of chaos and horror ensued as soldiers rampaged through the streets. Men were murdered for a loaf of bread, while heaps of silver and gold, looted from Moscow, were left untouched. Within twenty-four hours Smolensk was trashed and Napoleon, who had considered using the fort as a base for further operations, had no choice but to order the retreat to continue.

De Ségur picks up the story as the soldiers first catch sight of Smolensk, a city which, far from being their promised haven, was to be nothing but a mirage in a snowy desert.

AT LENGTH the army again came in sight of Smolensk. The soldiers pointed it out to each other: *there* was that land of promise where their famine was to find abundance, their fatigue rest; where bivouacs in a frost of nineteen degrees would be forgotten in houses warmed by good fires; *there* they should enjoy refreshing sleep, repair their rags; *there* they should be furnished with new shoes and clothing adapted to the climate.

At this sight, the *corps d'élite* and veteran regiments alone kept their ranks: the rest ran forward with all possible speed. Thousands of men, mostly unarmed, covered the two steep banks of the Dnieper. They crowded in masses round the walls and gates of the city: but their haggard faces, begrimed with dirt and smoke; their tattered uniforms (and the grotesque garb which they had substituted for them); their strange, hideous look and their extreme excitement, caused alarm. It was decided that if this crowd, maddened with hunger, was not barred, a general pillage would be the consequence and the gates were closed against it.[9]

It was also hoped that by this action the troops would be forced to rally. A horrid struggle between order and chaos then began in the remains of that unfortunate army. In vain did some beg, weep, threaten, battle to burst open the gates and drop down dead at the feet of their comrades: they were forced to await the arrival of the first troops who were still officered and in good order.

These were the Old and Young Guard. It was not till afterwards that the disbanded men were allowed to enter. They – and the other corps which arrived in succession, from the 8th to the 14th – believed that their entry had been delayed merely to give more rest and more food to the Guard. Were they then to be forever sacrificed to this privileged class, fellows kept merely for parade, who were never foremost but at reviews and distributions? Was the army always to put up with their leftovers? And in order to obtain them, was it always to wait till they had glutted themselves? It was impossible to tell them in reply, that to attempt to save all was the way to lose all; that it was necessary to keep at least one corps entire and to give preference to that which, in the end, would be capable of making the most powerful effort.

Meanwhile, these poor creatures were admitted into that Smolensk for which they had so warmly wished. They left the banks of the Dnieper strewed with the dying bodies of the weakest of their number, whom impatience and hours of waiting had brought to that state. They left others on the icy steep which they had to climb to reach the upper town. The rest ran to the magazines and there more of them dropped while they beset the doors, for there they were again repulsed: 'Who were they? To what corps did they belong? What had they to prove it?' The officials who had to distribute the provisions had orders to deliver them only to authorized officers bringing receipts. Those who applied had no officers, nor could they tell where their regiments were. Two-thirds of the army were in this predicament.

These unfortunate men then spread through the streets, having no longer any hope but pillage. However, horses dissected to the very bones told of famine. The doors and windows of the houses had all been broken and torn away to feed bivouac fires. They found no shelter, no winter quarters prepared, no wood. The sick and the wounded were left in the streets, in the carts which had brought them. It was again – it was always – the fatal highroad, passing through an empty name. It was a new bivouac among deceitful ruins, colder even than the forests which they had just quitted.

Only then did these disorganized troops seek their colours. They rejoined them for a moment in order to obtain food; but all the bread that could be baked had been distributed. There was no more biscuit nor butcher's meat. Rye flour, dry vegetables and spirits were dished out to them. It required the most strenuous efforts to prevent the different corps from murdering one another at the doors of the magazines; and when, after long formalities, their wretched fare was delivered to them, the soldiers refused to carry it to their regiments: they fell upon the sacks, snatched out a few pounds of flour and ran to hide themselves till they had devoured it. It was the same with the spirits. Next day the houses were full of the bodies of these unfortunate wretches.

In short, that fatal Smolensk, which the army had looked forward to as the term of its sufferings, marked only their beginning. Inexpressible hardships awaited us. We had yet to march forty days under that yoke of iron. Some, already overloaded with present miseries, sank under the alarming prospect of those which awaited them. Others revolted against their destiny: finding they had nothing to rely on but themselves, they resolved to live at any cost. Henceforward they plundered their dying companions – by violence or stealth – of their subsistence, their clothes and even the gold with which they had filled their knapsacks instead of food. These wretches, whom despair had made robbers, then threw away their weapons to save their booty, profiting by the general confusion, an unknown name, a uniform no longer recognizable and night.

The Emperor arrived on 9 November amid this scene of desolation. He shut himself up in one of the houses in the new square and never quitted it till the 14th, to continue his retreat. He had counted upon fifteen days' provisions and forage for an army of 100,000 men: there was not more than half the quantity of flour, rice and spirits and no meat at all. Cries of rage were set up against one of the persons appointed to provide these supplies. The commissary saved his life only by crawling for a long time on his knees at the feet of Napoleon. Probably the reasons which he gave did more for him than his pleas.

When he arrived, he said, bands of stragglers whom the army had left behind it had involved Smolensk in terror and destruction. The men died there of hunger as they had done upon the road. When some degree of order had been restored, the Jews alone had at first offered to furnish the necessary provisions. At length the foremost of the long convoys of provisions collected in Germany appeared: they brought no more than 200 quintals[10] of flour and rice. Several hundred German and Italian bullocks also arrived with them.

Meanwhile the accumulation of dead bodies in the houses, courts and gardens – and their unwholesome odours – infected the air. The dead were killing the living. The civil officers, as well as many of the military, were stricken: some had become to all appearance idiots, weeping or fixing their hollow eyes on the ground. There were others who, amidst a torrent of blasphemies, a horrid convulsion or a still more frightful laugh, had dropped down dead.

At the same time it had been found necessary to kill without delay the greatest part of the cattle brought from Germany and Italy. These animals would neither walk any farther nor eat. Their eyes, sunk in their sockets, were dull and motionless. They died without seeking to avoid the fatal blow. Other misfortunes followed: several convoys had been intercepted, magazines taken, and a drove of 800 oxen had just been carried off from Krasnoi.

This commissary added that regard ought also to be had to the great quantity of detachments which had passed through Smolensk; to the stay which Marshal Victor, 28,000 men and about 15,000 sick had made there. All had subsisted upon the magazines. It had been necessary to deal out nearly 60,000 rations per day. Lastly, provisions and cattle had been sent forward to Moscow as far as Mojaisk and towards Kaluga as far as Elnia.

Many of these allegations were well founded. A chain of other magazines had been formed from Smolensk to Minsk and Vilna. These two towns were in a still greater degree than Smolensk centres of provisioning, of which the fortresses of the Vistula formed the first line. The total quantity of provisions distributed over this space was incalculable; the efforts for transporting them there gigantic and the result little better than nothing. They were insufficient in that immensity.

Thus great expeditions are crushed by their own weight. Human limits had been surpassed. The genius of Napoleon, in attempting to soar above time, climate and distances had, as it were, lost itself in space: great as was its measure, it had gone beyond it. Accustomed to triumph over everything by the terror of his name and the wonder produced by his audacity, he had ventured his army, himself, his fortune, his all, on a first movement of Alexander's. He was still the same man as in Egypt, at Marengo, Ulm and Essling: it was Ferdinand Cortes; it was the Macedonian burning his ships and anxious, in spite of his troops, to penetrate still farther into unknown Asia; finally, it was Caesar risking his whole fortune in a fragile bark.

It was on 14 November, about five in the morning, that the imperial column at last quitted Smolensk. Its march was still firm but gloomy and silent as night. This army had left Moscow 100,000 strong: in five-and-twenty days it had been reduced to 36,000 men. The artillery had already lost 350 of their cannon and yet these feeble remains were always divided into eight armies, which were encumbered with 60,000 unarmed stragglers and a long train of cannon and baggage.

Whether it was the encumbrance of so many men and carriages or a mistaken sense of security which led the Emperor to order a day's interval between the departure of each marshal is uncertain: most probably it was the latter. Be that as it may, he, Eugène, Davout and Ney only quitted Smolensk in succession. Ney was not to leave it till the 16th or 17th. He had orders to make the artillery saw the trunnions off the cannon left behind and bury them; to destroy the ammunition, to drive all the stragglers before him and to blow up the towers which surrounded the city.

Kutusov, meanwhile, was waiting for us at some leagues' distance and preparing to cut in pieces successively those remnants of corps thus extended and parcelled out.

11 Men of Iron

> Although we were most wretched and dying of cold and hunger, we still possessed two things: courage and honour.
>
> Sergeant Bourgogne

Faced with the necessity of continuing the retreat, Napoleon knew he must reach the vital Dnieper bridges at Orsha ahead of the Russians or face entrapment. His objective, however, lay some seventy miles to the west down a single difficult road, obstructed by defiles, commanded by heights and caught in the grip of winter.

Napoleon ordered his 40,000 or so remaining effectives out of Smolensk piecemeal: Junot and Poniatowski left between 12 and 13 November; he followed on the 14th with the Guard; Eugène was to remain until the 15th; Davout and Ney until the 16th. If necessary Ney – who had been detailed as the new rearguard commander – was to linger yet another day, in order to complete the destruction of the city walls. Thus, rather than being concentrated into a single formidable force, the surviving soldiers were to remain in their individual, much weakened, army corps; strung out along the highroad, each unit separated from the other by a day's march.

Kutusov, however (who had been shadowing the Grand Army far to the south), was already closing in on Krasnoi, the next major settlement on the road to Orsha, some thirty miles west of Smolensk. In the words of Clausewitz, 'Near Krasnoi, Kutusov had fully gained the advance of the French army, so that it only depended upon him entirely to obstruct their retreat, for which the Dnieper afforded the greatest facilities.' Meanwhile, Miloradovich with a force of 20,000 men had quietly bypassed Smolensk and was preparing an ambush at a defile on the highroad, on the approaches to Krasnoi. According to de Ségur, this force 'took a position three leagues in advance of us, towards Merlino and Nikoulina, behind a ravine which skirts the left side of the great road; and there, lying in ambush on the flank of our retreat, it awaited our passage.' The Grand Army, divided into segments and dangerously extended along the Smolensk-Krasnoi highroad, was threatened with destruction piece by piece.

Napoleon, as yet unaware of the immediate danger and still anxious lest the Russians reach Orsha before him, pushed the pace, ordering fourteen hours' marching per day. The conditions on the road were atrocious: heavy snow, a biting wind and temperatures of around minus 30° Centigrade. It took his troops twenty-two hours to cover the first fifteen miles towards Krasnoi, men and horses falling away at an alarming rate; succumbing to frostbite, exposure, hunger and fatigue. Any soldiers who strayed from the column in search of food were butchered by Cossacks, partisans or peasants. Many were cruelly tortured before being murdered: those who died quietly in their sleep, carried away by the cold, were lucky by comparison.

On 15 November, having overtaken Junot, Napoleon entered Miloradovich's defile. The Russian commander, overawed by the Emperor's presence, failed to press home his attack and contented himself with raking Napoleon's column with artillery fire before letting it pass on, relatively unscathed, to Krasnoi. In the words of de Ségur, 'It appeared as if Miloradovich, from his elevated position, was satisfied with merely insulting the passage of the Emperor and of the Old Guard, which had been so long the terror of Europe. He did not dare to gather up its fragments until it had passed by; but then he became bold, concentrated his forces, and, descending from the heights, took up a strong position with 20,000 men, quite across the highroad. By this movement he separated Eugène, Davout and Ney from the Emperor and closed the road to Europe against these three leaders.'

Napoleon, meanwhile, having learned that the Russians held the villages to the south of Krasnoi, launched a surprise night attack, sending them flying. As for Kutusov, once he realized that he was facing Napoleon and his Imperial Guard – and not merely an isolated corps or rearguard, as previously suspected – he switched to the defensive. In the words of Clausewitz, 'Kutusov still feared his adversary.'

Eugène, having with difficulty rallied some 6,000 effectives (and dogged by double that number of unarmed stragglers), set off from Smolensk on schedule, only to stumble into Miloradovich's roadblock on 16 November. The gallant Viceroy rejected Russian calls to surrender and his Italian troops yelled defiantly as the enemy guns tore into their ranks. Effectively barred from Napoleon at Krasnoi, Eugène held out until nightfall when, under cover of darkness, he turned Miloradovich's flank. By a circuitous march, he arrived at Krasnoi later that night with a mere 4,000 survivors. His plight awoke Napoleon to the danger awaiting his corps commanders and he determined to seize the initiative.

Meanwhile, it was Davout's turn to march into Miloradovich's ambush. Realizing his desperate situation, Davout sent an urgent message to Ney for support but to no avail. (Ney later claimed never to have received Davout's message and heaped blame upon his fellow marshal for leaving him in the lurch!) The hard-pressed troops of I Corps were thus obliged to hold their line against overwhelming odds. Baron Lejeune, now serving as Davout's chief of staff, recorded in his memoirs that, 'Again and again our little army, reduced to 4,000 men bearing arms but hampered by numerous stragglers, halted to face the enemy and await Marshal Ney, who was to cover our retreat.' The spirits of the men were considerably lifted, however, by the incredible sangfroid of General Compans, commander of the 5th Division. Still suffering from a shoulder wound sustained at Borodino, Compans calmly wandered about under fire, constantly stopping to smile at the enemy. Help, however, was on its way.

Early on the morning of 17 November, Napoleon, displaying a breathtaking contempt for Kutusov's 80,000 Russians, sent Eugène on to Orsha, detailed General Claparède to hold Krasnoi, and ordered General François Roguet and the Guard to retrace their steps and pull Davout free. 'The Emperor,' wrote Lejeune, 'who was becoming very anxious about our fate, generously turned back and came to meet us, cutting a passage through our assailants at the head of the Old Guard.'

ON 17 NOVEMBER, before daylight, he issued his orders, armed himself and, going out on foot, at the head of his Old Guard, began his march. But it was not towards Poland, his ally, that it was directed, nor towards France, where he would still be received as the head of a new dynasty and the Emperor of the West. His words on taking up his sword on this occasion were, 'I have sufficiently acted the emperor; it is time that I should become the general.' He turned back into the midst of 80,000 enemies, plunged into the thickest of them, in order to draw all their efforts against himself, to make a diversion in favour of Davout and Ney and to wrest them from a country, the gates of which had been closed upon them.

Daylight at last appeared, revealing on one side the Russian battalions – which bounded the horizon – and on the other, Napoleon with his 6,000 guards[1] advancing with a firm step and proceeding to take his place in the middle of that terrible circle. At the same time Mortier, a few yards in front of his emperor, displayed in the face of the whole Russian army, the 5,000 men which still remained to him.

Their object was to defend the right flank of the highroad from Krasnoi to the great ravine in the direction of Stachova. A battalion of *chasseurs* of the Old Guard, formed in square like a fortress, was planted close to the highroad and acted as a support to the left wing of our young soldiers. On their right, in the snowy plains which surround Krasnoi, the remains of the cavalry of the Guard, a few cannon and the 400 troopers of Latour-Maubourg[2] (since they left Smolensk, the cold had killed or scattered 500 of them), occupied the place of the battalions and batteries which the French army no longer possessed.

The artillery of Mortier was reinforced by a battery commanded by Drouot; one of those men who are endowed with the whole strength of virtue, who think that duty embraces everything and are capable of making the noblest sacrifices simply and without the least effort.

Claparède remained at Krasnoi where, with a few soldiers, he protected the wounded, the baggage and the retreat. Prince Eugène continued his retreat towards Liadi. His engagement of the preceding day and his night march had entirely broken up his corps; his divisions only retained sufficient unity to drag themselves along in order to perish but not to fight.

Meantime Roguet had been recalled to the field of battle from Malievo. The enemy kept pushing columns across that village and was extending more and more beyond our right in order to surround us. The battle then commenced. But what kind of battle? The Emperor had here no sudden illumination to trust to, no flashes of momentary inspiration, none of these great strokes so unforeseen from their boldness, which ravish fortune, extort a victory and by which he has so often stunned, confused and crushed his enemies. All *their* movements were now free, all *ours* enchained and the genius of attack was reduced to defend himself.

Here, therefore, it became clear that Fame is not a vain shadow, that she is real strength and doubly powerful by the pride which she imparts to her favourites and the timid precautions which she suggests to such as venture to attack her. The Russians had only to march forward without manoeuvring – even without firing – their mass was quite sufficient of itself to crush Napoleon and all his troops; but they did not dare to come to close quarters with him. They were awed by the presence of the conqueror of Egypt and of Europe. The Pyramids, Marengo, Austerlitz, Friedland – an army of victories – seemed to rise between him and the whole of the Russians. We might almost fancy that, in the eyes of that submissive and superstitious people, a renown so extraordinary appeared like something supernatural;[3] that they regarded it as beyond their reach; that they believed they could only attack and demolish it from a distance; and in short that, against the Old Guard, that living fortress, that column of granite (as it had been styled by its leader), human efforts were useless and that cannon alone could destroy it.[4]

These made wide and deep breaches in the ranks of Roguet and the Young Guard but they killed without vanquishing. These young soldiers, one half of whom had never before been in an engagement, received the shock of death during three hours without retreating one step, without making a single movement to escape it, and without being able to return it: their artillery being broken and the Russians keeping beyond the reach of their muskets.

But every instant strengthened the enemy and weakened Napoleon. The noise of artillery told him that in the rear of Krasnoi and his army, Bennigsen was proceeding to take possession of the road to Liadi and cut off his retreat. The east, west and south were sparkling with the enemy's fires; one side only remained open, that of the north and the Dnieper, towards a hill at the foot of which were the highroad and the Emperor. We fancied we saw the enemy covering this hill with his cannon: in that situation they were just over Napoleon's head and might have crushed him at a few yards' distance. He was informed of his danger, cast his eyes for an instant upon it and merely uttered these words, 'Very well, let a battalion of my *chasseurs* take possession of it!' Immediately afterwards, without paying further attention to it, his whole attention reverted to the perilous situation of Mortier.

Then at last Davout made his appearance, forcing his way through a swarm of Cossacks, whom he drove away by a rapid march. At the sight of Krasnoi, this marshal's troops disbanded themselves and ran across the fields to get beyond the right of the enemy's line, in the rear of which they had come up. Davout and his generals could only rally them at Krasnoi.

I Corps was thus preserved but we learned at the same time that our rearguard could no longer defend itself at Krasnoi; that Ney was probably still at Smolensk and that we must give up waiting for him any longer. Napoleon, however, still hesitated: he could not determine on making this great sacrifice.

But at last, as all were likely to perish, his resolution was fixed. He called Mortier and, squeezing his hand sorrowfully, told him that he had not a moment to lose; that the enemy were overwhelming him in all directions; that Kutusov might already reach Liadi, perhaps Orsha and the last elbow of the Dnieper before him; that he would therefore proceed there rapidly with his Old Guard, in order to occupy that passage. Davout would relieve Mortier; but both of them must endeavour to hold out in Krasnoi until night, after which they must come and rejoin him. Then, with his heart full of Ney's misfortune and of despair at abandoning him, he withdrew slowly from the field of battle, traversed Krasnoi, where he again halted, and then cleared his way to Liadi.

Mortier was anxious to obey but at that moment the Dutch troops of the Guard lost, along with a third part of their number, an important post which they were defending,[5] which the enemy immediately covered with his artillery. Roguet, feeling the destructive effect of its fire, fancied he was able to extinguish it. A regiment which he sent against the Russian battery was repulsed; a second (the 1st Voltigeurs) got into the middle of the Russians and stood firm against two charges of their cavalry. It continued to advance, torn to pieces by their grapeshot, when a third charge overwhelmed it. Fifty soldiers and eleven officers were all of it that Roguet was able to preserve.[6]

That general had lost half of his men. It was now two o'clock and his unshaken fortitude still kept the Russians in astonishment, when at last, emboldened by the Emperor's departure, they began to press upon him so closely that the Young Guard was nearly hemmed in and very soon in a situation in which it could neither hold out nor retreat.

Fortunately, some platoons which Davout had rallied and the appearance of another troop of his stragglers attracted the enemy's attention. Mortier availed himself of it. He gave orders to the 3,000 men he had still remaining to retreat slowly in the face of their 50,000 enemies: 'Do you hear, soldiers?' cried General Laborde. 'The Marshal orders ordinary time! *Ordinary time,* soldiers!' And these brave troops, dragging with them some of their wounded under a shower of grapeshot, retired as slowly from this field of carnage as they would have done from a field of manoeuvre.

As soon as Mortier had succeeded in placing Krasnoi between him and Bennigsen, he was in safety. The communication between that town and Liadi was only interrupted by the fire of the enemy's batteries, which flanked the left side of the great road. Colbert and Latour-Maubourg kept them in check upon their heights. In the course of this march a most singular incident occurred. A howitzer shell entered the body of a horse and blew it to pieces without wounding the rider, who fell upon his legs and went on.

The Emperor, meanwhile, halted at Liadi, four leagues from the field of battle. When night came on, he learned that Mortier, who he thought was in his rear, had got before him. Uneasy, he sent for him and with an agitated voice said to him that he had certainly fought gloriously and suffered greatly, but why had he placed his emperor between him and the enemy? Why had he exposed him to be cut off?

The Marshal got the start of Napoleon without being aware of it. He explained that he had at first left Davout in Krasnoi (again trying to rally his troops) and that he himself had halted not far from that: but that I Corps, having been driven back upon him, had obliged him to retreat. That besides, Kutusov did not follow up his victory with vigour and appeared to hang upon our flank with no other view than to feast his eyes upon our distress and gather up our wreckage.

Next day the march was continued with hesitation. The impatient stragglers took the lead and all of them got the start of Napoleon. He was on foot with a stick in his hand, walking with difficulty and disgust and halting every quarter of an hour, as if unwilling to tear himself from Old Russia, whose frontier he was passing and in which he had left his unfortunate companion in arms.

In the evening he reached Dombrovna, a wooden town and inhabited as well as Liadi: a novel sight for an army which had for three months seen nothing but ruins. We had at last emerged from Old Russia and her deserts of snow and ashes and were entering into a friendly country, whose language we understood. The weather just then became milder, a thaw began and we received some provisions.[7]

Thus the winter, the enemy, solitude, famine, all ceased at once: but it was too late. The Emperor saw that his army was destroyed; every moment the name of Ney escaped from his lips with cries of grief. That night particularly he was heard groaning and exclaiming that the misery of his poor soldiers cut him to the heart; and yet he could not relieve them without fixing himself in some place. But where was it possible for him to rest without ammunition, provisions or artillery? He was no longer strong enough to halt. He must reach Minsk as quickly as possible.

He had hardly spoken these words when a Polish officer arrived with the news that Minsk itself – his magazine, his retreat, his only hope – had just fallen into the hands of the Russians, Chichagov having entered it on the 16th. Napoleon, at first, was mute and overpowered at this last blow; but immediately afterwards, elevating himself in proportion to his danger, he coolly replied, 'Very well! We have now nothing to do but clear ourselves a passage with our bayonets.'

But in order to reach this new enemy, who had escaped

from Schwarzenberg (or whom Schwarzenberg had perhaps allowed to pass, for we knew nothing of the circumstances) and to escape from Kutusov and Prince Wittgenstein, we must cross the Berezina at Borisov. With that view Napoleon sent orders on 19 November from Dombrovna to Dombrowski to give up all idea of fighting Hoertel and proceed with all haste to occupy that passage. He ordered Oudinot to march rapidly to the same point and to hasten to recover Minsk: Victor would cover his march. After giving these orders his agitation was appeased and his mind, worn out with suffering, sunk into depression.

It was still far from daylight when a singular noise drew him out of his lethargy. Some say that shots were at first heard, which had been fired by our own people, in order to draw out of the houses such as had taken shelter in them, that they might take their places; others assert that from a disorderly practice, too common in our bivouacs, of shouting to each other, the name of Hausanne, a grenadier, being suddenly called out in the midst of a profound silence, was mistaken for the alert cry of '*Aux armes*', which announced a surprise by the enemy.

Whatever might be the cause, everyone immediately saw – or fancied he saw – the Cossacks and a great noise of war and alarm surrounded Napoleon. Without disturbing himself he said to Rapp, 'Go and see: it is no doubt some rascally Cossacks, determined to disturb our rest!' But it became very soon a complete tumult of men running to fight or flee and who, meeting in the dark, mistook each other for enemies.

Napoleon for a moment imagined that a serious attack had been made. As an embanked stream of water ran through the town, he enquired if the remaining artillery had been placed behind that ravine and, being informed that the precaution had been neglected, he himself immediately ran to the bridge and caused his cannon to be hurried over to the other side.

He then returned to his Old Guard and stopping in front

of each battalion: 'Grenadiers!' he said to them, 'we are retreating without being conquered by the enemy, let us not be vanquished by ourselves! Set an example to the army! Several of you have already deserted your eagles and even thrown away your arms. I have no wish to have recourse to military laws to put a stop to this disorder but appeal entirely to yourselves! Do justice among yourselves. To your own honour I commit the support of your discipline!'

The other troops he harangued in a similar style. These few words were quite sufficient to the old grenadiers, who probably had no occasion for them. The others received them with applause but an hour afterwards, when the march was resumed, they were quite forgotten. As to his rearguard, throwing the greatest part of the blame for this hot alarm upon it, he sent an angry message to Davout on the subject.

At Orsha we found an abundant supply of provisions, a bridge equipage of sixty boats with all its accessories – which were entirely burnt – and thirty-six pieces of cannon with their horses, which were distributed between Davout, Eugène and Latour-Maubourg.

Here for the first time we met again with the officers and *gendarmes* who had been sent for the purpose of stopping the crowd of stragglers on the two bridges of the Dnieper and making them rejoin their columns. But those eagles, which formerly promised everything, were now looked upon as a fatal omen and deserted accordingly.

Disorder was already regularly organized and had enlisted in its ranks men who showed their ability in its service. When an immense crowd had been collected, these wretches called out, '*The Cossacks!*' with a view to quicken the march of those who preceded them and to increase the chaos. They then took advantage of it to carry off the provisions and cloaks of those whom they had thrown off their guard.

The *gendarmes*, who again saw this army for the first time since its disaster, were astonished at the sight of such misery, terrified at the great confusion, and became discouraged. This friendly frontier was entered riotously: it would have been given up to pillage, had it not been for the Guard and a few hundred who remained with Prince Eugène.

Napoleon entered Orsha with 6,000 guards, the remains of 35,000! Eugène with 1,800 soldiers, the remains of 42,000! Davout with 4,000, the remains of 70,000!

This marshal had lost everything, was without linen and emaciated with hunger. He seized upon a loaf which was offered him by one of his comrades and voraciously devoured it. A handkerchief was given him to wipe his face, which was covered with rime. He exclaimed that none but men of iron could support such trials, that it was physically impossible to resist them; that there were limits to human strength, the utmost of which had been exceeded.[8]

He it was who at first supported the retreat as far as Viasma. He was still, according to his custom, halting at all the defiles and remaining there the very last, sending everyone to his ranks and constantly struggling with the disorder. He urged his soldiers to insult and strip of their booty such of their comrades as threw away their arms; the only means of retaining the first and punishing the last. Nevertheless, his methodical and severe genius, so much out of its element in that scene of universal confusion, has been accused of being too much intimidated by it.

The Emperor made fruitless attempts to check this despondency. When alone, he was heard sympathizing with the sufferings of his soldiers; but in their presence, even upon that point, he wished to appear inflexible. He issued a proclamation ordering everyone to return to their ranks: if they did not, he would strip the officers of their grades and put the soldiers to death.

A threat like this produced neither a good nor bad impression upon men who had become indifferent or were reduced to despair: fleeing not from danger but from suffering; and less apprehensive of the *death* with which they were threatened than of the *life* that was offered to them.

But Napoleon's confidence increased with his peril; in his eyes and in the midst of these deserts of mud and ice, this handful of men was still the Grand Army and himself the conqueror of Europe! And there was no foolishness in this firmness: we were certain of it when in this very town, we saw him burning with his own hands everything belonging to him, which might serve as trophies to the enemy in the event of his fall.

There also were unfortunately consumed all the papers which he had collected in order to write the history of his life, for such was his intention when he set out for this fatal war. He had then determined to halt as a threatening conqueror on the borders of the Düna and the Dnieper, to which he now returned as a disarmed fugitive.

12 The Hero of the Retreat

> While the Emperor was agitated by gloomy uncertainty as to the fate of the rearguard and its intrepid leader, Ney was performing one of the most brilliant feats of arms recorded in military annals . . .
>
> Baron de Marbot

Napoleon entered Orsha on 19 November. There, at last, the troops were fed and an attempt was made to restore order to their devastated ranks. A number of fresh horses were found, as well as a few extra guns for the artillery. There was no time to rest, however, for Napoleon, having successfully gained the Dnieper, already had his eyes on the next and final obstacle between his army and comparative safety: the River Berezina, a further eighty miles or so to the west.

In order to lighten the army's load and so speed its journey, Napoleon gave orders to destroy all superfluous baggage, equipment and vehicles; but with no gendarmes *to see his instructions carried out, they went largely unheeded. Unfortunately, one particular imperial decree was executed: the destruction of the bridge-train. Believing the bridge at Borisov to be secure in the hands of his Polish troops, Napoleon decided to sacrifice this heavy, bulky equipment, in order to facilitate the coming march; and as de Ségur noted in the previous chapter, it was duly burned at Orsha. Fortunately, General Eblé of the Engineers, deliberately disobeying orders, managed to rescue two field forges and eight wagons of coal and tools from the flames. They would be sorely needed.*

Meanwhile, although Napoleon's reputation and the bayonets of the Guard had – for the moment at least – saved the retreat, Ney and the rearguard seemed lost for good. De Ségur tells us that, 'Napoleon was long before he could decide to quit the Dnieper. It seemed to him that this was like a second abandonment of the unfortunate Ney; and casting off for ever his intrepid companion-in-arms. There, as he had done at Liadi and Dombrovna, he was calling every hour of the day and night and sending to enquire if no tidings had been heard of that marshal. Four days this mortal silence had lasted and yet the Emperor still continued to hope.'

Michel Ney, Duke of Elchingen, Prince of the Moskva and Marshal of France, was born in Saarlouis, the son of a barrel-maker. Like so many of Napoleon's acolytes, he was a man of humble origins made good: for the Emperor's new aristocrats did not receive favours on account of their ancestry but on their merits as soldiers. Nicknamed 'Le Rougeaud' on account of his red hair, Ney enlisted as a hussar trooper in 1787. Thanks to the Revolution, which swept away the Ancien Régime in an avalanche of blood, he quickly rose to the rank of general; and in 1804, at the dawn of Napoleon's empire, his military talents were rewarded with a marshal's bâton. Prior to the 1812 campaign Ney had already earned himself the reputation of a hard-fighting front-line general; but his bravery in Russia at the head of III Corps would make him a legend. In the memoirs and journals of veterans we find Ney variously described as 'a God of war', 'a man of astonishing gallantry' and 'the real hero of this great catastrophe'.[1] *De Ségur, by recording the details of Ney's remarkable march to rejoin Napoleon at Orsha – as related to him by the survivors of III Corps – has ensured the legend's immortality.*

Ney left Smolensk on 17 November with about 6,000 troops and twelve guns. The next day, having come upon the scene of the recent fighting – or, in de Ségur's words, 'that field of snow reddened with blood, sprinkled with broken cannon and mutilated corpses' – he found his path blocked by Kutusov's army. An officer, sent by Kutusov to accept Ney's anticipated surrender, promptly made his appearance. According to de Ségur, 'The Russian had not finished his speech, when suddenly forty dis-

charges of grapeshot, proceeding from the right of his army and cutting our ranks to pieces, struck him with amazement and interrupted what he had to say. At that moment a French officer darted forward, seized, and was about to kill him as a traitor, when Ney, checking this fury, called to him angrily, "A marshal never surrenders; there is no parleying under an enemy's fire: you are my prisoner!"' And with that, knowing full well that 80,000 Russians stood between him and the rest of the Grand Army, Ney charged the enemy lines.

AND YET the French leader had no thought of surrendering – nor even of dying – but of cutting his way through the enemy (and without the least idea that he was attempting a sublime effort). Alone and looking nowhere for support, while all were supported by him, he followed the impulse of a fiery temperament and the pride of a conqueror, whom the habit of gaining unlikely victories had impressed with the belief that everything was possible.

Ricard and his 1,500 soldiers were in front. Ney pushed them against the enemy and prepared the rest of his army to follow them. That division descended into the ravine, but, ascending from it, was driven back, overwhelmed by the Russian first line.

The Marshal, without being intimidated – or allowing others to be so – collected the survivors, placed them in reserve and marched forward in their place: Ledru, Razont and Marchand seconded him. He ordered 400 Illyrians[2] to take the enemy on their left flank, and with 3,000 men he himself mounted a frontal assault. He made no speeches: he marched at their head, setting the example. All followed him. They attacked and overturned the first Russian line and without stopping were throwing themselves upon the second, but before they could reach it, a volley of grapeshot poured down upon them. In an instant Ney saw the greater part of his soldiers killed: their shapeless column whirled round, tottered, fell back and drew him along with it.

Ney found he had attempted the impossible and he waited till the flight of his men had once more placed the ravine between them and the enemy. That ravine was now his sole resource. There, equally hopeless and fearless, he halted and rallied them. He drew up 2,000 men against 80,000. He returned the fire of 200 cannon with six pieces and made Fortune blush that she should ever betray such courage.

She it was, doubtless, who then struck Kutusov with the palsy of inertia. To their infinite surprise, they saw this Russian Fabius running into extremes – like all imitators – persisting in what he called his humanity and prudence, remaining upon his heights with his pompous virtues, without allowing himself (or daring) to conquer, as if he was astonished at his own superiority. Seeing that Napoleon had been beaten by his own rashness, he pushed his horror of that fault to the very extreme of the opposite vice.

It required but an outburst of indignation in any one of the Russian corps to have completely extinguished us: but all were afraid to make a decisive movement. They remained stuck to their soil with the sluggishness of slaves, as if they had no boldness but in their obedience. This discipline, which formed their glory in *their* retreat, was their disgrace in *ours*.

They were for a long time hesitant, not knowing what enemy they were fighting: for they had imagined that Ney had retreated from Smolensk by the right bank of the Dnieper. They were mistaken, as is often the case, from supposing that their enemy had done what he ought to have done!

At the same time, the Illyrians had returned in disorder. They had had a most singular adventure: in their advance to the left flank of the enemy's position, these 400 men had met with 5,000 Russians returning from a fight and with a French eagle and several of our soldiers prisoners.

These two hostile troops – the one returning to its position, the other going to attack it – advanced in the same direction, side by side, measuring each other with their eyes but neither of them venturing to begin the engagement. They marched so close to each other that from the middle of the Russian ranks the French prisoners stretched out their arms towards their friends, begging them to come and deliver them. The latter called out to them to come across and they would receive and defend them: but no one moved on either side. Just then Ney was overthrown and they retreated along with him.

Kutusov, however, relying more on his artillery than his soldiers, sought only to conquer at a distance. His fire so completely commanded the ground occupied by the French that the same ball which levelled a man in the first rank proceeded to deal destruction in the last of the baggage train, among the women who had fled from Moscow.

Under this murderous hail, Ney's soldiers remained motionless, looking at their chief, awaiting his decision before being satisfied that they were lost: because in the midst of this extreme danger they saw his spirit calm and tranquil, like anything in its element. His expression became thoughtful; he was watching the enemy's army, which extended itself to a great distance on his flanks, in order to shut him out from all means of preservation.

The approach of night began to render objects indistinct. Winter – which in that one point was favourable to our retreat – brought it on quickly. Ney had been waiting for it; but the advantage he took of the respite was to order his men to return to Smolensk. They all said that at these words they remained frozen with astonishment. Even his aide-de-camp could not believe his ears and looked at his general with amazement. But the Marshal having repeated the same order in a commanding tone, they immediately obeyed and without hesitation turned their backs on their own army, on Napoleon and on France! They returned once more into that fatal Russia. Their retrograde march lasted an hour. They passed again over the field of battle marked by the remains of the Army of Italy. There they halted and their marshal, who had remained alone in the rearguard, then rejoined them.

Their eyes followed his every movement. What was he going to do? And whatever might be his plan, how would he direct his steps without a guide in an unknown country? But he, with his warlike instinct, halted on the edge of a ravine of such depth as to make it probable that a stream ran through it. He made them clear away the snow and break the ice, then, consulting his map, he exclaimed that this was one of the streams which flowed into the Dnieper: 'This must be our guide and we must follow it. It will lead us to that river, which we must cross, and on the other side we shall be safe!'

However, at a little distance from the highroad, which he had abandoned, he again halted in a village, the name of which they knew not (but believed it was either Fomina or Danikova). There he rallied his troops and made them light fires, as if he intended to take up his quarters for the night. Some Cossacks who followed him no doubt sent immediately to inform Kutusov of the spot where, next day, a French marshal would surrender his arms: for shortly after the noise of their cannon was again heard.

Ney listened: 'Is this Davout, who has remembered me at last?' And he listened a second time. But there were regular intervals between the firing. It was a salvo. Being then fully satisfied that the Russian army was celebrating in anticipation of his captivity, he swore he would give the lie to their joy and immediately resumed his march.

At the same time his Poles ransacked the country. A lame peasant was the only inhabitant they had discovered: this was an unlooked-for piece of good fortune. He informed them that they were within a league of the Dnieper; but that it was not fordable there and could not yet be frozen over: 'It will be so,' was the Marshal's remark. When it was observed to him that the thaw had just commenced, he added that it did not matter, we must pass, as there was no other resource.

At last, about eight o'clock, after passing through a village, the ravine ended and the peasant, who walked first, halted and pointed to the river. They imagined that this must have been between Syrokorenia and Gusinoë. Ney and those immediately behind him ran up to it. They found the river sufficiently frozen to bear their weight; the course of the ice which it bore along being thwarted by a sudden turn in its banks, the winter had completely frozen it over at that spot: both above and below, its surface was still moving.

This observation was enough to make their first sensation of joy give way to uneasiness. This hostile river might only offer them a deceitful appearance. One officer committed himself for the rest: he crossed to the other side with great difficulty, returned, and reported that the men and perhaps some of the horses might pass over; but that the rest must be abandoned; and there was no time to lose, as the ice was beginning to give way because of the thaw.

But in this nocturnal and silent march across fields, of a column composed of weakened and wounded men and women with their children, they had been unable to keep close enough to prevent their separating in the darkness. Ney realized that only a part of his people had come up; nevertheless, he might have surmounted the obstacle, thereby securing his own safety, and waited on the other side. The idea never entered his mind. Someone proposed it to him but he rejected it instantly. He allowed three hours for the rallying, and without suffering himself to be disturbed by impatience or the danger of waiting so long, he wrapped himself up in his cloak and passed the time in a deep sleep on the bank of the river.

At last, about midnight, the passage began. But the first persons who ventured on the ice called out that it was bending under them; that it was sinking; that they were up to their knees in water: immediately after which that frail support was heard splitting with frightful cracks, as in the breaking up of a frost. All halted in alarm.

Ney ordered them to pass one at a time. They advanced with caution, not knowing in the darkness if they were putting their feet on the ice or into a chasm: for there were places where they were obliged to clear large cracks and jump from one piece of ice to another, at the risk of falling between them and disappearing for ever. The first hesitated but those who were behind kept calling to them to make haste.

When at last, after several of these dreadful panics, they reached the opposite bank and fancied themselves saved, a vertical slope, entirely covered with rime, again opposed their landing. Many were thrown back upon the ice, which they broke in their fall or which bruised them. By their account, this Russian river appeared only to have contributed with regret to their escape.

But what seemed to affect them with the greatest horror was the distraction of the females and the sick, when it became necessary to abandon, along with all the baggage, the remains of their fortune, their provisions, and, in short, their whole resources against the present and the future. They saw them stripping themselves, selecting, throwing away, taking up again and falling with exhaustion and grief upon the frozen bank of the river. They seemed to shudder again at the recollection of the horrible sight of so many men scattered over that abyss, the continual noise of persons falling, the cries of such as sunk in, and, above all, the wailing and despair of the wounded who, from their carts, stretched out their hands to their companions and begged not to be left behind.

Their leader then determined to attempt the passage of several wagons loaded with these poor creatures; but in the middle of the river the ice sunk down and separated. Then were heard, proceeding from the abyss, cries of anguish long and piercing; then stifled, feeble groans and at last an awful silence. All had disappeared!

Ney was looking steadfastly at the void with an air of anxiety, when through the darkness, he imagined he saw an object still moving: it turned out to be one of those unfortunate persons, an officer named Briqueville, whom a deep wound in the groin had disabled from standing upright. A large piece of ice had borne him up. He was soon distinctly seen, dragging himself from one piece to another on his hands and knees; and on his getting near enough to the side, the Marshal himself caught hold of and saved him.

The losses since the preceding day amounted to 4,000 stragglers and 3,000 soldiers, either dead or missing. The cannon and the whole of the baggage were lost. There remained to Ney scarcely 3,000 soldiers and about as many disbanded men. Finally, when all these sacrifices were consumated and all that had been able to cross the river were collected, they resumed their march and the defeated river became once more their friend and their guide.

They proceeded at random, when one of them, happening to fall, recognized a beaten road: it was but too much so, for those who were marching first, stooping and using their hands as well as their eyes, halted in alarm, exclaiming that they saw the fresh marks of a great quantity of cannon and horses. They had, therefore, only avoided one hostile army to fall into the midst of another. At a time when they could scarcely walk, they must again be obliged to fight! The war was therefore everywhere! But Ney made them push on, and without disturbing himself continued to follow these menacing traces.

They brought them to a village called Gusinoé, into which they entered suddenly and seized everything. They found in it all that they had been in want of since they left Moscow: inhabitants, provisions, rest, warm houses and 100 Cossacks, who awoke to find themselves prisoners. Their reports and the necessity of taking some refreshment to enable them to proceed detained the Marshal there a few minutes.

About ten o'clock they reached two other villages and were resting themselves there, when suddenly the surrounding forests appeared to be filled with movement. They had scarcely time to call each other, to look about and to concentrate themselves in the village which was nearest to the Dnieper, when thousands of Cossacks came pouring out from between the trees and surrounded the unfortunate troops with their lances and their cannon.

These were Platov and his hordes, who were following the right bank of the Dnieper. They might have burnt the village, discovered the weakness of Ney's force and exterminated it; but for three hours they remained motionless, without even firing, for what reason is unknown. The account since given by themselves is that they had no orders; that at that moment their leader was not in a state to give any;[3] and that in Russia, no one dares to take upon himself a responsibility that does not belong to him.

The bold countenance of Ney kept them in check. He himself and a few soldiers were sufficient: he even ordered the rest of his people to continue their supper till night came on. He then caused the order to be circulated to decamp in silence, to give notice to each other in a low voice and to march as compact as possible. Afterwards, they all began their march together; but their very first step was like a signal given to the enemy, who immediately discharged the whole of his artillery at them: all his squadrons also put themselves in movement at once.

At the noise occasioned by this, the disarmed stragglers, of whom there were yet between 3,000 and 4,000, took the alarm. This flock of men wandered here and there; the great mass of them kept reeling about in uncertainty, sometimes attempting to throw themselves into the ranks of the soldiers, who drove them back. Ney contrived to keep them between him and the Russians, whose fire was principally absorbed by these useless beings. The most timid, therefore, in this instance served as a covering to the bravest.

At the same time that the Marshal made a rampart of these poor wretches to cover his right flank, he regained the banks of the Dnieper and by that covered his left flank. He marched on thus between the two, proceeding from wood to wood, from one turning to another, taking advantage of all the windings and of the least advantage of the ground. Whenever he ventured to any distance from the river, which he was frequently obliged to do, Platov then surrounded him on all sides.

In this manner, for two days and a distance of twenty leagues, did 6,000 Cossacks keep constantly buzzing about the flanks of their column, now reduced to 1,500 men in arms, keeping it in a state of siege, disappearing before its sallies, and returning again instantly.

The night brought some relief and at first they plunged into the darkness with a degree of joy; but then, if anyone halted for a moment to bid a last adieu to some worn-out or wounded comrade, who sank to rise no more, he ran the risk of losing the traces of his column. Under such circumstances there were many cruel moments and not a few instances of despair. At last, however, the enemy slackened his pursuit.

This unfortunate column was proceeding more calmly, groping its way through a thick wood, when all at once, a few paces before it, a brilliant light and several discharges of cannon flashed in the faces of the men in the first rank. Seized with terror, they fancied that there was an end of them, that they were cut off, that their last day was now come and they fell down terrified. Those who were behind got entangled among them and were brought to the ground. Ney, who saw that all was lost, rushed forward, ordered the charge to be beat, as if he had foreseen the attack and called out, 'Comrades, now is your time! Forward! They are our prisoners!' At these words his soldiers, who but a minute before were in dismay, believed they were about to surprise their foes: from being defeated, they rose up conquerors! They rushed upon the enemy, who had already disappeared and whose headlong flight through the forest they heard at a distance.

They passed quickly through this wood; but about ten

o'clock at night, they met with a small river embanked in a deep ravine, which they were obliged to cross one by one, as they had done the Dnieper. Intent on the pursuit of these poor fellows, the Cossacks again got sight of them and tried to take advantage of that moment: but Ney, by a few volleys of his musketry, again repulsed them. They surmounted this obstacle with difficulty and in an hour after reached a large village, where hunger and exhaustion compelled them to halt for two hours longer.

The next day, 19 November, from midnight till ten o'clock in the morning, they kept marching on, without meeting any other enemy than a hilly country. About that time Platov's columns again made their appearance and Ney halted and faced them, under the protection of the skirts of a wood. As long as the day lasted, his soldiers were obliged to resign themselves to see the enemy's shells overturning the trees which served to shelter them: for now they had nothing but small arms, which could not keep the Cossack artillery at a sufficient distance.

On the return of night, the Marshal gave the usual signal and they proceeded on their march to Orsha. During the preceding day, he had already despatched Pchébendowski there with fifty horsemen to demand assistance: they must have arrived there, unless the enemy had gained possession of that town.

Ney's officers concluded their narrative[4] by saying that during the rest of their march, they had met with several formidable obstacles but that they did not think them worth relating. They continued, however, speaking enthusiastically of their marshal and making us sharers of their admiration of him; for even his equals had no idea of being jealous of him. He had been too much regretted – and his preservation had excited too agreeable emotions – to allow envy to have any part in them. Besides, Ney had placed himself completely beyond its reach. As to himself, in all this heroism, he had gone so little beyond his natural disposition, that had it not been for the éclat of his glory in the eyes, the gestures, and the applause of everyone, he would never have imagined that he had performed a sublime action. Each of the latter days had had its remarkable men: among others, that of the 16th had Eugène, that of the 17th had Mortier; but after this time, Ney was universally proclaimed the hero of the retreat.

The distance between Smolensk and Orsha is hardly five days' march. In that short passage, what a harvest of glory had been reaped! How little space and time are required to establish an immortal renown! Of what nature then are these great inspirations, that invisible and impalpable germ of great devotion, produced in a few moments, issuing from a single heart, and which must fill time and eternity?

When Napoleon, who was two leagues farther on, heard that Ney had again made his appearance, he leaped and shouted for joy and exclaimed, 'I have then saved my eagles! I would have given 300 millions from my treasury, sooner than have lost such a man.'

13 'Behold My Star Reappear!'

> A dark rumour had spread that two new enemy armies were threatening our line of retreat . . . Without being pursued, we approached the Berezina, but on the march these rumours steadily gained substance, and the names 'Chichagov' and 'Berezina' passed from mouth to mouth . . .
>
> Captain von Borcke[1]

Chichagov's capture of Minsk scuppered any hope Napoleon may have had of heading south and linking up with Schwarzenberg's Austrian corps. Now the only option was a retrograde march to Vilna and the Polish frontier: the crucial thing being to get across the Berezina at Borisov, where – supposedly – the bridge was safe in the hands of Dombrowski's Poles. Chichagov, however, had other ideas.

Admiral Pavel Chichagov (Napoleon, defeated by this surname, simply referred to him as 'the Admiral' or 'that damned sailor') was not an experienced warrior but was popular at court; and at the commencement of hostilities had been given command of the Army of Moldavia. Freed from Balkan border duties by the Peace of Bucharest, Chichagov was initially sent north to link up with Tormassov's Third Army of the West, near the Pripet Marshes; by November, however, he was advancing to the line of the Berezina: his mission, to block Napoleon's expected escape route. Alexander, watching the wreck of the Grand Army crawl across his map in St Petersburg, wanted 'the modern Attila' snared.

As previously stated, responsibility for Napoleon's southern flank lay in the hands of Prince Schwarzenberg and his Austrian contingent. Austria's participation in the war was, however, nominal; and Schwarzenberg was committed just enough to satisfy the demands of honour. Thus, when Chichagov – having edged his way round the western tip of the Pripet Marshes – sent General Sacken to menace Polish territory in the Grand Army's rear, Schwarzenberg felt obliged to act. Falling for Chichagov's feint, he went scampering after Sacken, leaving Napoleon's main supply depot at Minsk uncovered and vulnerable in the process.[2] *Although Schwarzenberg defeated Sacken at Volkovisk on 16 November, he could do nothing to stop Chichagov from taking Minsk and its well-stocked magazines the following day. The Grand Army's southern flank was now left hanging: Alexander's trap was closing.*

Bronikowski, Napoleon's governor of Minsk (who had foolishly ignored rumours of a Russian attack), managed to escape Chichagov's coup with 2,000 garrison troops. He made directly for Borisov, fifty miles or so to the north-east, determined to hold the all-important bridge over the Berezina. It was here that he was joined – at midnight on 20 November – by General Dombrowski and his mixed force of French, Poles and Würtembergers. With Schwarzenberg far away to the south-west and Napoleon at Orsha, some seventy miles to the east, the defenders – around 5,000 in all – could do little but prepare to sell their lives dearly.

Early next morning, advanced elements of Chichagov's army arrived at Borisov and the battle for the bridge began. Dombrowski's heroes hung on for as long as humanly possible but were eventually overwhelmed by superior numbers. According to Edward Foord, 'The fight raged obstinately well into the afternoon, the 1st and 6th Polish regiments with their French and German comrades resisting with magnificent courage.' But by nightfall, with over half his men either dead or wounded, Dombrowski was evicted from the town and sent flying down the Orsha road.

Meanwhile, on 22 November, according to de Ségur, 'The army had a disagreeable march from Orsha towards Borisov, on a wide road in which the snow had melted and through a deep and liquid mud.' It was on this 'disagreeable' march that Napoleon received the news of Borisov's capture by 'that damned sailor'. Having literally burned his bridges at Orsha, Napoleon now faced entrapment and annihilation. In the words of de Ségur, 'The Emperor, striking the ground with his stick and darting a furious look to heaven, pronounced these words, "Is it then written above that we shall now commit nothing but faults?"' In spite of all his plans and precautions, 'every disaster which Napoleon could anticipate had occurred.'

With the situation getting grimmer by the hour, Napoleon – with personal safety uppermost in his mind – created the legendary Sacred Squadron: a unit consisting of the few remaining cavalry officers still mounted (having lost their horses to the cold or the cooking-pot, most troopers were now marching with the footsore infantry). In it – according to Napoleon's own 29th Bulletin – 'Generals served as captains, the colonels as non-commissioned officers. This sacred squadron, commanded by General Grouchy under the orders of the King of Naples, did not lose sight of the Emperor wherever he went.'[3]

It was at this point, however, that Marshal Oudinot – not one of Napoleon's brightest lieutenants but surely one of his boldest – began to make his mark on the campaign. As commander of II Corps, he had spent most of the campaign north of the main column, scrapping with Prince Wittgenstein's Army of Finland along the banks of the River Drissa. Ordered by Napoleon to retake Minsk, Oudinot had been nearing Borisov with his 8,000 relatively fresh troops, when he learned of Chichagov's recent success. Without further ado – and picking up Dombrowski's survivors on the way – he set off to recover the town and its vital bridge.

On 23 November the intrepid Marshal caught Chichagov's advanced guard completely off balance. Panic ensued as the Russians, abandoning their baggage, fled back through Borisov and over the Berezina to the safety of its western bank. Chichagov had just been about to sit down to a silver service dinner in town when Oudinot's attack went in: he bolted across the Borisov bridge on foot, leaving his supper to the grateful French soldiery.

Despite Oudinot's best efforts, however, he could not prevent the Russians from destroying the real prize: the bridge over the Berezina. According to Baron de Marbot, serving with II Corps, 'A battalion of grenadiers came up at the double and forced us at the bayonet's point to abandon the bridge, which was presently covered with lighted torches and became a huge furnace.'

Nevertheless, Oudinot was able to comfort Napoleon with a scrap of hope; for, thanks to General Corbineau, commander of his 6th Cavalry Brigade, a ford had been discovered eight miles north of Borisov at the village of Studzianka, where, according to de Ségur, 'the river was only fifty-four fathoms wide and six feet deep.'[4] *The situation was still desperate; for bridges would have to be improvised in order to save the army and its impedimenta, but at least the possibility of a miracle now existed. Napoleon's star began to glimmer again.*

Meanwhile, as the Grand Army approached the Berezina, it was joined by the men of Marshal Victor's IX Corps, who had been pushed back on to the main column from their position on its northern flank by Prince Wittgenstein's army. Although Victor's men – like Oudinot's – were still fresh, the survivors of Napoleon's column were, by now, nothing but spectres – mere shadows of their former selves. Captain von Borcke, a German serving with the Grand Army who survived the nightmare, later noted: 'Gloomy, silent and with downcast eyes, this rabble of dying men walked from Orsha to the Berezina like a funeral procession.'[5]

IN THIS last stage of weakness and confusion, as we were approaching Borisov, we heard loud cries before us. Some rushed forward, thinking it was an attack. It was Victor's army, which had been driven back by Prince Wittgenstein to the right side of our road, where it remained waiting for the Emperor to pass by. Still quite complete and full of fire, it received the Emperor as soon as he made his appearance with the customary but now long-forgotten acclamations.

Of our disasters it had heard nothing: they had been carefully concealed even from its leaders. When, therefore, instead of that grand column which had conquered Moscow, its soldiers saw behind Napoleon only a train of spectres covered with rags, female pelisses, pieces of carpet or dirty cloaks – half burnt and riddled by fire – and with nothing on their feet but rags of all sorts, their consternation was extreme. They looked terrified at the sight of those unfortunate soldiers, as they defiled before them with lean carcasses, faces black with dirt and hideous bristly beards, unarmed, shameless, marching confusedly with their heads bent, their eyes fixed on the ground and silent, like a troop of captives.

But what astonished them more than all was to see the number of colonels and generals scattered about and isolated, who seemed only occupied about themselves, thinking of nothing but saving the wrecks of their property or their persons. They were marching pell-mell with the soldiers, who did not notice them, to whom they no longer had any commands to give, and of whom they had nothing to expect: all ties between them being broken and all distinction of ranks obliterated by the common misery.

The soldiers of Victor and Oudinot could not believe their eyes. Moved with compassion, their officers with tears in their eyes detained such of their companions as they recognized in the crowd. They first supplied them with clothes and provisions and then asked them where were their corps. And when the others pointed them out, seeing, instead of so many thousand men, only a weak platoon of officers and NCOs, their eyes still kept on the lookout.

The sight of so great a disaster struck the II and IX Corps with discouragement from the very first day. Disorder – the most contagious of all evils – attacked them; for it would seem as if order was an effort against nature. And yet the unarmed and even the dying, although they were now fully aware that they had to fight their way across a river and through a fresh enemy, never doubted of their being victorious.

It was now merely the shadow of an army: but it was the

shadow of the Grand Army! It felt conscious that Nature alone had defeated it. The sight of the Emperor revived it. It had been long accustomed to look to him, not for its means of support but solely to lead it to victory. This was its first unfortunate campaign and it had had so many fortunate ones! It only required to be able to follow him. He alone, who had raised his soldiers so high and now sunk them so low, was yet able to save them. He was still, therefore, cherished in the heart of his army, like hope in the heart of man.

Thus, amid so many men who might have reproached him with their misfortunes, he marched on without the least fear, speaking to one and all without affectation, certain of being respected as long as glory could command our respect. Knowing perfectly that he belonged to us, as much as we to him – his fame being a sort of national property – we should have sooner turned our arms against ourselves (which was the case with many) than against him.

Some of them fell and died at his feet; and though in the most frightful delirium, their suffering never gave its wanderings the turn of reproach but of entreaty. And in fact did he not share the common danger? Which of them all risked so much as he? Who suffered the greatest loss in this disaster? If any curses were uttered, it was not in his presence. It seemed that of all misfortunes, that of stirring his displeasure was still the greatest: so rooted were their confidence in, and submission to, that man who had given the world to them.

We were now approaching the most critical moment: Victor was in the rear with 15,000 men; Oudinot in front with 5,000 and already close to the Berezina; the Emperor between them with 7,000 men, 40,000 stragglers and an enormous quantity of baggage and artillery, the greatest part of which belonged to the II and IX Corps.

On the 25th, as he was about to reach the Berezina, he appeared to linger on his march. He halted every instant on the highroad, waiting for night to conceal his arrival from the enemy and to allow Oudinot time to evacuate Borisov.

This marshal, when he entered that town upon the 23rd, found the bridge, which was 300 fathoms in length,[6] destroyed at three different points; and that the presence of the enemy rendered it impossible to repair. He had learned that on his left, two miles lower down the river, there was, near Oukoholda, a deep and unsafe ford; that at the distance of a mile above Borisov, at Stadhof, there was another but of difficult approach. Finally, he had learned within the last two days that at Studzianka, two leagues above Stadhof, there was a third passage. For this knowledge he was indebted to Corbineau's brigade.

This was the same brigade which the Bavarian general, von Wrede, had taken from II Corps on his march to Smoliantzy. He had retained it until he reached Dokszitzi, whence he sent it back to II Corps by way of Borisov. When Corbineau arrived there, he found Chichagov already in possession of it and was forced to make his retreat by ascending the Berezina and concealing his force in the forests which border it. Not knowing at what point to cross the river, he accidentally saw a peasant, whose horse seemed to be quite wet, as if he had just come out of it. He laid hold of this man and made him his guide. He got up behind him and crossed the river at a ford opposite to Studzianka. He immediately rejoined Oudinot and informed him of the discovery he had made.

As Napoleon's intention was to retreat directly upon Vilna, the Marshal saw at once that this passage was the most direct, as well as the least dangerous. It was also observed that even if our infantry and artillery should be too closely pressed by Prince Wittgenstein and Kutusov, and prevented from crossing the river on bridges, there was at least a certainty – from the ford having been tried – that the Emperor and the cavalry would be able to pass; that all would not then be lost – both peace and war – as if

Napoleon himself remained in the enemy's hands. The Marshal, therefore, did not hesitate. In the night of the 23rd, the general of artillery, a company of *pontonniers*, a regiment of infantry and Corbineau's brigade, took possession of Studzianka.

At the same time the other two passages were reconnoitred and both found to be strongly observed. The object, therefore, was to deceive and displace the enemy. As force could do nothing, recourse was had to stratagem; in furtherance of which, on the 24th, 300 men and several hundred stragglers were sent towards Oukoholda with instructions to collect there, with as much noise as possible, all the necessary materials for the construction of a bridge; the whole division of the cuirassiers was also made to promenade on that side within view of the enemy.

In addition to this, General Lorencé had several Jews sought out and brought to him: he interrogated them with apparent minuteness with regard to the ford and the roads leading from it to Minsk. Then, pretending to be mightily pleased with their answers, and to be satisfied that there was no better passage to be found, he detained some of these rascals as guides and had the others conveyed beyond our outposts. But to make still more sure of the latter *not* keeping their word with him, he made them swear that they would return to meet us, in the direction of the lower Berezina, in order to inform us of the enemy's movements.

While these attempts were making to draw Chichagov's attention entirely to the left, the means of effecting a passage were secretly preparing at Studzianka. It was only on the 25th, at five in the evening, that Eblé[7] arrived there, followed only by two field forges, two wagons of coal, six covered wagons of tools and nails, and some companies of *pontonniers*. At Smolensk he had made each workman provide himself with a tool and some cramp irons.

But the trestles, which had been made the day before out of the beams of the Polish cabins, were found to be too weak. The work was to do all over again. It was found to be quite impossible to finish the bridge during the night: it could only be fixed during the following day, the 26th, in full daylight and under the enemy's fire; but there was no room for hesitation.

On the first approach of that decisive night, Oudinot gave up to Napoleon the occupation of Borisov and went to take position with the rest of his corps at Studzianka. They marched in the most profound darkness, without making the least noise.

By eight o'clock at night Oudinot and Dombrowski had taken possession of the heights commanding the crossing, while General Eblé descended from them. That general placed himself on the bank of the river with his *pontonniers* and a wagonload of the irons and abandoned wheels, which at all hazards he had made into cramp irons. He had sacrificed everything to preserve that feeble resource and it saved the army.

At the close of the night of the 25th, he made them sink the first trestle in the muddy bed of the river. But to crown our misfortunes, the rising of the waters had made the traces of the ford entirely disappear. It required the most incredible efforts on the part of our unfortunate sappers, who were plunged in the water up to their mouths and had to contend with the floating pieces of ice which were carried along by the stream. Many of them perished from the cold or were drowned by the ice floes, which a violent wind drove against them.

They had everything to conquer but the enemy. The severity of the temperature[8] was just at the degree necessary to render the passage of the river more difficult without suspending its course or sufficiently fixing the moving ice upon which we were about to venture. On this occasion the winter showed itself more Russian than even the Russians themselves. The latter failed their season, which never failed them.

The French[9] laboured during the whole night by the light of the enemy's fires, which shone on the heights of the opposite bank and within reach of the artillery of Tchaplitz's division. The latter, having no longer any doubt of our intentions, sent to inform his commander-in-chief.

The presence of a hostile division deprived us of all hope of deceiving the Russian admiral. We expected every instant to hear the whole fire of his artillery directed upon our workmen; and even if he did not discover them until daylight, their labours would not then be sufficiently advanced and the opposite bank, being low and marshy, was too much commanded by Tchaplitz's positions to make it possible for us to forge a passage.

When he quitted Borisov therefore, at ten o'clock at night, Napoleon imagined that he was setting out for a most desperate contest. He took up his quarters for the night with the 6,400 guards which still remained to him, at Staroi-Borisov, a chateau belonging to Prince Radzivil, situated on the right of the road from Borisov to Studzianka and equidistant from these two points.

He passed the remainder of that night on his feet, going out every moment to the passage where his destiny was accomplishing: for the magnitude of his anxieties so completely filled his hours, that as each revolved, he fancied that it was morning. Several times he was reminded of his mistake by his attendants.

Darkness had scarcely disappeared when he joined Oudinot. The sight of danger tranquillized him – as it always did – but on seeing the Russian fires and their position, his most determined generals, such as Rapp, Mortier and Ney, exclaimed that if the Emperor escaped from this danger, they must absolutely believe in the influence of his star! Murat himself thought it was now time to think of nothing but saving Napoleon.

The Emperor was waiting for the approach of daylight in one of the houses by the river, on a steep bank which was crowned by Oudinot's artillery. Murat obtained access to him; he declared to his brother-in-law that he looked upon the passage as impossible; he urged him to save himself while there was yet time. He informed him that he might, without danger, cross the Berezina a few leagues above Studzianka; that in five days he would reach Vilna; that some brave and determined Poles, perfectly acquainted with all the roads, had offered themselves for his guards and to be responsible for his safety.

But Napoleon rejected this proposition as an outrageous plan, as a cowardly flight, and was indignant that anyone should dare to think for a moment that he would abandon his army, so long as it was in danger. He was not, however, at all displeased with Murat, probably because that prince had afforded him an opportunity of showing his firmness, or rather, because he saw nothing in his proposal but a mark of devotion and because the first quality in the eyes of sovereigns is attachment to their persons.

At that moment the appearance of daylight made the Russian fires grow pale and disappear. Our troops stood to their arms, the artillerymen placed themselves by their guns and the looks of all were steadily directed to the opposite bank, preserving that silence which betokens great expectations and is the forerunner of great danger.

Since the day before, every blow struck by our *pontonniers*, echoing among the woody heights, must, we concluded, have attracted the whole attention of the enemy. The first dawn of the 26th was therefore expected to display to us his battalions and artillery, drawn up in front of the weak scaffolding, to the construction of which Eblé had yet to devote eight hours more. Doubtless they were only waiting for daylight to enable them to point their cannon with better aim. When day appeared, we saw their fires abandoned, the bank deserted and upon the heights thirty pieces of artillery in full retreat. A single shell of theirs would have been sufficient to annihilate the only plank of safety, which we were about to fix in order to unite the two banks: but that artillery gradually retreated, as our batteries were placed.

Farther off, we perceived the rear of a long column which

was moving off towards Borisov without ever looking behind it. One regiment of infantry, however, and twelve cannon remained but without taking up any position; we also saw a horde of Cossacks wandering about the outskirts of the wood. They formed the rearguard of Tchaplitz's division, 6,000 strong, which was thus retiring, as if for the purpose of delivering up the passage to us.

The French at first could hardly believe their eyes. At last, transported with joy, they clapped their hands and uttered loud shouts. Rapp and Oudinot rushed headlong into the house where the Emperor was: 'Sire,' they said to him, 'the enemy has just raised his camp and quitted his position!' 'It is not possible!' he replied. But Ney and Murat just then entered and confirmed the report. Napoleon immediately darted out; he looked and could just see the last files of Tchaplitz's column getting farther off and disappearing into the woods: 'I have outwitted the Admiral!' he exclaimed.

During this first movement, two of the enemy's guns reappeared and fired. An order was given to remove them by a discharge of our artillery. One salvo was enough: it was an act of imprudence which was not repeated, for fear of recalling Tchaplitz. The bridge was as yet scarcely begun: it was eight o'clock and the first trestles were only then being fixed.

The Emperor, however, impatient to get possession of the opposite bank, pointed it out to the bravest. Jacqueminot, aide-de-camp to Oudinot, and the Lithuanian Count Predziecski were the first who threw themselves into the river and in spite of the ice, which cut the chests and sides of their horses, succeeded in reaching the other side. Sourd, chief of the squadron, and fifty *chasseurs* of the 7th Regiment, each carrying a *voltigeur*, followed them, as well as two frail rafts which transported 400 men in twenty trips. The Emperor having expressed a wish to have a prisoner to interrogate, Jacqueminot, who overheard him, had scarcely crossed the river, when he saw one of Tchaplitz's soldiers;

he rushed after, attacked, and disarmed him; then seizing and placing him on the bow of his saddle, he brought him through the river and the ice to Napoleon.

About one o'clock the bank was entirely cleared of Cossacks and the bridge for the infantry finished. Legrand's division crossed it rapidly with its cannon, the men shouting, *'Vive l'Empereur!'* in the presence of their sovereign, who was himself actively pressing the passage of the artillery and encouraging his brave soldiers by his voice and example.

When he saw them in possession of the opposite bank he exclaimed, 'Behold my star reappear!' For he was a believer in fate, like all conquerors; those men who, having the largest accounts with Fortune, are fully aware how much they are indebted to her and who, moreover, having no intermediate power between themselves and heaven, feel themselves more immediately under its protection.

14 In the Midst of This Horrible Bedlam

> At the approaches to the bridge all semblance of order had ceased. Officers and orderlies had either fled before the raging mob or, if they stood their ground, had been cut to pieces. By now there were many trying to swim the river but few succeeded: most perished in the icy water.
>
> Heinrich Vossler

Originally, there were to be three bridges built at Studzianka but materials were lacking and the army had to make do with two: one for the troops and one for the guns and wagons. The fact that the army was able to bridge the Berezina at all was entirely due to the foresight of General Eblé: having preserved – against Napoleon's orders – two field forges and several wagons of coal and tools, his 400 pontonniers *were able to strip Studzianka of its timber and begin the task of saving the Emperor's skin.*

The bridges were placed some 200 yards apart, each one supported by twenty-three sets of trestles; there were no handrails and the rickety boardwalks – made primarily from roofing timbers – were almost level with the water. Eblé's engineers worked around the clock to construct the bridges – and keep them functioning – doing fifteen-minute shifts in the freezing water. Sergeant Bourgogne was just one of many veterans who later paid tribute to the sappers: 'We saw the brave pontonniers *working hard at the bridges for us to cross. They had worked all night, standing up to their shoulders in ice-cold waters, encouraged by* their general. These brave men sacrificed their lives to save the army. One of my friends told me as a fact that he had seen the Emperor himself handing wine to them.' Weakened by their ordeal, some were swept away and drowned; others died of exposure; while yet more – including the fifty-four-year-old Eblé himself – succumbed to tuberculosis soon afterwards. Of the 400 pontonniers who built the Berezina bridges, a mere forty made it home.

As soon as the infantry bridge was completed at 1.00 p.m. on 26 November, Marshal Oudinot was rushed across with II Corps to secure the bridgehead; and when the artillery bridge was finished around 4.00 p.m., the passage began in earnest. Napoleon, who for so long had been a mere spectator to the disasters accumulating around him, suddenly came alive, relishing the drama and danger of the situation and hitting something like his old form. He crossed with the Guard on the 27th and remained at the bridges, keeping a tally of the troops as they stepped onto the western bank. An eyewitness described the Emperor as being 'as calm as if he were taking a review at the Tuileries'.[1]

Meanwhile, cluttering up the approaches to the bridges, swarmed the congregation of stragglers and non-combatants: denied access until the fighting men had crossed. The operation was covered by Marshal Victor's IX Corps, acting as rearguard and holding the Studzianka perimeter.

What news, then, of the Russian armies closing in on Napoleon? Strange to say, when the hour of victory was upon them, each of the Russian commanders was suddenly struck with inertia: Kutusov, who had wasted precious time hunting Marshal Ney, was thirty miles behind the battlefront and effectively out of the picture; Prince Wittgenstein, advancing upon the bridges from the north and outnumbering Victor's rearguard by two to one, mistook the mass of stragglers for effective troops and declined to press home his attack; while Admiral Chichagov – whose brain, according to one of his generals,[2] was 'like a volcano: every minute it produced some new project . . . which was either absurd or impracticable' – simply dithered. According to Clausewitz, 'Chichagov thought it probable that Bonaparte would take his direction more to the south, as there he would draw nearer to

Schwarzenberg. Starting from this too strongly conceived opinion and confirmed in it by false reports which came from Kutusov himself, he considered Victor's preparations as demonstrations and believed Bonaparte already on his march south.' In other words, he fell for the ruse designed to draw him away from Studzianka and make him focus his attention on Borisov.

When, on 27 November, he finally realized his error, Chichagov – inexperienced and out of his depth – did little to recover the situation. In the words of de Ségur: 'Thus it was, that the Admiral lost the remainder of the 26th and the whole of the 27th in consultations, in feeling his way and in preparations. The presence of Napoleon and his Grand Army, of the weakness of which it was impossible for him to have any idea, dazzled him.'

The only real setback for Napoleon during the Berezina operation – collapsing bridges aside – came when General Partouneaux, commander of the 12th Division of IX Corps, managed to get himself captured. He had been stationed at Borisov as part of Victor's rearguard, when ordered to quit his position during the night of 27–28 November and make his way to Studzianka to cover the passage. He set off at 3.00 a.m. but took a wrong turn and marched straight into Prince Wittgenstein's army: thus, in a matter of hours, 4,000 precious troops were lost.

AFTER TWO days feeling his way, the report of a prisoner and the recapture of Borisov by Platov had opened Chichagov's eyes. From that moment the three Russian armies of the north, east and south felt themselves united: their commanders had mutual communications. Prince Wittgenstein and Chichagov were jealous of each other but they detested us still more. Hatred not friendship was their bond of union. These generals were therefore prepared to attack in conjunction the bridges of Studzianka on both sides of the river.

This was on 28 November. The Grand Army had had two days and two nights to effect its passage; it ought to have been too late for the Russians. But the French were in a state of complete disorder and materials were deficient for the two bridges. Twice during the night of the 26th the one for the carriages had broken down and the passage had been set back by seven hours. It broke a third time on the 27th at about four in the afternoon.[3] On the other hand the stragglers, who had been scattered in the woods and surrounding villages, had not taken advantage of the first night; and on the 27th, when daylight appeared, they all presented themselves at once in order to cross the bridge.

This was particularly the case when the Guard, by whose movements they regulated themselves, began its march. Its departure was like a signal: they rushed in from all parts and crowded upon the bank. Instantly there was seen a deep, broad and confused mass of men, horses and carriages, besieging the narrow entrance of the bridge and overwhelming it. The first, pushed forward by those behind them and driven back by the guards and *pontonniers* (or stopped by the river), were crushed, trodden underfoot or thrown among the ice floes of the Berezina. From this immense and horrible rabble there arose at times a confused buzzing noise, at others a loud clamour, mingled with groans and dreadful oaths.

The efforts of Napoleon and his lieutenants to save these desperate men by establishing order among them were for a long time completely fruitless. The disorder was so great that about two o'clock, when the Emperor presented himself in his turn, it was necessary to use force to open a passage for him. A corps of grenadiers of the Guard and Latour-Maubourg, out of pure compassion, declined clearing themselves a way through these poor wretches.

The imperial headquarters were established at the hamlet of Zanivki, which is situated in the midst of the woods, within a league of Studzianka. Eblé had just then made a survey of the baggage with which the bank was covered; he informed the Emperor that six days would not be sufficient to enable so many carriages to pass over. Ney, who was present, immediately called out that in that case they had better be burnt immediately. But Berthier opposed this: he assured the Emperor that the army was far from being reduced to that extremity and Napoleon was led to believe him, from a preference for the opinion which flattered him the most; and from a wish to spare so many men – for whose misfortune he reproached himself as the cause – and whose provisions these carriages contained.

In the night of the 27th the disorder ceased by the effect of an opposite distraction. The bridges were abandoned and the village of Studzianka attracted all these stragglers: in an instant, it was pulled to pieces, disappeared and was converted into an infinite number of bivouacs. Cold and hunger kept these wretched people fixed around them: the whole of that night was again lost for their passage.[4]

Meantime Victor, with 6,000 men, was defending them against Prince Wittgenstein. But with the first dawn of the 28th, when they saw that marshal preparing for a battle, when they heard the cannon of Prince Wittgenstein thundering over their heads and that of Chichagov rumbling at the same time on the opposite bank, they all rose at once, ran headlong from the heights and returned to the bridges.

Their terror was not without foundation: the last day for many of these unfortunate men was come. Prince Wittgenstein and Platov, with 40,000 Russians of the armies of the north and east, attacked the heights on the left bank, which Victor and his small force defended. On the right bank, Chichagov with his 27,000 Russians of the army of the south debouched from Stachova against Oudinot, Ney and Dombrowski. These three could hardly count 8,000 men in their ranks, which were supported by the Sacred Squadron, as well as by the Old and Young Guard, which then consisted of 3,800 infantry and 900 cavalry.

The two Russian armies attempted to possess themselves at once of the two exits from the bridges and of all who had been unable to push forward beyond the marshes of Zembin. More than 60,000 men, well clothed, well fed and completely armed, attacked 18,000 who were half-naked, badly armed, dying of hunger, separated by a river and encumbered with more than 50,000 stragglers, sick or wounded. During the last two days the cold and misery had been such that the Old Guard had lost one-third and the Young Guard one-half of their effective men.

This fact and the calamity which had overtaken Partouneaux's division sufficiently explain the frightful reduction of Victor's corps; and yet that marshal kept Prince Wittgenstein in check during the whole of that day, the 28th. As to Chichagov, he was beaten. Marshal Ney, with his 8,000 French, Swiss and Poles, was a match for 27,000 Russians.

The Admiral's attack was slow and feeble. His cannon cleared the road but he dared not venture to follow his bullets and penetrate the gap which they made in our ranks. Opposite to his right, however, the Legion of the Vistula gave way to the attack of a strong column. Oudinot, Albert, Dombrowski, Claparède and Kosikowski were then wounded. Some uneasiness began to be felt but Ney hastened forward; he made Doumerc and his cavalry dash through the woods upon the flank of the Russian column: they broke through it, took 2,000 prisoners, cut the rest to pieces and by this vigorous charge decided the fate of the battle, which was dragging on in uncertainty. Chichagov, thus defeated, was driven back into Stachova.

On our side, most of the generals of II Corps were wounded; for the fewer troops they had, the more they were obliged to expose their persons. Many officers on this occasion took the muskets and the places of their wounded men. Among the losses of the day, that of young Noailles, Berthier's aide-de-camp, was remarkable. He was struck dead by a ball.[5] He was one of those meritorious but too zealous officers who are incessantly exposing themselves and are considered sufficiently rewarded by being employed.

During this combat Napoleon, at the head of his Guard, remained in reserve at Brilova, covering the exit of the bridges between the two armies but nearer to that of Victor. That marshal, although attacked in a very dangerous position and by a force quadruple his own, lost very little ground. The right of his corps, disfigured by the capture of Partouneaux's division, was protected by the river and supported by a battery which the Emperor had erected on the opposite bank. His front was defended by a ravine but his left was in the air, without support and in a way lost, in the elevated plain of Studzianka.

Prince Wittgenstein's first attack was not made until ten o'clock in the morning of the 28th, across the road to Borisov and along the Berezina, which he endeavoured to ascend as far as the passage; but the French right wing stopped him and kept him back for a considerable time, out of reach of the bridges. He then deployed and extended the engagement with the whole front of Victor, but without effect. One of his attacking columns attempted to cross the ravine but it was attacked and destroyed.

At last, about the middle of the day, the Russian general discovered the point where his superiority lay: he overwhelmed the French left wing. Everything would then have been lost had it not been for a memorable effort by Fournier and the devotion of Latour-Maubourg. That general was passing the bridges with his cavalry: he saw the danger and immediately retraced his steps. On his side, Fournier charged at the head of two regiments of Hesse and Baden. The Russian right wing, already victorious, was obliged to halt: it was attacking but he forced it to defend itself; and three times were the enemy's ranks broken by three bloody charges.

Night came on before Prince Wittgenstein's 40,000 men could make any impression on the 6,000 of Victor. That marshal remained in possession of the heights of Studzianka and still preserved the bridges from the attacks of the Russian infantry; but he was unable to conceal them from the artillery of the left wing.

During the whole of that day the situation of IX Corps was so much more critical, as a weak and narrow bridge was its only means of retreat; in addition to which, its path was obstructed by baggage and the stragglers. By degrees, as the action got warmer, the terror of these poor wretches increased their disorder. First of all they were alarmed by the rumours of a serious engagement, then by seeing the wounded returning from it and, last of all, by the batteries of the Russian left wing, some bullets of which began to fall among their confused mass.

They had already been crowding one upon the other, and the huge mass heaped upon the bank pell-mell with the horses and carriages formed a most alarming encumbrance. It was about the middle of the day that the first Russian shells fell in the midst of this chaos: they were the signal for universal despair.[6]

Then it was, as in all cases of extremity, that dispositions showed themselves without disguise and actions were witnessed, some most base, and others most sublime. According to their different characters, some furious and determined with sword in hand cleared for themselves a horrible passage. Others, still more cruel, opened a way for their carriages by driving them without mercy over the crowd of unfortunates who stood in the way, whom they crushed to death. Their detestable greed made them sacrifice their companions in misfortune to the preservation of their baggage. Others, seized with a disgusting terror, wept, pleaded and sunk under the influence of that passion, which completed the exhaustion of their strength. Some were observed (and these were principally the sick and wounded) who, renouncing life, went aside and sat down resigned, looking with a fixed eye on the snow which was shortly to be their tomb.

Many of those among this crowd of desperadoes missed the bridge and attempted to scale it by the sides: but the greater part were pushed into the river. There were seen women in the midst of the ice with their children in their arms, raising them by degrees as they felt themselves sinking; and even when completely submerged their stiffened arms still held them aloft.

In the midst of this horrible bedlam, the artillery bridge burst and broke down. The column that was entangled in this narrow passage, attempted to retreat in vain. The crowds which came behind, unaware of the calamity and not hearing the cries of those before them, pushed them on and threw them into the gulf, into which they were tossed in their turn.

Everyone then attempted to pass by the other bridge. A number of large wagons, heavy carriages and cannon crowded to it from all parts. Directed by their drivers and carried along rapidly over a rough and unequal slope, in the midst of heaps of men, they ground to powder the poor wretches who were unlucky enough to get between them. After which, the greater part, driving violently against each other and getting overturned, killed in their fall those who surrounded them. Nothing was heard but cries of rage and suffering. In this frightful medley, those who were trodden and stifled under the feet of their companions struggled to lay hold of them with their nails and teeth but were repelled without mercy, like so many enemies.

Among them were wives and mothers, calling in vain for their husbands and children, from whom they had been separated but a moment before, never more to be united. They stretched out their arms and begged to be allowed to pass in order to rejoin them; but being carried backwards and forwards by the crowd and overcome by the pressure, they sank without even being noticed. Amidst the tremendous noise of a violent hurricane, the firing of cannon, the explosion of shells, shouts, groans, and the most frightful oaths, this wild and chaotic crowd heard not the cries of the victims whom it was swallowing up.

The more fortunate gained the bridge by scrambling over the heaps of wounded, women and children, thrown down and half suffocated, and whom they again trod down in their attempts to reach it. When at last they got to the narrow defile, they fancied they were safe, but the fall of a horse or the breaking of a plank again stopped all.

There was also, at the exit of the bridge, on the other side, a bog into which many horses and carriages had sunk: a circumstance which again embarrassed and slowed the clearance. Then it was, that in that column of desperadoes, crowded together on that single plank of safety, there arose a wicked struggle, in which the weakest and worst situated were thrown into the river by the strongest. The latter, without turning their heads and hurried away by the instinct of self-preservation, pushed on towards the goal with fury, regardless of the curses of rage and despair uttered by their companions or their officers, whom they had thus sacrificed.

But on the other hand, how many noble instances of devotion! There were seen soldiers and even officers, harnessing themselves to sledges to snatch from that fatal bank their sick and wounded comrades. Farther off and out of reach of the crows, were seen soldiers watching over their dying officers, who had entrusted themselves to their care. In vain did the latter beg them to think of nothing but their own lives: they refused and sooner than abandon their leaders, were content to take the chance of slavery or death.

Above the first passage, while the young Lauriston threw himself into the river in order to execute the orders of his sovereign more promptly, a little boat, carrying a mother and her two children, was upset and sank under the ice. An artilleryman, who was struggling like the others on the bridge to open a passage for himself, saw the accident. All at once, forgetting himself, he threw himself into the river and, by great exertion, succeeded in saving one of the three victims: it was the youngest of the two children. The poor little thing kept calling for his mother with cries of despair and the brave artilleryman was heard telling him not to cry, that he had not saved him from the water merely to desert him on the bank; that he should want for nothing; that he would be his father and his family.

The night of the 28th added to all these calamities. Its darkness was insufficient to conceal its victims from the artillery of the Russians. Amidst the snow, which covered everything, the course of the river, the dark mass of men, horses, carriages, and the noise proceeding from them, were sufficient to enable the enemy's gunners to direct their fire.

About nine o'clock at night there was a still further increase of desolation, when Victor commenced his retreat and his divisions came and opened themselves a horrible breach through these unhappy wretches, whom till then they had been protecting. A rearguard, however, having been left at Studzianka, the multitude – benumbed with cold or too concerned to preserve their baggage – refused to avail themselves of the last night for passing to the opposite side. In vain were the carriages set on fire in order to tear them from them. It was only the appearance of daylight which brought them all at once – but too late – to the entrance of the bridge, which they again besieged. It was half past eight in the morning when Eblé, seeing the Russians approaching, at last set fire to it.[7]

The disaster had reached its utmost bounds. A multitude of carriages and of cannon, several thousand men, women and children, were abandoned on the hostile bank. They were seen wandering in desolate groups on the bank of the river. Some threw themselves into it in order to swim across; others ventured themselves on the pieces of ice which were floating along; some there were also who threw themselves headlong into the flames of the burning bridge, which sank under them: burnt and frozen at one and the same time, they perished under two opposite punishments. Shortly after, the bodies of all sorts were seen collecting together against the trestles of the bridge.[8] The rest awaited the Russians. Prince Wittgenstein did not show himself upon the heights until an hour after Eblé's departure, and without having gained a victory reaped all the fruits of one.

While this catastrophe was accomplishing, the remains of the Grand Army on the opposite bank formed nothing but a shapeless mass, which unravelled itself confusedly as it took the road to Zembin. The whole of this country is a high and woody plain of great extent, where the waters, flowing in uncertainty between different inclinations of the ground, form one vast morass. Three consecutive bridges of 300 fathoms[9] in length are thrown over it: along these the army passed with a mingled feeling of astonishment, fear and delight.

15 Sauve-Qui-Peut

> Death in his most terrible forms pursued men who were nothing but skeletons.
>
> Captain Rigau[1]

'On 29 November,' writes de Ségur, 'the Emperor quitted the banks of the Berezina, pushing before him the crowd of disbanded soldiers and marching with IX Corps, which was already disorganised . . .' The passage – a mixture of luck and heroism – could be said to have both saved the Grand Army, yet also finally killed it off as a cohesive force. The losses incurred during the three-day battle for the bridgeheads were enormous: perhaps as many as 20,000 fighting troops and 36,000 stragglers and non-combatants. The fate of the latter was particularly appalling: stranded on the wrong side of the river, those who did not perish attempting to swim its icy waters – or in the massacre which followed the arrival of the Cossacks – simply died of cold and hunger.

Despite the carnage, however, the Berezina represented a massive moral victory for Napoleon. According to Clausewitz, serving with the Russians, 'It was his reputation which chiefly saved him and he traded in this instance on a capital amassed long before. Prince Wittgenstein and Chichagov were both afraid of him here, as Kutusov had been afraid of him at Krasnoi.' The latter, having arrived at the Berezina two days too late for the fighting, saw his mission as largely accomplished: the invading army, reduced to a rabble, had been evicted from Russia proper and it only remained to prod its survivors back over the Polish border. Alexander, however, deprived of his prey, never forgave Kutusov for dragging his heels and allowing Napoleon to escape. But in the eyes of the Russian people, Kutusov was the hero and Chichagov the chief bungler; and it was the latter who took the rap. Unable to elude the disgrace, the Admiral eventually renounced Russian nationality and emigrated to Britain.

Having crossed the Zembin marshes, over bridges which the Russians had obligingly failed to destroy, Napoleon set out on the long road to Vilna, some 120 miles to the north-west. The remains of his army marched – in the words of Captain Coignet – 'like prisoners, without arms or knapsacks. There was no longer any discipline or any human feeling for one another. Each man looked out for himself.' Meanwhile, a Russian division under Major-General Chaplitz followed on their heels, 'attacking at every opportunity, picking up abandoned guns and vehicles mile by mile and disarming prisoners, who were then left to live or die as they might'.[2] *The pursuit of the Russian regulars, however, was running out of steam. Having taken around 10,000 casualties at the Berezina and suffering from the cold almost as much as their enemies, the prosecution of the war passed almost entirely into the hands of the Cossacks, who were now only in it for the plunder.*

On 30 November Napoleon arrived at the village of Plechenitzi, a day too late to witness a singular act of heroism, which has since passed into legend. Marshal Oudinot, wounded in the side by a musket ball during the fighting at the Berezina bridgehead (he was replaced as head of II Corps by General Nicholas-Joseph Maison), had been evacuated to this place under the guard of a small escort. While having his wound dressed at the house of a local Jew, the village was occupied by a detachment of 400 Cossacks and 150 hussars. Half-naked and brandishing a brace of pistols, the forty-five-year-old marshal (who once claimed he never had time to experience fear) made a successful dash for a nearby house which contained General Pino and a handful of Italian grenadiers. There the small party held out against repeated attacks. At one point, having brought up a cannon, the Russians succeeded in bringing down the roof of the building and Oudinot was wounded yet again by splinters. Eventually, the tiny band of heroes (which included the Marshal's son) was rescued by reinforcements and the enemy horsemen fled.

On 3 December Napoleon reached Molodechno, a mere 13,000 troops remained with the colours: 'the bulk of the men,' as Edward Foord states, 'already broken by misery and fatigue'. On this day Marshal Murat wrote a letter to his daughter which surely expressed the feelings of the whole army: it ended with the words, 'I am very unhappy at being so far from my dear family. When shall I see you all again, my dear ones?'[3]

ON 3 DECEMBER Napoleon arrived in the morning at Molodechno, which was the last point where Chichagov was likely to have got the start of him. Some provisions were found there, the forage was abundant, the day beautiful, the sun shining and the cold bearable. There also the couriers, who had been so long delayed, arrived all at once. The Poles were immediately directed forward to Warsaw through Olita and the dismounted cavalry by Merecz to the Niemen. The rest of the army was to follow the highroad, which they had again regained.

Up to that time, Napoleon seemed to have entertained no idea of quitting his army.[4] But about the middle of the day, he suddenly informed Daru and Duroc of his determination to set off immediately for Paris.

Daru did not see the necessity of it. He objected that communication with France was again opened and the most dangerous crisis passed; that at every step he would now be meeting the reinforcements sent him from Paris and Germany. The Emperor's reply was that he no longer felt himself sufficiently strong to leave Prussia between him and France. What need was there for him to remain at the head of a routed army? Murat and Eugène would be sufficient to direct it and Ney to cover its retreat.

But in order to achieve his object, it was necessary that he should travel alone over 400 leagues, through the lands of his allies; his resolution unforeseen, his passage unknown, and the rumour of his retreat still uncertain; that he should precede the news of it and all the defections to which it might give rise. He had, therefore, no time to lose and the moment of his departure was at hand.

He only hesitated in the choice of the leader he should leave in charge of the army. He wavered between Murat and Eugène. He liked the caution and devotedness of the latter but Murat had greater prestige, which would give him more weight. Eugène would remain with that monarch: his youth and inferior rank would be a security for his obedience and his character for his zeal. He would set the example of these qualities to the other marshals.

Finally, Berthier, the channel to which they had been so long accustomed for all imperial orders, would remain with them: there would consequently be no change in the organization of the army; and this arrangement, while offering proof of his speedy return, would serve both to keep the most impatient of his officers in their duty, and the most ardent of his enemies in a salutary dread.

Such were the motives given by Napoleon. Caulaincourt immediately received orders to make secret preparations for departure. The rendezvous was fixed at Smorgonie and the time, the night of 5 December.

Although Daru was not to accompany Napoleon, who left him the heavy charge of the administration of the army, he listened in silence, having nothing to say in reply to motives of such weight; but it was quite otherwise with Berthier. This enfeebled old man,[5] who had for sixteen years never quitted the side of Napoleon, rebelled at the idea of this separation.

The private scene which took place was most violent. The Emperor was indignant at his resistance. In his rage he reproached him with all the favours with which he had loaded him. The army, he told him, stood in need of the reputation which he had made for him and which was only a reflection of his own. But to cut the matter short, he allowed him twenty-four hours to decide and if he still persisted in his disobedience, he might depart for his estates, where he should order him to remain, forbidding him ever again to enter Paris or his presence. Next day, 4 December, Berthier, excusing himself for his previous refusal by his advanced age and impaired health, resigned himself sorrowfully to his sovereign's pleasure.

But at the very moment that Napoleon determined on his departure, the winter became terrible, as if the Russian climate, seeing him about to escape, had redoubled its severity in order to overwhelm him and destroy us. On 4 December, when we reached Bienitza, the thermometer was at minus 26°.[6]

The Emperor had left Count Lobau and several hundred men of his Old Guard at Molodechno, at which place the road to Zembin rejoins the highroad from Minsk to Vilna. It was necessary to guard this point until the arrival of Victor, who in his turn would defend it until that of Ney.

For it was still to this marshal and to II Corps, commanded by Maison, that the rearguard was entrusted. On the night of 29 November, when Napoleon quitted the banks of the Berezina, Ney and the II and III Corps, now reduced to 3,000 soldiers, passed the long bridges leading to Zembin, leaving at their entrance Maison and a few hundred men to defend and to burn them.

Chichagov made a late attack – and not only with musketry but with the bayonet – but he was repulsed. Maison at the same time caused these long bridges to be loaded with the firewood which Chaplitz, some days before, had neglected to make use of. When everything was ready and night and the bivouacs well advanced, he rapidly passed the defile and set fire to them. In a few minutes these long causeways were burnt to ashes and fell into the marshes, which the frost had not yet rendered passable.

These quagmires stopped the enemy and compelled him to make a detour. During the following day, therefore, the march of Ney and of Maison was unmolested. But on the day after, 1 December, as they came in sight of Plechenitzi, lo and behold! The whole of the Russian cavalry were seen rushing forward impetuously and pushing Doumerc and his cuirassiers on their right. In an instant they were attacked and overwhelmed on all sides.

At the same time, Maison saw that the village through which he had to retreat was entirely filled with stragglers. He sent to warn them to flee directly; but these unfortunate and famished wretches, not seeing the enemy, refused to leave their meals which they had begun. Maison was driven back upon them into the village. Then only, at the sight of the enemy and the noise of the shells, the whole of them started up at once, rushed out and encumbered every part of the principal street.

Maison and his troops found themselves all at once lost in the midst of this terrified crowd which pressed upon them, almost stifled them, and deprived them of the use of their weapons. This general had no other remedy than to order his men to remain close together and wait till the crowd had dispersed. The enemy's cavalry then came up with this mass and got entangled with it; but it could only penetrate slowly and by hacking down. The crowd at last dispersed, revealing to the Russians Maison and his soldiers waiting for them with a determined countenance. But in its flight, the crowd had drawn along with it a portion of our combatants. Maison, in an open plain and with 700–800 men against thousands of enemies, lost all hope of safety. He was already seeking merely to gain a nearby wood, in order to sell their lives more dearly, when he saw coming out of it 1,800 Poles, a troop quite fresh, which Ney had met with and brought to his assistance. This reinforcement stopped the enemy and secured the retreat as far as Molodechno.

On 4 December, about four o'clock in the afternoon, Ney and Maison got within sight of that village, which Napoleon had quitted in the afternoon. Chaplitz followed them close. Ney had now only 600 men remaining with him. The weakness of his rearguard, the approach of night and the prospect of shelter excited the fervour of the Russian general: he made a warm attack. Ney and Maison, perfectly certain that they would die of cold on the highroad if they allowed themselves to be driven beyond the village, preferred perishing in defending it.

They halted at its entrance and as their artillery horses were dying, they gave up all idea of saving their cannon. Determined, however, that it should do its duty for the last, they formed every piece they possessed into a battery and made a tremendous fire. Chaplitz's attacking column was entirely broken by it and halted. But that general, availing himself of his superior forces, diverted a part of them to another entrance. His first troops had already crossed the enclosures of Molodechno, when all at once, they encountered a fresh enemy.

As good luck would have it, Victor with about 4,000 men – the remains of IX Corps – still occupied the village. The fury on both sides was extreme: the first houses were several times taken and retaken. The combat was much less for glory than to keep or acquire a refuge against the cold. It was not until half past eleven at night that the Russians gave up the contest and went from it half-frozen to seek shelter in the surrounding villages.

The following day, 5 December, Ney and Maison expected that Victor would replace them at the rearguard: but they found that that marshal had retreated, according to his instructions, and that they were left alone in Molodechno with only sixty men. All the rest had fled. The rigour of the climate had completely broken their soldiers, whom the Russians to the very last moment were unable to conquer.

Maison, who united great vigour of mind with a strong constitution, was not intimidated. He continued his retreat to Bienitza, rallying at every step men who were constantly escaping from him, but still continuing to give proofs of the existence of a rearguard with a few footsoldiers. This was all that was required, for the Russians themselves were frozen and obliged to disperse before night into the neighbouring houses, which they dared not quit until daylight. They then recommenced their pursuit of us but without making any attack; for with the exception of some numbed efforts, the cruelty of the cold was such as not to allow either party to halt with the view of making an attack or of defending themselves.

In the meantime Ney, being surprised at Victor's departure, went after him, overtook him and tried to prevail upon him to halt; but the Marshal, having orders to retreat, refused. Ney then wanted him to give up his soldiers, offering to take the command of them; but Victor would neither consent to that, nor to take the rearguard, without express orders. In the quarrel which arose between these two, Ney gave way to his passion in a most violent manner, without producing any effect on the coolness of Victor. At last an order of the Emperor arrived: Victor was instructed to support the retreat and Ney was summoned to Smorgonie.

Napoleon had just arrived there amidst a crowd of dying men, devoured with disappointment but not allowing the least emotion to show itself at the sight of these unhappy men's sufferings; who, on the other hand, had allowed no complaints to escape them in his presence. It is true that a rebellious movement was impossible: it would have required an additional effort, as the strength of every man was fully occupied in struggling with hunger, cold and fatigue; it would have required unity, agreement and mutual understanding; while famine and so many evils separated and isolated them, by concentrating every man's feelings completely in himself. Far from exhausting themselves in provocations or complaints, they marched along silently, exerting all their efforts against a hostile climate and diverted from every other idea by a state of continual action and suffering. Their physical wants absorbed their whole moral strength. Thus they lived mechanically in their sensations, continuing in their duty from habit, from the impressions which they had received in better times, and in no slight degree from that sense of honour and glory which had been inspired by twenty years of victory: the warmth of which still survived and struggled within them.

The authority of the commanders also remained complete and respected, because it had always been highly paternal; and because the dangers, the triumphs and the calamities had always been shared in common. It was an unhappy family, the head of which was perhaps the most to be pitied. The Emperor and the Grand Army, therefore, preserved towards each other a melancholy and noble silence: they were both too proud to utter complaints and too experienced not to feel the uselessness of them.

Meantime, however, Napoleon had entered his last imperial headquarters. There he finished his final instructions, as well as the 29th and last bulletin of his expiring army.[7] Precautions were taken in his inner apartment that nothing of what was about to take place there should transpire until the following day.

But the presentiment of a last misfortune seized his officers: all of them would have wished to follow him. Their hearts yearned for France, to be once more in the bosom of their families and to flee from this terrible climate. But not one of them ventured to express a wish of the kind: duty and honour restrained them.

While they affected a tranquillity which they were far from tasting, the night and the moment which the Emperor had fixed for declaring his resolution to the commanders of the army arrived. All the marshals were summoned. As they successively entered, he took each of them aside in private and first of all gained their approval of his plan.

Thus it was that on noticing Davout, he ran forward to meet him and asked him why it was that he never saw him, and if he had entirely deserted him. And upon Davout's reply that he fancied he had incurred his displeasure,[8] the

Emperor explained himself mildly, received his answers favourably, confided to him the road he meant to travel and took his advice respecting its details.

His manner was kind and flattering to them all. Afterwards, having assembled them at his table, he complimented them for their noble actions during the campaign. As to himself, the only confession he made of his audacity was couched in these words: 'If I had been born on the throne, if I had been a Bourbon, it would have been easy for me not to have committed any faults.'

When their entertainment was over, he made Eugène read to them his 29th Bulletin; after which, declaring aloud what he had already confided to each of them, he told them that he was about to depart that very night with Duroc, Caulaincourt and Lobau for Paris; that his presence there was indispensable for France as well as the remains of his unfortunate army. It was only there he could take measures for keeping the Austrians and Prussians in check.

He added that he had ordered Ney to proceed to Vilna, there to reorganize the army. That Rapp would second him and afterwards go to Danzig, Lauriston to Warsaw and Narbonne to Berlin; that his household would remain with the army but that it would be necessary to strike a blow at Vilna and stop the enemy there. There they would find Loison, von Wrede, reinforcements, provisions and ammunition of all sorts. Afterwards they would go into winter quarters on the other side of the Niemen . . .

In conclusion: 'I leave the King of Naples to command the army. I hope that you will give him the same obedience as you would to myself and that the greatest harmony will prevail among you.'

It was now ten o'clock at night. He rose, squeezed their hands affectionately, embraced them all and departed.

Napoleon passed through the crowd of his officers, who were drawn up in an avenue as he passed, bidding them adieu merely by forced and melancholy smiles. Their good wishes, equally silent and expressed only by respectful gestures, he carried with him. He and Caulaincourt shut themselves up in a carriage, his Mameluke and Wonsowitsch, captain of his guard, occupied the box. Duroc and Lobau followed in a sledge.[9]

His escort at first consisted only of Poles, afterwards of the Neapolitans of the Royal Guard. This corps consisted of between 600 and 700 men when it left Vilna to meet the Emperor: it perished entirely in that short journey. The winter was its only adversary. That very night the Russians surprised and afterwards abandoned Youpranui (or as others say, Osmiana), a town through which the escort had to pass. Napoleon was within an hour of falling into that affray.

He met Maret, Duke of Bassano,[10] at Miedniki. His first words to him were that he no longer had an army; that for several days past he had been marching in the midst of a troop of disbanded men, wandering to and fro in search of subsistence; that they might still be rallied by giving them bread, shoes, clothing and weapons; but that the Duke's administration had anticipated nothing and his orders had not been executed. But upon Maret replying by showing him a statement of the immense magazines collected at Vilna, he exclaimed that he gave him fresh life! That he would give him an order to transmit to Murat and Berthier to halt for eight days in that capital, there to rally the army and breathe into it sufficient life and strength to continue the retreat less deplorably.

The subsequent part of Napoleon's journey was made without molestation. He went round Vilna by its suburbs, crossed the Wilkowiski, where he exchanged his carriage for a sledge, stopped during the 10th at Warsaw to ask the Poles for a levy of 10,000 Cossacks, to grant them subsidies and to promise them he would return speedily at the head of 300,000 men. From there he rapidly crossed Silesia, visited Dreden and its monarch, passed through Hanau,

Metz and finally got to Paris, where he suddenly made his appearance on 19 December, two days after the appearance of his 29th Bulletin.

From Maloyaroslavets to Smorgonie, this master of Europe had been no more than the general of a dying and disbanded army. From Smorgonie to the Rhine, he was an unknown fugitive, travelling through a hostile country; beyond the Rhine he again found himself the master and conqueror of Europe. A last breeze of the wind of prosperity once more swelled his sails.

Meanwhile his generals, whom he left at Smorgonie, approved of his departure; and far from being discouraged, placed all their hopes in it. The army had now only to flee. The road was open and the frontier at a very short distance. They were within reach of reinforcements, of a great city and immense magazines. Murat and Berthier, left to themselves, fancied themselves able to control the flight. But in the midst of the acute disorder, it required a colossus for a rallying point and he had just disappeared. In the great chasm which he left, Murat was scarcely perceptible.

The very first night, a general refused to obey. The marshal who commanded the rearguard was almost the only one who returned to the royal headquarters. Three thousand men of the Old and Young Guard were still there. This was the whole of the Grand Army and of that gigantic body there remained nothing but the head. But at the news of Napoleon's departure these veterans, spoiled by the tradition of being commanded by the conqueror of Europe and scorning to act as guards to another, gave way in their turn and voluntarily fell into disorder.

Most of the colonels of the army, who had hitherto been such subjects of admiration and had marched on with only four or five soldiers around their eagle, preserving their place of battle, now followed no order but their own. Each of them imagined himself entrusted with his own safety and looked only to himself for it. There were men who marched 200 leagues without even looking round. It was an almost general *sauve-qui-peut*.[11]

The Emperor's disappearance and Murat's incapacity were not, however, the only causes of this dispersion. The principal certainly was the severity of the winter, which at that moment became extreme. It aggravated everything and seemed to have planted itself firmly between Vilna and the army.

Till we arrived at Molodechno and up till 4 December, the day when it set in upon us with such violence, the march – although painful – had been marked by a smaller number of deaths than before we reached the Berezina. This respite was partly owing to the vigorous efforts of Ney and Maison, which had kept the enemy in check, to the then milder temperature, to the supplies which were obtained from a less ravaged country and, finally, to the circumstance that they were the strongest men who had escaped from the passage of the Berezina.

The partial organization which had been introduced into the disorder was kept up. The mass of runaways kept on their way, divided into a number of petty associations of eight or ten men. Many of these bands still possessed a horse, which carried their provisions and was himself finally destined to be converted to the same purpose. A covering of rags, some utensils, a knapsack and a stick formed the accoutrements of these poor fellows. They no longer possessed either the weapons or the uniform of a soldier, nor the desire of combating any other enemies than hunger and cold; but they still retained perseverance, firmness and a spirit always ready and quick in making the most of their situation. Finally, among the soldiers still under arms, the dread of a nickname,[12] by which they themselves ridiculed their comrades who had fallen into disorder, retained some influence.

But after leaving Molodechno and the departure of Napoleon, when winter with all its force attacked each of us, there was a complete dissolution of all those associations against misfortune. It was no longer anything but a multitude of isolated and individual struggles. The best no longer respected themselves; nothing stopped them; no speaking looks detained them; misfortune was hopeless of assistance and even of regret; discouragement had no longer judges to condemn or witnesses to prove it: all were its victims.

Henceforward there was no longer fraternity in arms. There was an end to all society, to all ties: the excess of evils had brutalized them. Hunger, devouring hunger, had reduced these unfortunate men to the instinct of self-preservation – all which composes the understanding of the most ferocious animals – and which is ready to sacrifice everything to itself. A rough and barbarous nature seemed to have communicated to them all its fury. Like savages, the strongest despoiled the weakest. They rushed round the dying and frequently waited not for their last breath. When a horse fell, you might have fancied you saw a famished pack of hounds: they surrounded him, they tore him to pieces, for which they quarrelled among themselves like ravenous dogs.

The greater number, however, preserved sufficient moral strength to consult their own safety without injuring others; but this was the last effort of their virtue. If either leader or comrade fell by their side or under the wheels of the cannon, in vain did they call for assistance, in vain did they invoke the names of a common country, religion and cause: they could not even obtain a passing look. The cold inflexibility of the climate had completely passed into their hearts; its rigour had contracted their feelings equally with their countenances. With the exception of a few commanders, all were absorbed by their sufferings and terror left no room for compassion.

Thus it was that the same egotism with which excessive prosperity has been reproached was produced by the excess of misfortune, but much more excusable in the latter: the first being voluntary and the last compulsive; the first a crime of the heart and the other an impulse of instinct entirely physical. And certainly it was risking one's life to stop for an instant. In this universal shipwreck, the stretching forth of one's hand to a dying comrade was a wonderful act of generosity. The least movement of humanity became a sublime action.

16 Here Come the Cossacks!

> Although the retreat from Moscow was a bloody catastrophe for Napoleon, it was also glorious for him and the troops who were at Krasnoi and the Berezina, because the skeleton of the army was saved, when not a single man should have returned . . .
>
> Baron Antoine Henri de Jomini[1]

Thus, while his soldiers 'flitted along in this empire of death like unhappy spirits', Napoleon began his long trip back to the Tuileries. Ever since, he has stood accused of deserting the Grand Army; of saving his own skin and leaving his troops to their fate. Even at the time, many of his men viewed the disappearance of 'our comrade' as a betrayal: according to Marbot, 'His departure produced a great effect on the troops'; while Major Pion, of the Guard artillery, went so far as to declare his emperor, 'the greatest fool in the world', and claimed that the soldiers 'cursed Napoleon at the tops of their voices'.[2] The fact remains, however, that having led the Grand Army across the Berezina – its last major obstacle before the Polish frontier – Napoleon's job as a general was largely done. With Austria and Prussia itching to switch sides, however – and rumours of his death causing mayhem – it was time to retrieve the reins of power in Paris. One thing is sure: Napoleon's exit was not motivated by cowardice. Before starting out he handed the captain of his escort a brace of pistols, with orders to shoot him rather than let him be taken alive. As Bourrienne states,

'Napoleon a coward! They know nothing of his character who say so. Tranquil in the midst of danger, he was never more happy than on the field of battle.'

Within twenty-four hours Napoleon was nearing Vilna. At the dead of night and with the thermometer at minus 37.5°C, Caulaincourt was sent into town to organize fresh horses and to buy fur-lined boots for his companions (Napoleon, travelling incognito, was posing as Caulaincourt's secretary); but the good people of Vilna, unaware of the sufferings of the Grand Army or Napoleon's sudden departure, were sleeping soundly after the excitement of a grand ball. Caulaincourt, banging on the windows and doors for attention, later observed: 'They danced while others froze to death. The inhabitants of Vilna had no conception of our situation, of what had already happened, or of what was to come.'

And so with Napoleon gone, discipline at breaking-point and worsening winter weather, the survivors of the Grand Army marched from Smorgonie to Vilna: down a cruel stretch of road which would claim 20,000 lives.

Firstly, there was the cold: 'The very day after Napoleon's departure,' writes de Ségur, 'the sky showed a still more dreadful appearance. You might see icy particles floating in the air; birds fell from it quite stiff and frozen. The atmosphere was motionless and silent: it seemed as if everything which possessed life and movement in nature – the wind itself – had been seized, chained and, as it were, frozen by a universal death.' Baron Lejeune, in less poetic but more immediate terms, describes how, 'We were all covered with ice. Our breath, looking like thick smoke, froze as it left our mouths and hung in icicles from our hair, eyebrows, moustaches and beards, sometimes quite blinding us.'

With the cold came frostbite: 'Lack of sound and suitable footwear cost thousands of lives,' wrote Lieutenant Heinrich Vossler. 'In many cases extremities simply broke off, in others fingers and toes, and often whole arms and legs had to be amputated.' And there was also dysentery which, according to Lejeune, 'worked terrible ravages amongst us . . . its victims, with their dry and livid skin and emaciated limbs, looked like living skeletons'. There was blindness as well: caused by snow, ice and the smoke from fires which the soldiers in an attempt to keep warm insisted upon hugging. Weak-sightedness became so prevalent that Dr Heinrich von Roos recorded: 'One saw men dragging their comrades along by sticks, like beggars.'[3]

Meanwhile, rumours of cannibalism and horror stories of men reduced to drinking their own blood sapped the moral strength of even the strongest. According to Marbot, 'One of the stoutest and bravest officers in my regiment was so distracted by what he had seen in the last few days that he laid himself down on the snow and no persuasions being able to make him rise, died there. Many soldiers of all ranks blew out their brains to put an end to their misery.'

Even in death there was no peace. Soldiers stripped the bodies of their dying comrades: one fallen warrior turned to his tormentor and begged, 'Let me, do let me die in peace.'[4]

The horses, meanwhile, were simply eaten alive. According to a sergeant of cuirassiers, 'It was too cold to kill and cut up those we destined for our rations; our hands, exposed for so long to the cold air, would have refused to perform this service . . . So we cut a slice from the quarters of the horses still on their feet and walking, and the wretched animals gave not the least sign of pain, proving beyond doubt the degree of numbness . . . caused by the extreme cold.'[5]

At the head of this ice-bound funeral cortège rode the army's new commander-in-chief, Joachim Murat: the man among Napoleon's deputies who was, perhaps, least suited for the task. The son of an innkeeper turned King of Naples, Murat was famously brave and charismatic. He had come to Napoleon's notice during the Revolutionary Wars as a dashing cavalry captain and quickly became a trusted aide-de-camp. Marriage to Napoleon's sister Caroline followed and with it – as a member of the Bonaparte clan – titles, honours, riches and the Neapolitan throne. Yet, despite oozing flair and courage, Murat lacked discipline and common sense. At his happiest at the head of a charge or in his palace, designing outlandish uniforms, by December 1812 Murat was, according to his biographer, A.H. Atteridge, 'broken in spirit and worn out with fatigue and cold'. Even worse, he no longer believed in Napoleon's star and – determined to hold on to his own kingdom at all costs – was planning his own departure.

The reaction among the troops to Murat's appointment was lukewarm. He was seen by many – and with much justification – as having wrecked the army's cavalry through mismanagement. In the words of Captain Coignet, 'We remained under the command of the King of Naples and were not too happy in our minds.' Many favoured Eugène who, in fact, penned a letter of complaint to Napoleon over Murat's appointment: though he was sensible enough not to labour the point, claiming, 'I don't look for glory now, the price is too high.'[6] *Meanwhile Murat, according to Lejeune, 'recognised that the task the Emperor had left him was beyond his powers and his efforts were restricted to escaping, being taken alive by the Cossacks, whom he had so often defied and so many of whom he had cut down.'*

On 8 December Murat reached Vilna and was met by Hugues-Bernard Maret, the town's governor. When Maret, in accordance with Napoleon's instructions, began discussing plans for holding off the Russians and wintering the troops, Murat curtly exclaimed, 'No, no! I don't mean to get myself caught in this hole!' And when Berthier – on the verge of a breakdown – asked Murat for orders, he simply replied, 'You know better than me what ought to be done. Give the orders yourself!'[7]

Next day the frozen, famished survivors of the Grand Army hit Vilna, 'wandering the streets in rags and dying of hunger; some paying its weight in gold for wretched food, others begging for a morsel of bread'.[8]

THE ARMY was in this last state of physical and moral distress when it reached Vilna. Vilna! Its name alone still supported the courage of a few.

On 9 December, the greatest part of these poor soldiers at last arrived within sight of that capital. Instantly – some dragging themselves along, others rushing forward – they threw themselves headlong into its suburbs; pushing obstinately before them and crowding together so tightly that they formed but one mass of men, horses and vehicles.

For the space of ten hours, with the cold at 27 and even 28°,[9] thousands of soldiers who fancied themselves in safety died – either from cold or suffocation – just as had happened at the gates of Smolensk and at the bridges across the Berezina. Sixty thousand men had crossed that river and 20,000 recruits had since joined them: of these 80,000 half had already perished, the greater part within the last four days, between Molodechno and Vilna.[10]

The capital of Lithuania was still ignorant of our disasters, when all at once 40,000 famished soldiers filled it with groans and lamentations. At this unexpected sight its inhabitants were terrified and shut their doors. It was shocking to see these troops of wretched wanderers in the streets – some furious, others desperate – threatening, begging, attempting to break open the doors of the houses or dragging themselves to the hospitals. Everywhere they were repulsed (at the magazines, from most inappropriate formalities as, from the collapse of the corps and the mixture of the soldiers, all regular distribution had become impossible).

There had been collected sufficient flour and bread to last 100,000 men forty days (with butcher's meat enough for thirty-six). Not a single officer ventured to step forward and give orders for distributing these provisions. Those in charge were afraid of being made responsible for them and the others dreaded the excesses to which the famished troops would give themselves up to, when everything was at their mercy. Besides, these officials were ignorant of our desperate situation and as there was scarcely time for pillage (had they been so inclined) our unfortunate comrades were left for several hours to die of hunger at the very doors of these immense stores, all of which fell into the enemy's hands the following day.[11]

At the barracks and the hospitals they were equally

repulsed but not by the living, for there death held sway supreme. The few who still breathed[12] complained that for a long time they had been without beds – even without straw – and almost deserted. The courts, the passages and even the apartments were filled with heaps of dead bodies. They were so many charnel houses of infection.

At last, the exertions of several commanders, such as Eugène and Davout, the compassion of the Lithuanians (and the greed of the Jews), opened some places of refuge. Nothing could be more remarkable than the surprise which these unfortunate men displayed at finding themselves once more in inhabited houses. How delicious did a loaf of leavened bread appear to them and how inexpressible the pleasure of eating it seated! And afterwards, with what admiration were they struck at seeing a scanty battalion still under arms, in regular order and uniformly dressed! They seemed to have returned from the very ends of the earth: so much had the violence of their sufferings torn and cast them from all their habits; so deep had been the abyss from which they had escaped!

But scarcely had they begun to taste these sweets, when the guns of the Russians commenced thundering over their heads. These threatening sounds, the shouts of the officers, the drums beating to arms and the wailings and clamour of an additional multitude of unfortunates which had just arrived, filled Vilna with fresh confusion. It was the vanguard of Kutusov and Chaplitz, commanded by O'Rourke,[13] Lanskoi and Seslavin, that had attacked Loison's division, which was protecting the city, as well as the retreat of a column of dismounted cavalry on its way to Olita, by way of Novi-Troki.

At first an attempt was made to resist. Von Wrede and his Bavarians had also just rejoined the army by Naroc-Zwiransky and Niamentchin. They were pursued by Prince Wittgenstein, who from Kamen and Vileika hung upon our right flank, at the same time that Kutusov and Chichagov were pursuing us. Von Wrede had not 2,000 men left under his command. As to Loison's division and the garrison of Vilna, which had come to meet us as far as Smorgonie and render us assistance, the cold had reduced them from 15,000 men to 3,000 in the space of three days.

Von Wrede defended Vilna on the side of Rukoni: he was obliged to fall back after a gallant resistance. Loison and his division, which was nearer to Vilna, kept the enemy in check. They had succeeded in making a Neapolitan division take arms and even go out of the city; but the muskets slipped from the hands of these children of the sun: in less than an hour they returned disarmed and the best part of them maimed.

At the same time, the General was ineffectually beat in the streets. The Old Guard itself, now reduced to a few platoons, remained scattered. Everyone thought much more of disputing life with hunger and the cold than with the enemy. But when the cry of *'Here come the Cossacks!'* was heard – which for a long time had been the only signal which the greater number obeyed – it echoed immediately throughout the whole city and the rout began again.

Von Wrede presented himself unexpectedly before the King of Naples. He said that the enemy were close at his heels; that his Bavarians had been driven back into Vilna, which they could no longer defend. At the same time, the noise of the clamour reached the King's ear. Murat was astonished. Fancying himself no longer master of the army, he lost all command of himself. He instantly quitted his palace on foot and was seen forcing his way through the crowd. He halted at the last house in the suburbs, from where he despatched his orders and waited for daylight and the army, leaving Ney in charge of the rest.

Vilna might have been defended for twenty-four hours longer and many men might have been saved. This fatal city retained nearly 20,000, including 300 officers and seven generals. Most of them had been wounded by the winter more than by the enemy (who took the credit of the triumph). Several others were still in good health – to all appearance at least – but their moral strength was completely exhausted. After courageously battling with so many difficulties, when they were near their haven they lost heart at the prospect of four days' march. They had at last found themselves once more in a civilized city and, sooner than make up their minds to return to the desert, they placed themselves at the mercy of Fortune: she treated them cruelly.

It is true that the Lithuanians, although we had compromised them so much and were now abandoning them, received into their houses and assisted several; but the Jews, whom we had protected, repelled the others. They did even more: the sight of so many sufferers excited their avarice. Had their greed been content with speculating upon our miseries and selling us some meagre supplies for their weight in gold, history would scorn to sully her pages with the disgusting detail; but they enticed our wounded men into their houses, stripped them, and on seeing the Russians, threw the naked bodies of these dying victims from the doors and windows of their houses into the streets and left them to perish of cold.[14]

On 10 December Ney, who had again voluntarily taken upon himself the command of the rearguard, left that city, which was immediately flooded by the Cossacks of Platov, who massacred all the poor wretches in their path. In the midst of this butchery, there suddenly appeared a *piquet* of thirty French, coming from the bridge of the Vilia, where they had been left and forgotten. At sight of this fresh prey, thousands of Russian horsemen came hurrying up, besetting them with loud cries and assailing them on all sides.

But the officer commanding this *piquet* had already drawn up his soldiers in a circle. Without hesitation, he ordered them to fire and then, making them present bayonets, proceeded at the *pas de charge*. In an instant all fled before him: he remained in possession of the city but without feeling more surprise about the cowardice of the Cossacks than he had done at their attack, he took advantage of the moment, turned sharply round and succeeded in rejoining the rearguard without loss.

Napoleon had given no regular order for retreat: he was anxious that our defeat should have no forerunner but that it should proclaim itself and take our allies by surprise and that, taking advantage of their astonishment, we might pass through those nations before they might be able join the Russians and overpower us. This was the reason why the Lithuanians and everyone at Vilna – even to the minister himself – had been deceived. They did not believe our disaster until they saw it and in that, the almost superstitious belief of Europe in the infallibility of the genius of Napoleon was of use to him. But the same confidence had buried his own officers in a profound security: at Vilna, as well as at Moscow, not one of them was prepared for a movement of any description.

This city contained a large proportion of the baggage of the army and its treasures, its provisions, a glut of enormous wagons loaded with the Emperor's equipage, a large quantity of artillery and a great number of wounded men. Our retreat had come upon them like an unexpected storm, almost like a thunderbolt. Some were terrified and thrown into confusion, while consternation kept others motionless. Men, horses and carriages were running about in all directions, crossing and overturning each other.

In the midst of this tumult, several commanders pushed forward out of the city towards Kovno with all the troops they could muster; but at the distance of a league from the latter place, this column encountered the height and defile of Ponari.

During our conquering march, this woody hillock had only appeared to our hussars a fortunate accident of the ground, from which they could survey the whole plain of Vilna. Its rough, steep slope had then hardly been noticed. During a regular retreat it would have presented an excellent position for turning round and stopping the enemy: but in a disorderly flight, where everything that might be of service became injurious, where in our haste and disorder everything was turned against ourselves, this hill and its defile became an insurmountable obstacle, a wall of ice, against which all our efforts were powerless. It stopped everything: baggage, treasure and wounded.

It was here that money, honour and all remains of discipline were completely lost. After fifteen hours of fruitless efforts, when the drivers and soldiers of the escort saw the King of Naples and the whole column of deserters passing them by the sides of the hill; when they turned their eyes at the noise of the cannon and musketry which was coming nearer every instant; and they saw Ney himself retreating with 3,000 men (the remains of von Wrede's and Loison's divisions); when at last, turning their eyes back to themselves, they saw the hill completely covered with cannon and carriages, broken or overturned, men and horses fallen to the ground and dying one upon the other; then it was that they gave up all idea of saving anything and determined only to beat the enemy to the plunder.

One of the covered wagons of treasure, which burst open of itself, served as a signal: everyone rushed to the others; they were instantly broken and the most valuable effects taken from them. The soldiers of the rearguard, who were passing at the time of this disorder, threw away their weapons to join in the plunder. They were so eagerly engaged in it as neither to hear nor pay attention to the whistling of the bullets and the howling of the Cossacks in pursuit of them.

It is even said that the Cossacks got mixed among them. For some minutes, French and Tartars, friends and foes, forgetting they were at war, were seen pillaging together the same treasure wagons: ten millions in gold and silver then disappeared.[15]

But amidst these horrors there were noble acts of devotion. Some there were who abandoned everything to save some of the wounded by carrying them on their shoulders; several others, being unable to extricate their half-frozen comrades from this jumble, lost their lives in defending them from the attacks of their countrymen and the blows of their enemies.

On the most exposed part of the hill an officer of the Emperor, Colonel the Count de Turenne, repulsed the Cossacks and in defiance of their cries of rage, he distributed before their eyes the private treasure of Napoleon to the guards whom he found within his reach. These brave men, fighting with one hand and collecting the spoils of their leader with the other, succeeded in saving them. Long afterwards, when they were all out of danger, each man faithfully restored the items which had been entrusted to him.

This catastrophe at Ponari was the more disgraceful as it was easy to foresee and equally easy to prevent, for the hill could have been turned by its sides. The wreckage which we abandoned, however, was at least of some use in arresting the pursuit of the Cossacks. While these were busy in collecting their prey, Ney, at the head of a few hundred French and Bavarians, supported the retreat as far as Evé. As this was his last effort, we must not omit the description of his method of retreat, which he had followed ever since he left Viasma on 3 November, during thirty-seven days and nights.

Every day at five o'clock in the evening he took his position, stopped the Russians, allowed his soldiers to eat and take some rest and resumed his march at ten o'clock. During the whole of the night he pushed the mass of stragglers before him by dint of cries, entreaties and blows. At daybreak, which was about seven o'clock, he halted again, took position and rested under arms and on guard until ten o'clock; the enemy then made his appearance and he was compelled to fight until the evening.

For a long time this rearguard did not consist of more than 2,000, then of 1,000, afterwards about 500, and finally of sixty men; and yet Berthier – either on purpose or from mere routine – made no change in his instructions. These were always addressed to the commander of a corps of 35,000 men. In them he coolly detailed all the positions which were to be taken up and guarded until the next day, by divisions and regiments which no longer existed. And every night when, in consequence of Ney's urgent warnings, he was obliged to go and awake the King of Naples and compel him to resume his march, he showed the same surprise.

In this manner did Ney support the retreat from Viasma to Evé and a few leagues beyond it. There, according to his usual custom, he had stopped the Russians and was giving the first hours of the night to rest, when about ten o'clock, he and von Wrede realized that they had been left alone. Their soldiers had deserted them, as well as their arms, which they saw piled together close to their abandoned fires.

Fortunately the intensity of the cold, which had just completed the discouragement of our people, had also benumbed their enemies. Ney overtook his column with some difficulty. It was now only a band of fugitives which a handful of Cossacks chased before them, without attempting either to take or kill them: either from compassion – for one gets tired of everything in time – or that the enormity of our misery had terrified even the Russians and they believed themselves sufficiently revenged; or, finally, that they were satiated and overloaded with booty. (It might also be that in the darkness they did not realize that they only had to do with unarmed men.)

Winter, that terrible ally of the Russians had sold them his assistance dearly. Their disorder pursued our disorder. We often saw prisoners who had escaped several times from their frozen hands. There were some of them who, taking advantage of a favourable moment, ventured to attack the Russian soldiers when isolated and strip them of their provisions, uniforms and even their weapons, with which they covered themselves. Under this disguise they mingled with their conquerors; and such was the disorganization, carelessness and numbness into which their army had fallen, that these prisoners marched for a whole month in the midst of them without being recognized. The 120,000 men of Kutusov's army were then reduced to 35,000. Of Prince Wittgenstein's 50,000, scarcely 15,000 remained. Wilson asserts that of a reinforcement of 10,000 men sent from the interior of Russia, with all the precautions which they know how to take against the winter, not more than 1,700 arrived at Vilna. But a head of a column was quite sufficient against our disarmed soldiers. Ney attempted in vain to rally a few of them: and he who had hitherto been almost the only one whose commands had been obeyed in the rout was compelled to follow it.

He arrived along with it at Kovno, which was the last town of the Russian empire. Finally, on 13 December, after marching forty-six days under a terrible yoke, they once more came in sight of a friendly country. Instantly, without halting or looking behind them, the greater part plunged into the forests of Prussian Poland. Some there were, however, who, on their arrival on the Allied bank of the Niemen, turned round: there, when they cast a look on that land of suffering from which they were escaping, when they found themselves on the same spot where, five months previously, their countless eagles had taken their victorious flight, it is said that tears flowed from their eyes and that they uttered cries of grief.

This then was the bank which they had studded with their bayonets! This the country which had disappeared only five months before under the steps of an immense united army and seemed to them to be metamorphosed into moving hills and valleys of men and horses! These were the same valleys from which, under the rays of a burning sun, poured forth the three long columns of dragoons and cuirassiers, resembling three rivers of glittering iron and brass. And now men, arms, horses – the sun itself and even this frontier river, which they had crossed filled with enthusiasm and hope – all have disappeared. The Niemen is now only a long mass of ice, caught and chained by the increasing severity of the winter. Instead of the three French bridges, a Russian bridge is alone standing. Finally, in the place of these innumerable warriors, of their 400,000 comrades who had been so often their partners in victory and who had dashed forward with such joy and pride into the territory of Russia, they saw issuing from these pale and frozen deserts only 1,000 infantry and horsemen still under arms, nine cannon and 20,000 miserable wretches covered with rags. This was the whole of the Grand Army!

All were fleeing and Murat himself, quitting Kovno as he had done Vilna, first gave and then withdrew the order to rally at Tilsit and subsequently fixed on Gumbinnen. Ney then entered Kovno, accompanied only by his aides-de-camp, for all besides had given way or fallen around him. From the time of his leaving Viasma, this was the fourth rearguard which had melted in his hands. But winter and famine, still more than the Russians, had destroyed them. For the fourth time he remained alone before the enemy, and still unshaken he searched for a fifth rearguard.

At Kovno the Marshal found a company of artillery, 300 German soldiers who formed its garrison and General Marchand with 400 men. Of these he took the command. He first walked over the town to reconnoitre its position and rally some additional forces, but he found only some sick and wounded who were struggling in tears to follow our retreat. For the eighth time since we left Moscow, we were obliged to abandon these en masse in their hospitals, as they had been abandoned singly along the whole march, on all our fields of battle and at all our bivouacs.

Several thousand soldiers covered the marketplace and the neighbouring streets; but they were laid out stiff before the liquor shops which they had broken open and where they drank the cup of death, from which they supposed they were to inhale fresh life. These were the only reinforcements which Murat had left. Ney found himself alone in Russia with 700 foreign recruits. At Kovno, as it had been after the disasters of Viasma, Smolensk, the Berezina, Vilna, it was to him that the honour of our arms and all the danger of the last steps of the retreat were again confided.

On the 14th, at daybreak, the Russians commenced their attack. One of their columns made a hasty advance from the Vilna road, while another crossed the Niemen on the ice above the town, landed on Prussian territory and, proud of being the first to cross its frontier, marched to the bridge of Kovno, to close that exit upon Ney and completely cut off his retreat.

The first firing was heard at the Vilna gate. Ney ran there with a view to drive away Platov's artillery with his own: but he found his cannon had already been spiked and that his artillerymen had fled! Enraged, he dashed forward and, raising his sword, would have killed the officer who commanded them had it not been for his aide-de-camp who warded off the blow and enabled this miserable fellow to make his escape.

Ney then summoned his infantry but only one of two feeble battalions had taken up arms: it consisted of the 300 Germans of the garrison. He drew them up, encouraged them and, as the enemy was approaching, was just about to give them the order to fire, when a Russian cannon ball, grazing the palisade, broke the thigh of their commanding officer. He fell and without hesitation, finding that his wound was mortal, he coolly drew out his pistols and blew out his brains before his troop. Terrified at this act of despair, his soldiers at once threw down their arms and fled.

Ney, abandoned by all, neither deserted himself nor his post. After vain efforts to stop these fugitives, he collected their muskets, which were still loaded, became once more a common soldier and with only four others kept facing thousands of Russians. His audacity stopped them; it made some of his artillerymen ashamed, who imitated their marshal; it gave time to his aide-de-camp Heymès and General Gérard to personify thirty soldiers, bring forward two or three light guns, and to Generals Ledru and Marchand to collect the only battalion which remained.

But at that moment the second Russian attack commenced on the other side of the Niemen and near the bridge of Kovno: it was then half past two o'clock. Ney sent Ledru, Marchand and their 400 men forward to retake and secure that passage. As to himself, without giving way or troubling himself further as to what was passing in his rear, he kept on fighting at the head of his thirty men and maintained himself until night at the Vilna gate. He then crossed the town and the Niemen, constantly fighting – retreating but never flying – supporting to the last the honour of our arms; and for the hundredth time during the last forty days and nights, putting his life in jeopardy to save a few more Frenchmen. Finally, he was the last of the Grand Army who quitted that fatal Russia: showing to the world the impotence of fortune against great courage and proving that with heroes everything turns to glory, even the greatest disasters.

Epilogue

> Ordinary men died, men of iron were taken prisoner: I only brought back with me men of bronze.
>
> Napoleon[1]

At midnight on 14 December – four hours after Ney had thrown his musket from the Kovno bridge and quit Russian territory – Napoleon entered Dresden, scene of his dazzling display of might and authority the previous May. Then, he had entered the Saxon capital in glory, pomp and triumph, at the head of an army half a million strong; then, the crowned heads of Europe had gathered at his command and the people of the city, electrified by his presence, had crowded his route, straining to catch a glimpse of the conqueror of Europe. Now he stood alone in the shadows, while Caulaincourt, in an attempt to find the French minister's house, banged on the door of a local doctor who, opening a window and peering out in his nightcap, ignored requests for directions and promptly slammed it shut again. In Napoleon's own words, 'Between the sublime and the ridiculous, there is but one step.'[2]

Napoleon did not tarry at Dresden. The minister's house was found – thanks to a helpful passer-by – and there he caught up with his correspondence, took some supper and snatched a little sleep. Within a few hours he was on his way westward again, in a coach fitted with runners for the snow, provided by the King of Saxony.

Caulaincourt was now the Emperor's only companion (his escort having been left behind once the safety of the Polish frontier had been reached) and finding himself with a captive audience, Napoleon combated the cold with conversation. Unravelling the events of the past months, he heaped criticism upon Alexander and Kutusov and blame upon the weather, the fire at Moscow, his ministers – even the hapless General Partouneaux – and, of course, his arch-enemy England. Even at this late stage in the game, however, he remained optimistic: Vilna, he believed, could be held – 'If the King of Naples plays me no foolish tricks'[3] *– while Europe, he maintained, would rally to his cause being, in his view, more alarmed by Cossacks than the Continental System.*

Caulaincourt (who gives a fascinating account of this singular journey in his memoir of the campaign) soon tired of his master's apologia: 'As a matter of fact, it is Your Majesty they fear. It is Your Majesty who is the cause of everyone's anxiety and prevents them from seeing other dangers.' Unburdening his heart and speaking frankly, Caulaincourt informed Napoleon that the world saw him as a despot; that Europe was weary of him and that his Continental System had brought his allies to the brink of ruin. Napoleon listened good-humouredly, even attempting to pinch his equerry's ear: 'I am a reasonable being, who does no more than he thinks will profit him,' he countered. As for the catastrophic outcome of the campaign, 'We are victims of the climate. The fine weather tricked me. If I had set out a fortnight sooner, my army would be at Vitebsk and I should be laughing at the Russians and your prophet Alexander . . . Everything turned out badly because I stayed too long at Moscow . . . all will be retrieved within three months.'[4]

As Napoleon sped homeward through the snow, the survivors of his army, 'shod with sheepskin or bits of cloth; heads bound with rags; wrapped in horse-cloths or women's petticoats',[5] *stumbled into East Prussia, harassed by their sole remaining enemy, the cold. Riddled with disease and ravaged by hunger, the sight of these 'walking ghosts'*[6] *aroused feelings of pity – for the most part – among a population exasperated by French domination: although the dread of meeting with* les mutilés *– as soldiers horribly disfigured by frostbite had become known – kept peasant women* *and their children housebound for weeks. Sadly, after so much suffering and so many privations, the shock of civilization upon the shattered constitutions of many returning soldiers proved lethal: according to de Ségur, 'This sudden change was fatal to us . . . Lariboissière, general-in-chief of the artillery, fell a sacrifice; Eblé, the pride of the army, followed him. Every day and every hour, our consternation was increased by fresh deaths.'*

Meanwhile, Murat's flight from the Cossacks continued as far as Gumbinnen, some sixty miles west of Kovno, on the River Pregel. It was here that General Dumas, a staff officer, encountered at an inn a man 'in a long brown cloak, wearing a long beard, his face blackened with powder, his whiskers half burned by fire but his eyes sparkling with brilliant lustre. "Well, here I am at last," he said. "What, General Dumas, do you not know me?" "No, who are you?" "I am the rearguard of the Grand Army – Marshal Ney. I have fired the last musket on the bridge of Kovno: I have thrown into the Niemen the last of our arms and I have walked hither, as you see, across the forests."'[7]

Despite the dramatic entry, Ney's reappearance did little to lift the morale of Murat, whose command now consisted of around 15,000 enfeebled men. On 18 December he called a council of war, at which he declared the line of the Niemen untenable. He proposed pulling back a further sixty miles or so to Königsberg, on the Baltic coast; but some chiefs – aware that Napoleon expected them to hold their ground – remained unconvinced and the meeting grew stormy. Murat, carried away by high emotion, gave vent to his exasperation in a verbal assault upon Napoleon which astounded his listeners. De Ségur maintains that Murat 'exclaimed that it was no longer possible to serve such a madman! That there was no safety in supporting his cause; that no monarch in Europe could now place any reliance on his word or in the treaties concluded with him.' He ended his tirade by predicting Napoleon's fall and declaring that, as for himself, he wished he'd joined the English. Davout, Murat's bête noir of the campaign, was aghast. Accusing the King of Naples of 'black ingratitude', he continued, 'You are only a king by the grace of Napoleon and at the cost of French blood.' 'I am as much King of Naples as Francis is Emperor of Austria,' retorted Murat, adding, 'and I can do as I please!'[8] *The next day saw him duly ensconced at Königsberg.*

By now, Napoleon was back in Paris, having arrived just before midnight the previous evening. It was only with the greatest difficulty that the unshaven, travel-weary Caulaincourt could gain admittance to the Tuileries: 'The porter, who had gone to bed, came out with a lamp in his hand and dressed only in his shirt, to see who was knocking. Our faces looked so strange to him that he called his wife. I had to repeat my name three or four times over before I could persuade them to open the door.' Meanwhile, a crowd of footmen and ladies-in-waiting had gathered and proceeded to gape at Napoleon from head to foot, until eventually the penny dropped: '"It's the Emperor!" one of them shouted . . . They could scarcely contain themselves.'

Napoleon arrived at Paris only twenty-four hours behind his 29th Bulletin, which had announced disaster and defeat in Russia. Needless to say, the capital was still in a state of shock; the atmosphere fearful and gloomy. Napoleon immediately threw himself into a damage-limitation exercise; but his attempt to lift morale backfired: misjudging the public mood, he ordered a round of balls and parties but the Parisians, shocked at the scale of the human tragedy unfolding in the east, fancied themselves dancing on graves.

No such qualms, however, in Vilna where, on 24 December, a grand ball was held in honour of Alexander's birthday. The Tsar had arrived at the ice-bound capital of Lithuania the day before, quipping that 'It has cost me the end of my nose to come here!'[9] *He danced once more with Countess Tiesenhausen, his partner at the moonlit ball of 24 June, when Balashov first broke the news of Napoleon's invasion; and greeted Field Marshal Kutusov, the two men shedding tears of relief at Russia's deliverance. (In public, Alexander heaped honours upon the old warrior, recognizing the need for a national hero, but in private he never forgave Kutusov for suffering Napoleon to escape at the Berezina.)*

Alexander – by now in a state of religious ecstasy – was deeply shocked by conditions at Vilna, where convents and hospitals were choked with the dead and dying of both sides. De Ségur states that 'at Vilna, more than 16,000 of our prisoners had already perished. The convent of St Basil contained the greatest number; from 10 to 23 December they had only received some biscuits but not a stick of wood nor a drop of water had been given them.' While Foord writes, 'Gangrened wounds, frostbite and typhus produced by filth, hunger and putrefaction swept them away. In three weeks 15,000 are said to have died.' Careless of his own safety, Alexander pitched in, personally supervising a humanitarian relief operation. He was aided by his brother, Grand Duke Constantine and, as de Ségur observes, 'If a few escaped out of the 20,000 of our unfortunate comrades who were made prisoners, it was to these two princes they owed their preservation.'

Indeed, preservation was the order of the day; and with the destruction of the Grand Army's central column, its flanking forces – the Austrians to the south and MacDonald's X Corps (including a strong Prussian contingent) to the north – sought to extricate themselves from the mess. The Austrians quickly came to an understanding with Kutusov, promising not to fight if allowed to march home unmolested. In the north, however, things took a more dramatic turn.

Marshal MacDonald had spent almost the entire campaign far to the north of the main action, blockading the Baltic port of Riga. He led a mixed force of Bavarians, Poles, Würtembergers and Prussians: the latter, some 18,000 strong, being under the direct command of their chief, Major-General von Yorck. On 19 December MacDonald quit Riga with his Poles and Germans and retreated on Tilsit: Yorck's Prussians, given the job of rearguard, were to follow in due course. However, having successfully reached his goal with minimal losses (mainly men who 'got drunk and perished, removed by the cold into eternal sleep'[10]), MacDonald was perturbed to learn that his rearguard had apparently disappeared into thin air. Despite numerous attempts to make contact, no one, it seemed, could find any trace of Yorck or his men. MacDonald, gradually suspecting some kind of foul play, decided, nevertheless, to await definite news of Yorck before making any further move, 'that my life and career should never have to bear upon them the blot of having abandoned, on account of fears which were perhaps imaginary, the troops committed to my care'.[11]

A capable and highly professional soldier, Yorck was, nevertheless, too strong-willed and independent to be a good subordinate. More importantly, he was a patriot, who viewed his country's humiliating enthralment to Napoleon with disdain. When, therefore, on 25 December, he found himself separated from MacDonald by a screen of Cossacks, commanded by the Prussian émigré General Diebitsch, he opted for discussion rather than combat. Diebitsch, anxious to persuade his countryman to defect, informed Yorck of the extent of Napoleon's defeat and, in the words of Edward Foord, 'boldly proposed . . . a conference in order to prevent useless bloodshed'. Yorck – who could have cut through Diebitsch's Cossacks with ease – hinted that he might be amenable to an agreement, so long as it might be achieved without loss of honour. The dialogue continued for the next five days, all the while Yorck hoping that the arrival of Russian reinforcements would enable him to legitimately accept Diebitsch's offer. By 30 December, however, Yorck realized that he could wait no longer and – committing what MacDonald later described as 'an act of treachery unparalleled in history'[12] *– signed the Convention of Tauroggen. In exchange for the return of captured men and baggage, and the safe-conduct of Prussian stragglers, Yorck agreed to declare his neutrality: effectively taking his men out of the Grand Army and, as a consequence, his country out of the campaign. Initially frowned upon by Berlin, Yorck's defiance of the French caught the mood of the Prussian people and helped kindle the War of German Liberation, which would set Europe ablaze the following year.*

Thus, with both wings of the Grand Army gone and Kutusov poised to cross the Niemen with 40,000 troops, Murat was obliged to retreat on the River Oder, leaving Rapp to garrison the key Baltic port of Danzig. For Murat, Yorck's defection was the last straw. Out of his depth, demoralized and 'troubled by rumours that had reached him as to Caroline's private conduct in his absence',[13] *he penned a string of letters to Napoleon, declaring his unstinting loyalty, while attempting to wheedle permission to return to Naples. Sensing the shift in the balance of power, Murat also entered into a secret dialogue with Vienna, in a treacherous bid to keep his Neapolitan crown come what may. By 17 January, however, his nerve finally broke: pleading sickness as his excuse ('I have fever and the beginning of a marked attack of jaundice'[14]), Murat quit. He did not even wait to personally hand over command to Eugène, but simply bolted for it, taking a fast coach for Naples, which he reached on 31 January. 'Not bad for a sick man,' commented Eugène dryly[15].*

On 28 February, King Frederick William III of Prussia signed the Convention of Kalisch, thus entering into a formal pact with Russia. In return for Alexander's help in regaining territory taken from him by Napoleon at Tilsit, he undertook to join the Tsar's holy war against Napoleon the Antichrist. Prussian resistance to Napoleon was slow to mobilize: 'It should be remarked that the Prussian nation,' writes de Ségur, 'which drew its sovereign towards Yorck, only ventured to rise successively as the Russians came in sight, and, by degrees, as our feeble remains quitted their territory.' Nevertheless, as news of Frederick's defection became known, Eugène was obliged to withdraw the remains of the Grand Army – bolstered by the arrival of sundry raw recruits – to the line of the River Elbe. This constituted the last manoeuvre of the campaign: thereafter a lull ensued as Napoleon and Alexander braced themselves for battle in Germany. This brief respite – so dearly bought and so desperately needed by Napoleon's army – was not, as de Ségur observes, seized upon as a chance for peace, 'but merely given to the premeditation of slaughter'.

And so ended Napoleon's expedition to Russia: a campaign of follies, fortitude and cruel calamities; a crushing defeat, made more bitter by the round of desertions, defections and squalid deaths which marked its denouement. The human cost of the conflict was immense: of the half-million men who crossed the Niemen with Napoleon, some 10,000 survived, making for a casualty rate of a staggering 98 per cent. Approximately 100,000 perished as prisoners of war in Russian hands. Alexander's army suffered a death-toll of around 150,000, while 300,000 more were crippled by wounds or frostbite: civilian casualties remain uncalculated. It should not be forgotten that the Grand Army also lost almost all its 150,000 horses during the six-month span of the campaign: they died of disease, exhaustion, hunger; or were simply eaten alive during the sub-zero trek from the Berezina to the Niemen. (Russians burned over 120,000 of their corpses in the clean-up operation.)

The greatest casualty of the campaign, however, was neither man nor beast: it was a reputation. 'A great reputation is but a great noise,' Napoleon had once said, 'the more there is of it, the further off it is heard.'[16] *He had begun his Russian adventure as the biggest of noises – a modern Caesar – whose military genius had set him apart as the greatest captain of the age: he ended it decidedly less fortissimo – a fallen idol – his record for invincibility shattered. Thus, the Russian campaign caused one of the most dramatic reversals in military history: before 1812 Napoleon had fought for conquest; after it, for political survival. In effect, his march on Moscow was merely the first leg of a longer journey, destined to end three years later on the South Atlantic island of St Helena. There, in perpetual exile as the Grand Disturber of the World, Napoleon reflected: 'I committed three great political faults. I ought to have made peace with England in abandoning Spain; I ought to have restored the Kingdom of Poland; and not have gone to Moscow . . . It was making war on Russia that ruined me.'*[17]

As de Ségur let the curtain fall on his epic, he declared: 'Everything in it was grand; it will be our lot to astonish future ages with our glory and our sorrow. Melancholy consolation! But the only one that remains to us; for doubt it not, comrades, the noise of so great a fall will echo in that futurity in which great misfortunes immortalize as much as great glory.' And finally, 'Comrades, my task is finished; it is now for you to bear your testimony to the truth of the picture. Its colours will no doubt appear pale to your eyes and to your hearts, which are still full of these great recollections. But which of you is ignorant that an action is always more eloquent than its description; and that if great historians are produced by great men, the first are still more rare than the last?'

Principal Personalities of Napoleon's Grand Army

Napoleon's motto of 'a career open to all talents, without distinction of birth', opened the door of opportunity to men of merit and ambition who, under the Ancien Régime, would have remained in obscure anonymity. As a rule, these men – often of humble origin – surfaced during the chaos of the French Revolution: attachment to Bonaparte, the Republican Hero, secured their fame; attachment to Napoleon, the Emperor of the French, secured their fortunes. For he made them his acolytes; and from these sons of brewers, bakers and barrel-makers created a new aristocracy of counts, dukes, princes and kings.

BEAUHARNAIS, Eugène de, Viceroy of Italy (1781–1824). Commander of the Italian contingent of the Grand Army and Napoleon's adopted son. (Josephine was his mother, General Alexandre de Beauharnais, an aristocratic victim of the Revolution, his natural father.) Eugène was honesty and decency personified. A popular commander and a steadfast lieutenant to his imperial stepfather, Eugène had been appointed Viceroy of Italy following Napoleon's accession to the Italian throne in 1805. Although lacking in military experience at the start of the Russian campaign, Eugène would emerge at its close with his reputation considerably enhanced.

BERTHIER, Marshal Louis-Alexandre, Prince of Neuchâtel (1753–1815). The Grand Army's chief of staff and Napoleon's main military collaborator since 1796. Berthier rarely left his master's side and was dubbed 'the Emperor's wife' by the troops. Napoleon, however, referred to Berthier as 'my chief clerk' and, though he showered his chief of staff with wealth, rarely credited him for his undoubted gifts as an administrator. Berthier's life was dominated by Napoleon (who worked him mercilessly) and his mistress, Madame Visconti, with whom he was totally infatuated: he would begin the campaign, therefore, both war-weary and lovesick.

BESSIÈRES, Marshal Jean-Baptiste, Duke of Istria (1768–1813). Commander of the cavalry of Napoleon's Imperial Guard, a corps which he had been instrumental in forming. A veteran of Bonaparte's early campaigns in Italy and Egypt, Bessières was a cautious, cool-headed commander: loyal to Napoleon and beloved by his men.

BONAPARTE, Jérôme, King of Westphalia (1784–1860). Commander of VIII Corps and Napoleon's profligate youngest brother. Jérôme had little military experience and in his short time as King of Westphalia had inspired mutiny among his own officers, while bringing the country to the brink of bankruptcy. He would quit the Grand Army after a row with his imperial brother.

CAULAINCOURT, General Armand de, Duke of Vicenza (1773–1827). As Napoleon's ambassador to St Petersburg, he had spoken out against war with Russia. Nevertheless, as Napoleon's grand equerry, he loyally accompanied his master to Moscow and back, becoming one of the Emperor's closest aides. Caulaincourt's brother, Auguste, would die at Borodino, leading the decisive cavalry charge of the day.

DARU, Count Pierre-Antoine (1767–1829). Napoleon's secretary of state, he was distinguished by his capacity for hard work and his role as a respected adviser.

DAVOUT, Marshal Louis-Nicholas, Duke of Auerstädt and Prince of Eckmühl (1770–1823). Commander of I Corps, the bald, bespectacled Davout – nicknamed 'the Iron Marshal' – was a model of military efficiency. The son of a professional soldier, Davout was perhaps the most talented of Napoleon's lieutenants: nevertheless, his performance in Russia would be marred by constant feuding with colleagues.

DUMAS, General Mathieu (1753–1837). The Grand Army's intendant general at the outset of the campaign, he would be replaced by Daru on the grounds of ill-health.

DUROC, General Géraud-Christophe-Michel, Duke of Frioul (1772–1813). The head of Napoleon's imperial household, Duroc was both soldier and diplomat and had served his master for many years as a senior aide. Napoleon once claimed that Duroc was the only person he had ever truly trusted.

JUNOT, General Jean-Andoche, Duke of Abrantès (1771–1813). One of Napoleon's principal aides, Junot would take over command of VIII Corps from Jérôme Bonaparte, upon the latter's desertion in a fit of pique. A hard-drinking, womanizing ex-law student, Junot was a veteran of the Egyptian campaign where, fighting like a whirlwind, he had picked up the sobriquet, 'la Tempeste'. His performance in Russia, however, would be lamentable, his mind being affected by the onset of syphilis.

MacDONALD, Marshal Jacques-Etienne, Duke of Tarentum (1765–1840). As commander of X Corps, MacDonald – the son of a Scottish Jacobite exile – would spend the bulk of the campaign detached far to the north of the main action, guarding the left flank of the Grand Army.

MORTIER, Marshal Edouard-Adolph, Duke of Treviso (1768–1835). Commander of Napoleon's Young Guard and destined to be governor of Moscow during the Grand Army's brief sojourn. A large, likeable man, Mortier was the son of a merchant and half-English on his mother's side. He was nicknamed 'the Big Mortar'.

MOUTON, Marshal Georges, Count Lobau (1770–1838). The son of a baker, Mouton (or Count Lobau, as he preferred to be known) was one of Napoleon's most trusted and courageous aides-de-camp.

MURAT, Marshal Joachim, King of Naples, Grand Duke of Berg (1767–1815). Commander of the Grand Army's cavalry reserve and brother-in-law to Napoleon. The son of an innkeeper, Murat came to Napoleon's notice as a dashing cavalry captain during the Revolutionary Wars. Having become Bonaparte's aide-de-camp, his future was further secured by marriage to his master's sister, Caroline, in 1800. Charismatic, vain and recklessly brave, Murat would drive the Grand Army's cavalry into the ground in pursuit of victory.

NEY, Marshal Michel, Duke of Elchingen (1769–1815). Commander of III Corps, Ney was a fiery front-line general with a reputation for insubordination. The son of a cooper and an ex-sergeant major, Ney would make his name in Russia as 'the Bravest of the Brave' and saviour of the Grand Army's rearguard.

OUDINOT, Marshal Nicolas-Charles, Duke of Reggio (1767–1847). The hard-fighting head of II Corps, Oudinot was a loyal subordinate but of limited ability in independent command. The son of a brewer, Oudinot was a veteran of the Revolutionary Wars who possessed an uncanny knack for getting himself wounded.

PONIATOWSKI, Marshal Jozef Anton, Prince (1763–1813). Commander of V Corps, Poniatowski was a nephew of

Stanislau II, the last King of Poland. Like many Poles, he saw Napoleon as the only hope for his country's salvation. Thus, for Poniatowski, the coming campaign held out the promise of a kingdom.

RAPP, General Jean (1771–1821). Napoleon's foremost aide-de-camp, Rapp originally enlisted as a cavalry trooper during the Revolutionary Wars. Devoted to Napoleon, he was destined to receive a total of twenty-five wounds in his master's service: four of which would be sustained within the space of ninety minutes, during the titanic clash with the Russians at Borodino.

VICTOR, Marshal Claude, Duke of Belluno (1764–1841). As commander of IX Corps, Victor would spend the first half of the campaign in reserve, but would play a crucial part in saving the Grand Army at the passage of the Berezina.

Napoleon's Expedition to Russia: a Chronology

1812

24 June: Napoleon crosses the Niemen with a Grand Army totalling some 500,000 men. No declaration of war is made and Alexander learns of the invasion while attending a moonlit ball at Vilna.

25 June: Napoleon enters the frontier town of Kovno and sets up his headquarters at the local convent.

26 June: Alexander and his staff having fled, Vilna is taken without a fight. Napoleon turns the Lithuanian capital into a major depot for his army.

29 June: A great storm strikes, throwing the Grand Army into a state chaos and demoralization. Meanwhile, the army's transport system becomes hopelessly bogged down: men and horses, constantly pushed forward on forced marches, begin to starve.

1 July: Napoleon receives General Balashov, sent by Alexander with a last minute call for peace: the overture is taken as a sign of weakness and Balashov is sent packing. Meanwhile, having failed to bring Russian generalissimo Barclay de Tolly to battle, Napoleon sends Marshal Davout south, to aid Jérôme Bonaparte in the entrapment of Prince Bagration's Second Army of the West.

6 July: Having dragged his heels, thereby inadvertently permitting Bagration's escape, Jérôme is relieved of his command by an incandescent Napoleon, who replaces him with Davout. Jérôme quits the army in a fit of pique. He is replaced by General Junot.

7 July: Napoleon orders the Grand Army out of Vilna and back on to the heels of the retreating Barclay.

24 July: Alexander, having (after much persuasion) abandoned the idea of commanding his troops in person, arrives at Moscow and calls out the militia.

25 July: Murat's advanced guard skirmishes with Barclay's rearguard at Ostrovno, a few miles west of Vitebsk. Napoleon, hoping for a major encounter, calls a halt to operations in order to better prepare for battle. Barclay, however, slips away once more and heads for the fortress of Smolensk and a junction with Bagration.

28 July: Napoleon, cheated of a decisive battle, enters Vitebsk. Leaving the pursuit of Barclay to Murat's advanced guard, he moves into the governor's house and announces a period of rest and recuperation.

31 July: Admiral Chichagov, a favourite of Alexander's with little military experience, leaves Bucharest at the head of the 38,000-strong Army of Moldavia and begins his long march to the front.

14 August: Having decided to march on Smolensk in search of battle, Napoleon approaches Krasnoi, on the south-western approaches to the city. Here, Ney's III Corps bloodies a Russian force under Neverovski.

15 August: Having gained the initiative, Napoleon

promptly loses it by spending this day, his birthday, reviewing the Imperial Guard rather than seizing Smolensk.

17 August: Napoleon's soldiers clear the suburbs of Smolensk at the point of the bayonet but make little impression on the city's massive defensive wall. Meanwhile, 130 miles to the north-west, Marshal Oudinot and General Gouvion St-Cyr engage Prince Wittgenstein's Army of Finland at the town of Polotsk.

18 August: Fearing encirclement, Kutusov and Bagration abandon Smolensk, leaving Napoleon master of the smouldering city. The Grand Army's losses are high and Napoleon talks of halting his advance. At Polotsk, Oudinot and St-Cyr defeat Prince Wittgenstein, thus securing the Emperor's northern flank.

19 August: Ney pursues the retreating Russians and a battle develops at the village of Valutino, a few miles north-east of Smolensk. Junot, however, bungles his command and, once again, the Russians are suffered to escape.

20 August: Although gradually grinding down the Grand Army through a policy of steady retreat, Barclay's unglamorous methods prove highly unpopular. Thus, responding to growing pressure for his removal, Alexander appoints the sixty-seven-year-old Kutusov as commander-in-chief of the Russian army.

25 August: Napoleon enters Dorogobuzh, having decided to march on Moscow where, he believes, ultimate victory awaits him. Despite having lost thousands of troops to dysentery, fatigue, heat exhaustion and hunger (plus some to combat and garrison duties), he is convinced that the Russians are on the brink of collapse and that 'Peace is in front of us.'

27 August: The Russian army is reinforced by 15,000 troops under Miloradovich.

29 August: Kutusov arrives at the front with orders to stem the retreat and start fighting. He selects the village of Borodino, seventy-five miles west of Moscow, to make his stand.

3 September: Marshal Victor crosses the Niemen with IX Corps in order to act as Napoleon's central reserve.

5 September: Napoleon comes upon Kutusov's outlying positions at Schivardino and takes them after a sharp engagement.

6 September: A day of calm preparation before the coming showdown. Although Napoleon's Grand Army has shrunk from half a million men to a mere 124,000 effectives, his only concern is that the Russians will elude him once more.

7 September: The inconclusive Battle of Borodino is fought with appalling losses on both sides. Kutusov withdraws under cover of darkness, uncovering the road to Moscow. For Napoleon, however, the battle has come too late and at too high a cost in blood for him to realistically achieve his goal of subjugating Alexander.

13 September: Kutusov takes the momentous decision to abandon Moscow in order to save the remnant of his army. Governor Rostopchin, who expected Kutusov to fight for the capital, orders fire-starters to torch the city upon Napoleon's arrival.

14 September: Napoleon enters an apparently deserted Moscow and takes up residence at the Kremlin. He fully expects his occupation of the city to bring Alexander to the bargaining table: within hours, however, fire breaks out in the merchants' quarter.

15 September: The fire quickly develops into an inferno and

Napoleon seeks refuge outside the city at the Petrovsky Palace. Martial law is declared at Moscow but the troops disregard orders and turn to pillage.

18 September: After destroying three-quarters of the city, the great fire dies down and Napoleon returns to the Kremlin, master of a heap of ashes. Meanwhile, Admiral Chichagov effects a junction with Tormassov's Third Army of the West, south of the Pripet Marshes.

20 September: Desperate to terminate the campaign and unsettled by Alexander's silence, Napoleon writes a letter, hinting that peace might be possible, so long as it could be secured without loss of honour. Alexander remains mute.

30 September: Napoleon holds a council of war and proposes marching on St Petersburg: he is shouted down by his marshals. Retreat is the only option.

4 October: Murat's advanced guard locates the Russian army encamped south-west of Moscow, behind the River Nara, at Tarutino. Finding Kutusov's position too strong to attack, Murat pulls back a few miles to Vinkovo.

18 October: The Russians counter-attack, Prince Wittgenstein hitting Gouvion St-Cyr at Polotsk and Kutusov catching Murat off guard at Vinkovo.

19 October: No longer dictating the course of events but merely reacting to them, Napoleon quits the capital, heading south for Kaluga and fertile territory untouched by war.

22 October: Kutusov learns of Napoleon's evacuation of Moscow.

23 October: Marshal Mortier quits Moscow, having largely ignored Napoleon's instructions to destroy the Kremlin. Meanwhile, Paris is thrown into momentary panic by an abortive coup perpetrated by General Malet, an escaped political agitator.

24 October: Napoleon's drive south is thwarted at the Battle of Maloyaroslavets. From this point the retreat begins in earnest, as Napoleon turns tail and makes for the Moscow-Smolensk highroad, still devastated by his incoming march of the previous summer. Unbeknown to him, Kutusov is also retreating, leaving the road to Kaluga open.

28 October: Kutusov learns of Napoleon's retreat. Turning his army about-face, he begins his pursuit, aiming merely to shepherd the Grand Army out of Russia and leaving the work of destruction to the coming winter.

3 November: A Russian force under Miloradovich attacks the Grand Army at Viasma, on the road to Smolensk. Davout's I Corps is cut off and has to be rescued by Eugène, Ney and Poniatowski. Already the Grand Army has entered the first stages of disintegration and Miloradovich takes 3,000 prisoners.

4 November: Winter arrives with the first fall of snow.

6 November: Napoleon learns of Malet's failed coup and realizes that he must return to Paris as soon as possible, in order to reassert his authority. Meanwhile the weather worsens: gales, snowstorms and sub-zero temperatures take their toll as thousands of troops fall out of the ranks and 5,000 horses die within a matter of days.

14 November: The Grand Army reaches Smolensk but only half of the troops who quit Moscow remain with the colours. Napoleon had hoped to use Smolensk as a base for further operations but the freezing, famished troops trash the place, consuming the city's supplies within twenty-four hours: Napoleon has no choice but to order the retreat to continue. His next goal is the crucial crossing-point over the Berezina at Borisov, some 150 miles to the west.

17 November: A Russian force under Miloradovich cuts the road six miles east of Krasnoi, separating Eugène, Davout and Ney from Napoleon and the rest of the army. Eugène extricates himself at a great cost in casualties, while Napoleon sends back the Guard to pull Davout free. Ney, however, who is still at Smolensk, is given up for lost.

18 November: Ney quits Smolensk with the rearguard and runs into the Russian troops bloodied at Krasnoi by the Guard. Although hopelessly outnumbered, Ney refuses to surrender and fights it out till nightfall; leaving his campfires burning, he slips away with the remains of III Corps under cover of darkness and heads for the Dnieper. Three days later, Ney catches up with the rest of the army at Orsha, accompanied by a mere 800 survivors.

22 November: Napoleon learns that the Borisov bridge has been cut. Having burned his bridge-train at Orsha, he now faces entrapment and destruction at the hands of three separate Russian armies under Chichagov, Kutusov and Prince Wittgenstein.

24 November: Napoleon approaches the Berezina with around 25,000 effective troops and a similar number of unarmed stragglers. With the bridge at Borisov down and the opposite bank in Chichagov's hands, he orders the construction of improvised bridges at a ford, eight miles upstream at the village of Studzianka. Chichagov, meanwhile, is hoodwinked into believing that the crossing will be attempted at Borisov and obligingly leaves the Studzianka sector relatively unguarded.

26 November: The two-day passage of the Berezina begins on extemporized bridges. Chichagov realizes his error and attacks along the western bank of the Berezina, as Prince Wittgenstein closes in on Studzianka from the east. Despite heavy losses – thousands were killed, captured or drowned – Napoleon escapes with some 20,000 survivors.

3 December: Napoleon composes the famous 29th Bulletin, in which he informs Paris of the Grand Army's destruction. He lays the whole burden of blame for the catastrophe on the Russian winter, while taking pains to assure the capital that 'His Majesty's health has never been better.'

5 December: Having seen the remains of the Grand Army safely over the Berezina – the last major obstacle between it and the safety of the Polish border – Napoleon departs for Paris, leaving his brother-in-law, Murat, in charge of the wreck of his army. Seen by some as a desertion, this exit was necessary if Napoleon was to raise a fresh army, rally public opinion, and at least attempt to forestall the defection of his allies.

9 December: The survivors of the Grand Army reach Vilna but within twenty-four hours Murat abandons the place to the Cossacks and the retreat – by now a rout – continues to Kovno.

13 December: Having abandoned Kovno, Murat crosses the River Niemen and orders the army – what's left of it – to concentrate around Gumbinnen. Meanwhile, Kutusov enters Vilna, having lost 90,000 casualties since the Berezina due to the severe cold.

14 December: The rearguard of the Grand Army reaches the Niemen, the original start-line for the invasion. The campaign – one of history's greatest military and human disasters – is effectively over. At 8.00 p.m. the last French soldier quits Russia: that man being the indefatigable Marshal Ney. Of the half-million men under arms who originally entered Russia, a mere 10,000 would live to tell the tale.

18 December: Murat holds a council of war at Gumbinnen. He insists that the line of the Niemen cannot be held and that the retreat must continue to Königsberg. He claims that Napoleon is a madman, whose cause is lost. Despite objections from Marshal Davout, Murat gets his way. Napoleon, blissfully ignorant of Murat's mounting insubordination, reaches Paris at a quarter to midnight. Next day, Alexander sets off for Vilna.

21 December: Murat enters into covert dialogue with the Austrian government in an attempt to retain his throne at Naples. Meanwhile, the line of the Niemen is abandoned and the Russians enter East Prussia.

30 December: Major-General von Yorck, commander of the Prussian contingent of the Grand Army, extricates himself and his entire corps from the war by signing the Convention of Tauroggen. In doing so, he strikes the spark which kindles the War of German Liberation of the following spring.

1813

2 January: Wth Murat constantly giving ground, Kutusov crosses the Niemen with 40,000 men. After further French retreats, Prince Wittgenstein crosses the Vistula twelve days later.

17 January: Murat quits the army, pleading sickness as his excuse. Eugène is left in command.

28 February: Prussia signs a treaty with Russia – the Convention of Kalisch – and Eugène has no choice but to retreat behind the Elbe. This is, effectively, the last manoeuvre of the campaign. Peace, however, is short-lived, as hostilities erupt with renewed vigour in the spring, when the battle for control of Germany begins.

Glossary

Battalion Infantry unit consisting of around 1,000 soldiers.

Brigade Cavalry or infantry unit made up of several regiments or battalions.

Carabinières Elite 'heavy' cavalry supplied with brass helmets and body-armour.

Carbine Short-barrelled musket carried by cavalrymen and clipped to a broad belt, worn over the shoulder.

Chasseur Literally meaning 'huntsman', this term applies both to mounted and foot soldiers who, lightly armed and fighting in loose order, fulfilled the role of scouts, snipers, etc.

Colours Flag or banner of a regiment, the loss of which was deemed shameful.

Corps Sub-division of an army into a smaller, self-contained force of all arms.

Cossack Irregular cavalryman loyal only to the person of the Russian Tsar.

Covered way Path or communication trench protected by a parapet on its outer side.

Cuirassier 'Heavy' cavalryman who wears a cuirass or breast-plate.

Debouch Deployment of troops into open ground.

Defile Narrow opening or way through which troops must march in file.

Division Large body of troops, either mounted or on foot, usually several thousand strong.

Dragoon Originally, an infantryman who rode into battle before deploying. By 1812, however, the term referred exclusively to a cavalryman, usually well armed and supplied with a steel helmet, but without body-armour.

Eagle Napoleon presented these regimental standards to most of his army units. Designed by the sculptor Chaudet in 1804 and based on the Roman imperial eagle, they were nicknamed 'cuckoos' by the troops.

Flêche V-shaped defensive work allowing troops to enter from the rear and facilitating fire on two protected flanks. The word literally means 'arrow'.

Grenadier Elite infantryman, supposedly over five feet eight inches tall.

Howitzer Short-barrelled artillery-piece used for high-angled firing.

Hussar 'Light' cavalryman, based on the extravagantly dressed Hungarian horsemen of tradition.

Line of communication Link between an army and its supplies.

Line of operation Direction taken by an army through hostile territory.

Outpost Outlying sentry-post.

Pelisse Fur-trimmed jacket, often festooned with buttons, braid and lace.

Platoon Small tactical unit, usually commanded by a lieutenant.

Piquet Sentry-post or lookout.

Pontoon Boat or cylinder, designed to float on water in order to support a temporary bridge.

Pontonnier Bridge-building military engineer.

Redoubt Fully enclosed bulwark or defensive fieldwork.

Sapper Private soldier in the Engineers.

Squadron Tactical unit of cavalry, most mounted regiments consisting of four squadrons.

Subaltern Junior officer.

Sutler Camp follower authorized to sell provisions to the troops.

Tirailleur Skirmisher.
Vedettes Cavalry scouts.
Voltigeur 'Light' infantryman, supposedly able to keep pace with a trotting horse.

Notes and Sources

Editor's Preface (pp. vii–xi)

1 De Ségur, General Count Philippe-Paul, *History of the Expedition to Russia, Undertaken by the Emperor Napoleon, in the Year 1812*, London 1827.
2 Quoted in Gleig, G.R., *Personal Reminiscences of the 1st Duke of Wellington*, London 1904.
3 This quotation from Virgil ('*Quamquam animus meminisse horret, luctuque refugit, Incipiam*') appears as an inscription on the title-page of the English translation of 1827.
4 De Ségur, General Count Philippe, *An Aide-de-Camp of Napoleon: Memoirs of General Count de Ségur*, London 1895.
5 *Ibid.*
6 *Ibid.*
7 This and all other quotations by Foord are taken from Foord, Edward, *Napoleon's Russian Campaign of 1812*.
8 Attached to the imperial headquarters staff, de Ségur's main function was to find and prepare suitable accommodation for Napoleon and his suite.
9 Quoted in the editor's introduction to de Ségur, *History of the Expedition to Russia*.
10 De Ségur, *History of the Expedition to Russia*.
11 This and all other quotations by Marbot are taken from de Marbot, Jean-Baptiste, *Memoirs of Baron de Marbot*, London 1900. In his memoirs, Marbot accuses de Ségur of exaggeration, and although he admits his book enjoyed great popularity, attributes this chiefy to 'the purity and elegance of its style'.
12 De Ségur, *History of the Expedition to Russia*.

13 In his introduction to the translation of 1827, de Ségur's English editor claims that the duel 'terminated without injury' to either man. It would appear to be generally accepted, however, that de Ségur was indeed wounded: thus, literally suffering for his art and becoming, in a sense, the last casualty of the Russian campaign. Incidentally, Gourgaud's book – the cause of the duel – was entitled, *Napoleon et la Grande Armée en Russie*, and was published in 1825. Although written as a direct riposte to de Ségur, it did little to dent public enthusiasm for the latter's work.

Introduction (pp. 1–9)

1 Herold, J. Christopher, *The Mind of Napoleon: a Selection from His Written and Spoken Words.*
2 Napoleon to the Bavarian minister, quoted in Wheeler, Harold F.B., *The Mind of Napoleon: as Revealed in His Thoughts, Speech and Actions.*
3 Herold, J. Christopher, *op.cit.*
4 Cohen, Louis, *Napoleonic Anecdotes.*
5 Quoted in Nafziger, George F., *Napoleon's Invasion of Russia.*
6 Herold, J. Christopher, *op. cit.*
7 This and all other Caulaincourt quotations are taken from Caulaincourt, Armand de, *With Napoleon in Russia.*
8 This and all other Bourrienne quotations are taken from Bourrienne, F. de, *Memoirs of Napoleon Bonaparte.*

Chapter 1 (pp. 11–20)

1 This and all other quotations by Lejeune are taken from Lejeune, Louis-François, *Memoirs of Baron Lejeune.*
2 Alexander's HQ was a hotbed of intrigue. He had surrounded himself with a coterie of foreign advisers and these 'scientific' soldiers were bitterly resented by the Russian top brass. Generally speaking, the Russian high command was riven by personal rivalries and petty jealousies. As Clausewitz – himself a Prussian émigré – observed, 'The head-

quarters of the Emperor were already overrun with distinguished idlers. To attain either distinction or usefulness in such a crowd would have required the dexterity of an accomplished intriguer.' (Unless otherwise stated, this and all other Clausewitz quotations are taken from Clausewitz, Carl von, *The Campaign of 1812 in Russia*.)

3 With hindsight, Napoleon's proclamation can be said to contain several cruel ironies: he announces a 'Polish war' while having no intention of helping the Poles regain their independence; he refers to Austria and Prussia as allies to be safeguarded against Russian aggression, yet both nations were secretly conniving with Alexander behind his back; and as for being 'still the soldiers of Austerlitz', Napoleon was but a shadow of his former self and his army, though strong in numbers, was weak in experience; finally, Napoleon would not 'put an end to' Russian influence, it would put an end to him! All in all, as Edward Foord points out, 'Despite the grim seriousness of the situation and the terrible drama which was soon to be acted, it is difficult not to see that Napoleon's position was a somewhat ludicrous one.'

4 The 'real object' of the war for Napoleon was to reassert his dominance over Alexander who, for his part, wished to break free from French interference in Russian affairs.

5 A French league was roughly equivalent to three English miles.

6 'A hare started out between the legs of his horse, Friedland, which swerved and threw him ... Berthier seized Caulaincourt's hand and murmured, "We had better not cross the Niemen. This fall is a bad omen."' Watson, S.J., *By Command of the Emperor: a Life of Marshal Berthier*.

7 Lejeune likened the sight of so many glittering bayonets to 'the quivering scintillations in the sunshine of the waters of some lake or river when ruffled by a passing breeze'.

8 Lejeune describes how 'A tremendous storm came up ... and the air became completely charged with electricity. The thunder and lightning were terrific and at about three o'clock two men and three horses were killed by lightning.' Storms followed the army over the succeeding days and the engineers, constantly employed in clearing obstructions and

constructing bridges in order to hurry the army forward, were permanently drenched: eventually, they simply stripped off and worked naked. As for the enormous loss of horses, this had more to do with hunger and forced marches than rain: pushed along at a punishing rate and reduced to eating green rye or thatch from village roofs, they dropped in their thousands from colic or exhaustion.

9 Marbot describes the incident thus: 'Beyond Kovno flows a small stream called the Vilia, the bridge over which had been cut by the enemy; and the storm having swollen it, Oudinot's leading scouts were stopped. The Emperor came up just as I reached the spot with my regiment. He ordered the Polish lancers to sound the ford and one man was drowned. I took down his name, which was Tzinski. If I emphasise this detail it is because the accident . . . has been vastly exaggerated.'

10 Fiery and tempestuous, *le beau* Montbrun, was a formidable cavalry commander. Napoleon ordered him to seize the enemy's supplies at Vilna but Murat, Montbrun's immediate superior, scotched the operation and the Russians quit town, taking their stores with them. Later, when a furious Napoleon publicly upbraided Montbrun for what, in truth, was Murat's blunder, the incandescent general drew his sabre and sent it spinning through the air, yelling, 'You can all go to the devil!' before galloping off to his tent.

11 Octave de Ségur, brother of the author, was captured by the Russians in this skirmish. Having survived his wounds and the ordeal of captivity, he returned home to Paris after the war where, in 1818, he drowned himself in the Seine on discovering his wife's infidelity. His son Eugène married Sophie Rostopchin, daughter of General Count Feodor Rostopchin, governor of Moscow in 1812.

Chapter 2 (pp. 21–29)

1 This and all other quotations by Vossler are taken from Vossler, H.A., *With Napoleon in Russia*.

2 Although Clausewitz informs us that von Pfuel 'passed in

Prussia for a man of much genius', he goes on to say that he 'never saw a man who lost his head so easily, who, intent as he ever was on great things, was soon overwhelmed by the least of little realities'.

3 According to Henry Lachouque and Anne S.K. Brown in *The Anatomy of Glory* (the standard work on Napoleon's Guard), pillagers from this elite unit discovered at Vilna were either returned to the line regiments or shot.

4 In *Human Voices from the Russian Campaign*, Arthur Chuquet describes the experiences of Major Boulart of the Guard artillery: 'On 30 June, when he reached Vilna, Boulart had lost ninety draft horses and seventy little ponies of the country . . . the poor beasts had nothing to eat but the still-green wheat, the most unwholesome food they could have had in the state of overwork in which they were constantly kept. The green food weakened them; the glacial rain finished them off.'

5 Balashov had been intercepted by French hussars on 26 June. Suspected of being a spy, he was detained under virtual arrest at Davout's headquarters, while the letter which he bore was forwarded to Napoleon. Four days later he was escorted to Vilna (via a different route to that taken by the army, that he might not see the pitiful state of the soldiers or the road lined with the carcasses of thousands of horses) and was received on 1 July in the very room where, a week earlier, Alexander had despatched him on his mission.

6 Jomini, General Antoine-Henri, Baron (1779–1869). He published the influential *Traité des Grande Operations Militaires* in 1805. Having served on the staffs of both Napoleon and Ney, Jomini was kept away from the front line during the 1812 campaign because of his Russian sympathies. When Smolensk fell to the French, however, he was appointed governor. The following year, as the balance of power lurched away from Napoleon, he switched sides, becoming adviser and aide-de-camp to the Tsar. Jomini's best known work is *Précis de l'Art de Guerre (The Art of War)*, published in 1836.

7 De Ségur's account tallies with Caulaincourt's own version of events. Apparently, Napoleon later told his grand equerry and former ambassador to St Petersburg, 'I know well

enough that you are an honest man. I was only joking. You are too touchy.'

8 Napoleon had attempted to intimidate Balashov by asking which was the best road to Moscow but the Russian answered dryly that Charles XII had gone via Poltava: a reference to the Swedish King's crushing defeat at the hands of Peter the Great in 1709. Balashov was returned to Alexander bearing a blame-laden letter from Bonaparte, in which he declared himself forced into war by the Tsar's intransigence. Now neither emperor could afford to back down: it would be a war to the death.

9 Murat has been much blamed by historians for his handling of the advanced guard and of his cavalry in particular. In *Joachim Murat*, A.H. Atteridge writes, 'It has been said that though none could excel him as a leader on the battlefield, he did not know how to take care of his horses on the march or in camp, or was careless on this all-important matter. He could conduct a campaign, say his critics, on condition of being allowed to use up some hundreds of horses every day. With scores of them at his own disposal, and a fresh mount every few hours, he did not realise that the heavily equipped cuirassier or dragoon had only one horse, and that horse could not work all day and all night without suffering for it.' (All other quotations by Atteridge are taken from this source.)

Chapter 3 (pp. 31–45)

1 This and all other quotations by Coignet are taken from Coignet, Jean-Roch, *The Narrative of Captain Coignet: Soldier of the Empire*.

2 Although sympathetic to the Polish cause, Napoleon dared not reconstitute the old Kingdom of Poland for fear of antagonizing Austria and Prussia who, along with Russia, had divided it up in 1795. As Lejeune states, 'Napoleon had no intention . . . of accepting the Polish proposal of co-operation with him and he needed all his diplomatic skill when at Vilna to evade destroying the hopes of the Poles or making any definite promises to them.'

3 Although Napoleon never forgave Jérôme for his blunder, the fault really lay with himself for, as a mere military novice, his youngest brother was way out of his depth. However, like some wary mafiosi, Napoleon insisted on keeping business within the family, often – as in this case – with catastrophic results.

4 One of Napoleon's rallying cries, it refers to the moment when, on a foggy 2 December 1805, the sun broke through the mist to reveal the sight of his most famous victory.

5 By the eighteenth century Russia had gained enough new territory to become a truly European power. She swallowed up Lithuania and much of Poland by the partitions of 1772, 1793 and 1795.

6 Without clean water or adequate fodder and worked to a standstill, many cavalry mounts were incapable of galloping, their riders being obliged to evade capture by fleeing on foot! A large proportion of the horses were too young for the rigours of an arduous campaign and simply gave up the ghost. No wonder Murat was keeping quiet.

7 Schwarzenberg, leader of Napoleon's Austrian contingent, successfully checked a clumsy advance by General Tormassov's Third Army of the West which, stationed south of the Pripet Marshes, briefly threatened Warsaw and the rear of the Grand Army.

8 According to Henry Lachouque and Anne S.K. Brown in *The Anatomy of Glory*, Napoleon made General Friant chief of the foot grenadiers of his Old Guard at a parade given on 9 August.

9 According to Bourrienne, Napoleon's 'natural impatience urged him forward as it were unconsciously, and he seemed to be under the influence of an invisible demon, stronger even than his own will'.

10 Another reference to the disastrous invasion of Russia undertaken by Charles XII of Sweden in 1708. The Russians, under Peter the Great, successfully pursued a scorched-earth policy before decisively beating a greatly reduced Swedish army at Poltava in June 1709. A catastrophe for Charles, it not only marked the end of his political and military career, he was actually lucky to escape with his life.

Chapter 4 (pp. 47–65)

1 This and all other quotations by Leroy-Dupré are taken from Leroy-Dupré, L.A.H., *Memoirs of Baron Larrey*.
2 Major Baron von Löwenstern, quoted in Brett-James, Anthony, *1812: Eyewitness Accounts of Napoleon's Defeat in Russia*.
3 Quoted in Nicolson, Nigel, *Napoleon 1812*.
4 Napoleon's attack went in shortly after midday and was, on the whole, successful: the Würtembergers and Poles being particularly effective in clearing the Russians from the suburbs opposed to them. Ney's assault on the royal citadel, however, was repelled with heavy loss. According to Foord, 'The French halted within musket-shot, sheltering as best they could behind the houses . . . but losing heavily by the fire from the battlements and especially from the light guns on the towers.'
5 Caulaincourt gives this vignette of Napoleon before Smolensk: 'His Majesty came up with the Prince of Neuchâtel and the Duke of Istria. They gazed at the flaming town. It lit up the whole horizon, already studded with the sparkle of our own bivouac fires. "An eruption of Vesuvius!" shouted the Emperor, clapping me on the shoulder and waking me from my stupor. "Isn't that a fine sight, my Master of Horse?" "Horrible, sire!" "Bah!" he said. "Gentlemen, remember the words of a Roman emperor: a dead enemy always smells sweet!"'
6 At 11.00 p.m., amid scenes of bitter acrimony and near-mutiny, Barclay ordered the evacuation of Smolensk. His officers were outraged at having to give up the city (as well as a battle which they felt they were winning) but Barclay was convinced that Napoleon would turn his flank and attack him from the rear. Having ordered Bagration out of Smolensk earlier in the day, he had the powder magazine blown and the holy icon of the Mother of God saved from the cathedral before marching his men – as the bells tolled and the city burned – over the bridge linking the Old City with the New Town. By 1.00 a.m. the last Russian soldier had crossed on to

the northern bank of the Dnieper: there Barclay regrouped, delaying his retreat in order to confuse the French advance guard as to his intentions. That same day, at St Petersburg, Alexander received a petition begging for Barclay's dismissal.

7 Digby Smith, in *The Greenhill Napoleonic Wars Data Book*, puts the French losses at 8,500 (most of them from Ney's III Corps) and those of the Russians at 6,000.

8 General Korv led the 2nd Cavalry Reserve Corps of Barclay's First Army of the West, consisting of some 3,000 dragoons and *uhlans* with attached artillery.

9 Voronzov commanded the 7th Grenadier Division in Bagration's Second Army of the West and this incident once again illustrates the poor level of co-operation between Bagration's and Barclay's forces.

10 General Charles-Etienne Gudin was an aristocratic soldier of the Ancien Régime. Having served in most of Napoleon's major battles, in 1812 he led the 3rd Division of Davout's I Corps. His loss at Valutina was deemed a catastrophe by the army.

11 Baron Lejeune superintended Gudin's funeral: 'I led the funeral procession to the large bastion on the south-east of the town, thinking that it would form a fitting mausoleum for the illustrious warrior. I ordered a tomb to be dug out in the bastion and above the corpse, arranged in the form of stars, were laid a number of muskets which had been broken in the struggle, for I thought to myself that some day perhaps Time, the all-destroyer, might expose the remains of the hero and this trophy of arms might win for him the same attention and respect as we ourselves pay to the bones of brave Gauls when the ancient tumuli concealing them are opened.'

12 One of Napoleon's oldest comrades-in-arms, General Jean-Andoche Junot, Duke of Abrantes, had held many positions of trust: aide-de-camp in 1796, front line general in 1799 and governor of Paris in 1806. In 1808 he led the French invasion of Portugal, returning home under a cloud after his defeat at the hands of the British at Vimeiro. Despite loyal services to Napoleon, he was never made a marshal and for this he bore a bitter grudge. In 1812 he replaced Jérôme in command of the Westphalians of VIII Corps.

13 Junot did not, as de Ségur suggests, lack experience in command, having been one of Napoleon's principal lieutenants for many years. He was, however – like most of Napoleon's generals – at a loss when removed from the guiding hand of his emperor. Matters were not helped by the onset of syphilis which, by 1812, had begun to undermine his reason. The following year, in a state of total derangement, Junot threw himself to his death from the upper storey window of his father's house.

14 The fight for Smolensk had claimed a total of over 14,000 casualties. When the Grand Army marched into the city on the morning of the 18th many of the French veterans literally threw up at the sight of the carnage. According to Dominique-Jean Larrey, Napoleon's chief surgeon, the streets were filled with Russian dead and dying, their numbers so great as to defy accurate computation.

Chapter 5 (pp. 67–87)

1 Uexküll, Detlev von, *Arms and the Woman: the Diaries of Baron Boris Uxkull 1812–1819*.
2 Chuquet, Arthur, *Human Voices from the Russian Campaign*.
3 Palmer, Alan, *Alexander I: Tsar of War and Peace*.
4 Field Marshal Suvarov (1729–1800) was a charismatic, aggressive, even brutal soldier, who came to personify bravery to the average Russian. He advocated the bayonet as the ultimate weapon and notched up a series of spectacular victories in his dramatic career.
5 Quoted in Caulaincourt, Armand de, *With Napoleon in Russia*.
6 Duffy, Christopher, *Borodino and the War of 1812*.
7 Caulaincourt, Armand de, *op. cit.*
8 Napoleon appears to have been suffering from a bladder complaint which caused him acute pain. He tried to keep this malady a secret, and as a consequence many officers were totally baffled by his apparent lack of interest in proceedings at Borodino. In general, his health was not good in 1812 and while in Russia he was dogged by colds and fevers.
9 The charismatic leader of II Cavalry Corps was hit in the

stomach by a shell splinter. An eyewitness heard him exclaim, 'Good shot!' as he slid from the saddle.

10 Baron Fain recalled that, on the eve of Borodino, 'Auguste de Caulaincourt was not asleep but half lying down on a camp mattress and wrapped in his coat, with his head propped up on his elbow: he was gazing sadly at a portrait of his young wife whom he had been forced to leave almost as soon as he had married her. One would have said he was bidding her eternal farewell.' Quoted in Brett-James, Antony, *1812: Eye-witness Accounts of Napoleon's Defeat in Russia.*

11 According to David Chandler in *The Campaigns of Napoleon,* the Grand Army fired approximately 90,000 artillery rounds and 2,000,000 musket rounds at Borodino.

12 Estimates vary in the literature but casualties among the top brass were severe enough for Caulaincourt to write, 'Generals who were killed or wounded were replaced without the least sensation being caused.'

13 De Ségur relates an almost identical incident when, on 29 October, the Grand Army recrosses the field of battle only to find a wounded Frenchman whose life had apparently been saved by this novel method (see Chapter 9).

Chapter 6 (pp. 89–106)

1 Faber du Faur, Christian Wilhelm von, *With Napoleon in Russia.*

2 Palmer, Alan, *Alexander I: Tsar of War and Peace.*

3 Foord, Edward, *Napoleon's Russian Campaign of 1812.*

4 Rostopchin later denied responsibility for the fire but only after public opinion condemned the act as a crime. Certain letters, however, written by Rostopchin on the eve of his departure, hint at a coming conflagration and of Moscow becoming Napoleon's 'tomb'. He later left Russia and took up residence at Paris, where his daughter Sophie married de Ségur's nephew, Eugène: a link which, perhaps, adds credence to de Ségur's version of events.

5 Uexküll, Detlev von, *Arms and the Woman: the Diaries of Baron Boris Uxkull 1812–1819.*

6 The two officers concerned were almost certainly de Ségur himself and Baron de Bausset, who, on 14 September, were sent into the Kremlin to prepare rooms for Napoleon. De Bausset later recalled that 'Ségur and I were obliged to spend the night fully clothed and stretched out on armchairs. We selected the room which had been reserved for the Emperor: here the windows had no shutters and no curtains . . . With such uncomfortable beds, I slept fitfully despite the exhausting day. Between midnight and one o'clock I noticed fairly bright glows, though they were some distance away. I went to the windows and saw flames leaping up in whichever direction I looked.' Quoted in Brett-James, Antony, *1812: Eyewitness Accounts of Napoleon's Defeat in Russia*.

7 The only reference I have found in the literature to a fire-balloon occurs in Alan Palmer's *Alexander I: Tsar of War and Peace*, and concerns a German inventor by the name of Leppich. Having failed to impress Napoleon with his madcap ideas, he travelled to Russia in June 1812. Alexander, fascinated by Leppich's talk of exploding balloons, welcomed him with open arms and funded experiments at a Moscow workshop. Leppich (now calling himself Schmidt) was soon exposed as a charlatan and fled: but when Napoleon's troops occupied the city, they came across his workshop and rumours of secret weapons, incendiary devices and fire-balloons soon spread throughout the Grand Army.

8 Sergeant Bourgogne describes how he and his comrades 'met several men with long beards and sinister faces looking still more terrible by the lurid light of the torches they carried; we let them pass us quietly . . . we then met a number of *chasseurs* of the Guard, who told us that the Russians themselves had set fire to the town and that the men we had just met did the business.' This and all other quotations by Bourgogne are taken from Bourgogne, Jean Baptiste, *Memoirs of Sergeant Bourgogne*, London 1899.

9 Bourgogne states that, 'During the 16th orders had been given to shoot everyone found setting fire to houses. This order was executed at once.'

10 Napoleon sought refuge at Petrovsky on 16 September. According to de Ségur, the fire had largely abated by the

19th and had ceased by the 20th; on which day, Napoleon took up residence in the Kremlin once more.

11 According to Captain Rigau, an officer on Berthier's staff, 'Moscow looked like a pit surrounded by a sea of flames; they reached from the north to the south, rising to the skies; the sound of sheets of iron crashing down from domes and houses onto the wide pavements struck sadness into the heart' (Chuquet, Arthur, *Human Voices from the Russian Campaign*).

12 Prince Wittgenstein, a Russian of German ancestry, commanded a force in the northern sector of the campaign. Although defeated at Polotsk on 18 August by General (afterwards, Marshal) Gouvion St-Cyr, he remained hovering on the edge of Napoleon's left flank.

13 De Ségur regards the saving of the Kremlin as unfortunate because it facilitated Napoleon's lengthy sojourn at Moscow which, arguably, led to the army's destruction in the icy grip of the Russian winter.

14 Pillage broke out almost as soon as the famished troops of the Grand Army entered Moscow: the fire served only to heighten the disorder. According to Bourgogne, 'as soon as it was known that the Russians themselves had fired the town, it was impossible to restrain the men.' The veteran campaigner, Captain Coignet, took advantage of the looting to augment his wardrobe: 'As I was crossing the square of the Kremlin, I met some soldiers loaded with fur robes and bearskins; I stopped them and offered to buy their furs. "How much is this one?" "Forty francs." I took it immediately and paid him the price he asked.'

Chapter 7 (pp. 107–122)

1 Palmer, Alan, *Alexander I: Tsar of War and Peace.*

2 According to Foord, Vereia was taken by the partisan leader, Dorokhov, who, reinforced by five battalions of regular infantry, plus some cavalry and artillery, 'stormed into Vereia, killing or capturing its garrison of over 500 Westphalians and thus establishing himself dangerously near the Moscow-Smolensk road'.

3 Napoleon was already referring to the Austrians and Prussians as 'enemies behind our backs'.
4 General Mikhail Miloradovich was an outstanding soldier: brave, cool-headed and experienced. He survived countless combats with his country's enemies only to be shot by his own men in the Decembrist Revolt of 1825.
5 According to Foord, 'No issue was made of clothing material until 17 October, nor were any preparations made for rough-shoeing the horses. In the general relaxation of discipline little was done by the men themselves.'
6 Murat's advanced guard was caught napping at Vinkovo, largely thanks to General Sébastiani who, according to Marbot, 'passed his days in slippers reading Italian poetry and never reconnoitring'. A.H. Atteridge describes Murat's unpleasant alarm call thus: 'At dawn on 18 October, he was surprised at Vinkovo and narrowly escaped destruction. He was asleep when Platov's Cossacks drove in his outposts. Half-dressed, he mounted and led more than one charge; but the most he could do was to drive the enemy from their position on his line of retreat and withdraw . . .'
7 Kutusov scored something of a lukewarm victory at Vinkovo: he lost around 1,500 killed and wounded, while inflicting 2,000 casualties upon Murat's much weaker force. He also bagged some 1,500 prisoners.

Chapter 8 (pp. 123–138)

1 Mortier did not approve of his mission and paid more attention to victualling his troops than destroying Moscow's famous citadel. Although the Kremlin was seriously damaged it was not destroyed. Mortier left Moscow on 23 October.
2 As a veteran of Austerlitz, Eylau and Borodino, General Dmitri Sergeivich Docturov was one of Kutusov's most experienced officers.
3 A hussar officer named Akinfov brought the glad tidings to Kutusov who, although he had retired to bed for the night, was still to be found bedecked with medals.

4 The population of Maloyaroslavets was around 10,000 in 1812.
5 Most sources concur that Napoleon had arrived on the scene by the early afternoon.
6 Although Docturov was reinforced by Raevski's advanced guard in the morning, Kutusov did not appear with the balance of his army until late afternoon: by which time Docturov had abandoned the town.
7 Delzons' 13th Infantry Division consisted of both French and Croatian troops.
8 Guilleminot was Eugène's chief of staff.
9 In fact, both sides committed around 24,000 men to the fight. The Grand Army sustained some 6,000 casualties; the Russians about 8,000.
10 De Ségur is perhaps a little harsh on Napoleon, for the Grand Army was now pitifully short of horses; and those which remained were mostly sick and half-starved. Meanwhile, the boggy nature of the ground (after heavy rains) and the abominable Russian roads further hindered the advance on Maloyaroslavets. Lastly, the sheer amount of baggage and booty carried by the army constituted a major encumbrance, as did the legion of camp-followers which had attached itself to the main column. As for being 'informed' of the Russians' march on Maloyaroslavets, Docturov had marched stealthily through the night, taking every precaution to avoid detection. His dawn attack on Delzons came as a complete surprise.
11 Russian guns were trained on the narrow bridge, making any attempt to cross an act of suicide. Napoleon was not, at this late stage of the campaign, prepared to take the necessary losses for an attack on Kutusov's position.
12 De Ségur pays tribute to Kutusov but the real credit goes to Docturov and Raevski: their quick thinking and determination actually saved Kutusov at Maloyaroslavets.
13 These audacious horsemen were, apparently, regular Tartar lancers or *uhlans*, though most eyewitnesses refer to them as Cossacks.
14 Le Coulteux joined in the mad scramble to save Napoleon from capture and was accidentally run through by a French grenadier for his trouble: fortunately, he survived. Although

Sergeant Bourgogne claims to have heard Napoleon joking with Murat shortly after his escapade, the Emperor took the event seriously enough to order his physician, Dr Yvan, to prepare a vial of poison in case of further dire emergencies. Capture, for Napoleon, was not an option.

Chapter 9 (pp. 139–152)

1 Clausewitz summed up Kutusov's strategy thus: 'Kutusov still feared his adversary and would not commit himself in a decisive battle; but resolved to do him all the mischief he could without himself incurring the risk of defeat' (Clausewitz, General Carl von, *The Campaign of 1812 in Russia*).

2 Wilson, General Sir Robert (1777–1849). Described by Wellington as 'a very slippery fellow,' Wilson was a British cavalry officer turned diplomat who, having been sent to Constantinople in 1812, decided to join the Russians in their fight against Napoleon. He enjoyed some popularity with Alexander and was highly critical of Kutusov.

3 Quoted in Chuquet, Arthur, *Human Voices from the Russian Campaign*.

4 Quoted in Wheeler, Harold F.B., *The Mind of Napoleon: as Revealed in His Thoughts, Speech and Actions*.

5 Some authorities estimate the total number of dead and wounded at Borodino to have been as many as 76,000.

6 On 19 May 1798 General Bonaparte set sail from Toulon with the Army of the Orient: his goal, the conquest of Egypt. Although victorious at the Battle of the Pyramids, Bonaparte's expedition was stranded after Nelson destroyed his invasion fleet, lying at anchor, at the Battle of the Nile. A foray into Syria was thwarted before the walls of Acre and Bonaparte, leaving his plague-ridden army to its fate, returned to France to stage the coup which would eventually give him absolute power.

7 Despite de Ségur's rhetoric, most of the men on the expedition were simply there as conscripts.

8 This episode would appear to be an echo of the incident described in Chapter 5, in which a Russian soldier 'lived for

several days in the carcase of a horse, which had been gutted by a shell'. Marbot, who was not at Borodino, was unconvinced by de Ségur's vignette: 'It was pointed out to him that the man would have been stifled by the gases of decomposition and that he would probably have preferred to cover his wounds with fresh earth or even grass, than to make them worse by bringing them into contact with putrid flesh . . .'

9 According to Leroy-Dupré, 'Larrey, on quitting Kolotskoi, gave the wounded Russians money, as he observed many itinerant dealers from whom these convalescents might purchase such things as were indispensable for their complete restoration. Having done this good work to the Russian officers, Larrey then commended to their care in that foreign land those wounded among his own countrymen who, such was the severity of their wounds, could not be removed.'

10 French wounded left in Moscow hospitals were murdered and then dumped in the river.

11 De Ségur makes several references to the psychological strain on Davout. A conscientious professional and stern disciplinarian, the 'Iron Marshal' must have been particularly distressed at the army's disintegration. Matters were not helped by Napoleon's harsh treatment of him and feuds with Berthier, Murat and Ney.

Chapter 10 (pp. 153–161)

1 Quoted in Chuquet, Arthur, *Human Voices from the Russian Campaign*.

2 General Hulin was the governor of Paris. Although shot and wounded by Malet, he survived his ordeal.

3 Malet was given the honour of commanding his own firing squad. The first volley felled his eleven hapless colleagues – innocent scapegoats for the most part – but left Malet standing: he calmly put the squad through its paces a second time.

4 Watson, S.J., *By Command of the Emperor*.

5 Chuquet, Arthur, *op. cit.*

6 Quoted by Bourrienne, who claimed to have it from Rapp.

7 General Augereau, younger brother of Marshal Augereau,

Duke of Castiglione, was captured by partisans on the road between Elnia and Smolensk.

8 On 9 November Eugène's corps reached the River Vop. With no bridging equipment, the soldiers were obliged to wade up to their waists through the freezing water: Eugène, surrounded by his Italian Royal Guard, led the way. Once across, the troops had to chase away Platov's Cossacks. Chaos ensued, however, when Eugène attempted to get his artillery and baggage across: guns and wagons stuck in the mud and had to be abandoned; the troops then fought over the pickings and pillage and murder followed. That night, many of Eugène's men died of exposure as, harassed by Cossacks, IV Corps was driven back to Smolensk. Eugène arrived on 13 November with about 6,000 effective troops and twenty guns.

9 Bourgogne states, 'Thousands of men were there already from every corps and of every nation. They were waiting at the gates and ramparts till they could gain admission and this had been refused them on the grounds that, marching as they were without officers or order, and already dying of hunger, they might pillage the town for provisions. Many hundreds of these men were already dead or dying. When we arrived there with the rest of the Guard in an orderly fashion and taking the utmost precaution for our sick and wounded, the gates were opened and we entered. The greater number broke ranks and spread on all sides, anxious to find some roof under which to spend the night and eat the food promised us.'

10 A quintal is equal to one hundredweight or 112 pounds or 50 kilos.

Chapter 11 (pp. 162–175)

1 Most authorities seem to agree that the total number of troops available to Napoleon at Krasnoi was 16,000, against Kutusov's 35,000.

2 Latour-Maubourg was an intrepid cavalry general. He survived the Russian campaign only to lose a leg at the Battle of Leipzig the following year: his stoical reaction was simply to

inform his servant that in future there would only be one boot to polish!

3 As previously mentioned, many ordinary Russians believed Napoleon to be the Antichrist. Kutusov's soldiers claimed numerous simultaneous sightings of him over vast distances, and in some instances this was claimed as proof of his supernatural powers! Murat, too, was considered to possess magical qualities as, although he was always first into battle, he never failed to emerge miraculously unscathed.

4 Davidov, the Russian partisan leader described how 'The Guard with Napoleon passed through our Cossacks like a 100-gun ship through a fishing fleet.'

5 According to Foord, 'A murderous cannonade was directed upon the thin French line south of Krasnoi and under cover of it the Russian infantry advanced. The Dutch Grenadiers, shattered by artillery fire, fell out of the line.'

6 Bourgogne tells how 'These poor fellows, nearly all very young, having their hands and feet mostly frostbitten, had no power to defend themselves and were absolutely massacred.'

7 According to Foord, 'Though a thaw was setting in this brought little relief to the sufferings of the Grande Armée. Snow fell heavily and the fatigue of tramping through it was enormous, while the damp foggy weather told almost as heavily upon the men as the bitter cold of the previous days.'

8 His nose frostbitten, his servants dead, his baggage gone, his marshal's *bâton* lost, Davout must have cut a sorry figure. Stoical to the last, the Marshal blamed the army's misfortunes on the severity of the weather: 'No power or genius on earth could prevent the harm the weather is doing us.' Quoted in Chuquet, Arthur, *Human Voices from the Russian Campaign*.

Chapter 12 (pp. 177–189)

1 All quoted in Chuquet, Arthur, *Human Voices from the Russian Campaign*.

2 These troops were drawn from territories along the Adriatic coast, ceded to France by Austria in 1809. The so-called

Illyrian Provinces included parts of modern-day Croatia and Slovenia.

3 Presumably de Ségur means that he was drunk. Marbot observes that the Russian officers of that time all shared 'the bad habit of drinking too much brandy'.

4 De Ségur describes how, when Ney's troops were met by Eugène's, 'They all proceeded together in company towards Orsha, all impatient, Eugène's soldiers to hear and Ney's to tell their story.' His account of III Corps' adventures, therefore, is based on the testimony of its survivors.

Chapter 13 (pp. 191–203)

1 Johann von Borcke, quoted in Brett-James, Antony, *1812: Eyewitness Accounts of Napoleon's Defeat in Russia.*

2 Schwarzenberg's victory over Sacken counted for little among the hard-pressed troops of the Grand Army: when the news of Minsk's capture broke, they blamed the Austrians for the catastrophe and accused Schwarzenberg of betraying them. According to de Ségur, 'Although the treachery of Schwarzenberg was by no means so evident, it is certain that with the exception of the three French generals who were with him, the whole of the Grand Army considered it as beyond a doubt.'

3 Quoted in Herold, J. Christopher, *The Mind of Napoleon: a Selection from His Written and Spoken Words.*

4 A fathom being roughly equal to a measurement of two metres, this makes the river crossing at this point 108 metres wide.

5 Johann von Borcke, quoted in Brett-James, Antony, *op. cit.*

6 Thus making the bridge 600 metres long.

7 General Jean-Baptiste Eblé (1758–1812) has gone down in history as the man who saved the Grand Army on the banks of the River Berezina. An artilleryman by profession, he was given charge of the army's pontoon-train in 1812. His foresight in preserving – against Napoleon's direct orders – at least some of his bridging equipment enabled him to effect the passage of the Berezina. In January 1813 Napoleon pro-

moted him, unaware that he had died of tuberculosis a month before as a result of his exertions in Russia.

8 The temperature was recorded at around minus 25° Centigrade.

9 In fact, a quarter of Eblé's engineers were Dutch. Incidentally, the sappers did not work naked at Studzianka, as has occasionally been stated, and were not permanently submerged: much of the work was carried out with the aid of makeshift rafts.

Chapter 14 (pp. 205–216)

1 This eyewitness was Louise Fusil, a French actress who had thrown in her lot with the Grand Army at Moscow, in the hope of gaining a safe passage home. She claimed that Napoleon waved her carriage over the bridge, telling her not to be afraid, while Murat strutted about 'like the hero of a melodrama'. Her adventures at the Berezina are briefly described in Johnson, David, *The French Cavalry, 1792–1815*.

2 General Count de Langeron commanded an infantry division in Chichagov's army. His critical pen-portrait of Chichagov is quoted in Brett-James, Antony, *1812: Eyewitness Accounts of Napoleon's Defeat in Russia*.

3 The artillery bridge was constantly giving way: completed around 4.00 p.m. on 26 November, three of its trestles had given way within four hours but the bridge was functional again by 8.00 p.m. The centre of the bridge broke at 2.00 a.m. on the 27th but, once more, repairs were quickly effected and the bridge was functioning again by 6.00 a.m. It gave way again, as de Ségur says, around 4.00 p.m. on the 27th but was repaired within the space of two hours. Although the infantry bridge held, its boardwalk kept breaking and needed constant attention.

4 Marbot notes that the thousands of stragglers stranded on the eastern bank could simply have walked across the bridges on the night of 27 November: 'These men, sitting calmly in front of enormous fires, were grilling horseflesh without a notion that they had in front of them a river, the passage of which

would cost many of them their lives on the next day, while they could at the present time cross it without hindrance in a few minutes and finish preparing their supper on the other bank.'

5 According to Marbot, Noailles ventured too far in the direction of the Russian positions at the village of Stachova and 'was surrounded by a group of Cossacks, who threw him from his horse and dragged him along by the collar, striking him as they went. I sent a squadron to his assistance but my effort was fruitless, for a brisk fire from the houses prevented the troopers from entering the village and from that day nothing was ever heard of M. de Noailles.'

6 According to Vossler, the shells of the Russian artillery awoke the unfortunates still waiting to cross to the danger of Cossacks: 'Around one o'clock the cry went up, "The Cossacks are coming!" Those on the periphery knew they would be the first victims. Any speeding up of the movement towards the bridge seemed utterly impossible but the cry electrified the rabble and spurred everybody to a final effort.'

7 Eblé delayed burning the bridges for as long as possible, in the hope that the stragglers would cross, but to no avail. Eventually, according to Lejeune, 'General Eblé, charged with the painful duty of burning the bridges after Marshal Victor's corps had passed over, had the greatest difficulty in cutting his way to them; and many of our own people were piteously struck down by the hatchets of his men before they were able to perform the task assigned to them.'

8 The Russians later claimed to have dragged 36,000 bodies from the river.

9 As already stated, a fathom is roughly equal to a measurement of two metres, making each bridge 600 metres long. Neglecting to burn the bridges over the Zembin marshes was a major blunder on the part of the Russians, as de Ségur himself observes: 'Caught between the morass and the river, in a narrow space, without provisions, in the midst of a tremendous hurricane, the Grand Army and its Emperor must have been compelled to surrender without striking a blow.' The French rearguard did not make the same mistake: once safely over the marshes, they set fire to the bridges, thus

thwarting their pursuers. The Russians eventually crossed the freezing marshes on planks.

Chapter 15 (pp. 217–231)

1 Captain Rigau, quoted in Chuquet, Arthur, *Human Voices from the Russian Campaign*.
2 Foord, Edward, *Napoleon's Russian Campaign of 1812*.
3 Quoted in Atteridge, A.H., *Joachim Murat*.
4 Ever since hearing of the Malet Conspiracy on 6 November, Napoleon's mind had been fixed on returning to Paris. Having seen his army across the Berezina, its last major obstacle before reaching the Niemen, there remained nothing to detain him.
5 Berthier was fifty-eight in 1812 and as Napoleon's chief of staff had been virtually worked to death. Caulaincourt records that Berthier 'was greatly upset at having to remain behind'.
6 De Ségur would seem to be giving temperatures in degrees Réaumur, a system used by the Russians up to the outbreak of the First World War. A temperature of minus 26° Réaumur is roughly equivalent to minus 33° Centigrade. The famous statistical chart produced by Charles Joseph Minard in 1861, showing the losses of the Grand Army in relation to the increasing cold, gives the temperature for 6 December, a mere two days later, as minus 37.5° Centigrade.
7 The famous 29th Bulletin was Napoleon's synopsis of the campaign, intended for public consumption. He paid tribute to his troops and lieutenants, highlighting their glorious deeds and hinting at their sufferings and losses. He was careful to overplay the effects of the Russian winter (which only became unusually severe after his departure, by which time the army was already wrecked), thus laying the foundation for the subsequent mythology of the campaign. He concluded the bulletin with the phrase, 'His Majesty's health has never been better,' words which have been taken ever since for gross cynicism, bearing in mind the scale of the human tragedy unfolding around him. In the aftermath of

the Malet Conspiracy, however, Napoleon was keen to quash any rumours of his death or capture. It was not so much cynicism as realpolitik.

8 Davout managed to make an enemy of almost every colleague by quarrelling and issuing unwanted advice. A loyal, methodical, professional soldier, his character was diametrically opposed to showy adventurers like Murat. Unfortunately for him, both Napoleon and the army in general heartily approved of such charismatic *sabreurs*, and Davout, largely unpopular and unfairly blamed for having deserted Ney in his hour of need, spent much of the campaign out of favour at imperial headquarters.

9 According to Caulaincourt, he and Napoleon occupied a 'sleeping coach' while Wonsowitsch and Roustam, the Emperor's Mameluke bodyguard, rode alongside with two other outriders; Duroc and Count Lobau followed, not in a sledge, but 'in one calèche, Baron Fain and M. Constant in a second'. Once safely out of Russian territory, it was Napoleon and Caulaincourt who took to a sledge, bought by the latter for a few gold pieces. This novel conveyance took the Emperor and his grand equerry as far as Dresden, where they once again took to a coach.

10 Hugues-Bernard Maret, Duke of Bassano, was Napoleon's foreign minister and one of the Emperor's chief diplomats and advisers. He later became Napoleon's private secretary.

11 *Sauve-qui-peut* roughly translates as 'a stampede' or 'every man for himself'.

12 Lejeune records that stragglers were referred to as *fricoteurs* or revellers; while Marbot calls them *rôtisseurs*, a derogatory term meaning 'sellers of roast meat'.

Chapter 16 (pp. 233–248)

1 Jomini, Baron Antoine Henri de, *The Art of War*.

2 Quoted in Chuquet, Arthur, *Human Voices from the Russian Campaign*.

3 Quoted in Brett-James, Antony, *1812: Eyewitness Accounts of Napoleon's Defeat in Russia*.

4 Chuquet, Arthur, *op. cit.*
5 Auguste Thirion, quoted in Brett-James, Antony, *op. cit.*
6 Quoted in Johnson, David, *Napoleon's Cavalry and its Leaders.*
7 Atteridge, A.H., *Joachim Murat.*
8 Chuquet, Arthur, *op. cit.*
9 Presumably degrees Réaumur or almost minus 35° Centigrade.
10 According to Foord, between 5 and 9 December 20,000 men 'dropped away from the column'.
11 Napoleon kept the plight of his army a secret so as not to spread panic: thus Vilna, like Smolensk, was totally unprepared for a sudden influx of freezing, starving soldiery. Although the stores were immense – 4,000,000 rations of biscuit, plus meat, clothing, boots (30,000 pairs) and weapons (27,000 muskets) – Marbot records how 'There, as at Smolensk, the commissaries required, before giving out provisions and clothing, that regular receipts should be handed to them, a thing which, in the disorganised state of all the regiments, was impossible to do.' According to Chuquet in *Human Voices from the Russian Campaign,* a certain Lieutenant Jacquemont was detailed to blow up the stores before the Russians arrived but the Cossacks stormed into town and the good lieutenant's men ran away: thus, 'Jacquemont missed the opportunity of connecting his name with an event that doubtless would have been one of the memorable episodes of the campaign.'
12 At Vilna the hospitals were already full of casualties from the earlier stages of the campaign.
13 Major-General O'Rourke was a Russian soldier of Irish ancestry.
14 De Ségur's account of the sufferings of Napoleon's soldiers at the hands of the Jews of Vilna finds parallels in other contemporary accounts. According to Marbot – who is so often at odds with de Ségur – the Jews received such soldiers as could pay for their hospitality and then, with the arrival of the Cossacks, robbed them and 'pitched them naked out of the window'.
15 Marbot claims that Marshal Ney ordered the treasure chests to be opened and plundered, in preference to the loot falling into the hands of the Cossacks. Captain Coignet of the

Imperial Guard, however, merely states that 'All the material of the army and the Emperor's carriages were on the ground. The soldiers helped themselves to gold and silver plate. All the chests and caskets were burst open. What a quantity of plunder was left on that spot!' The Cossacks rooting through Napoleon's belongings apparently drank his eau de Cologne, mistaking it for spirits!

Epilogue (pp. 249–256)

1 Johnson, David, *Napoleon's Cavalry and its Leaders.*
2 Knowles, Elizabeth (editor), *Oxford Dictionary of Quotations.*
3 Caulaincourt, Armand de, *With Napoleon in Russia.*
4 *Ibid.*
5 Chuquet, Arthur, *Human Voices from the Russian Campaign.*
6 Napoleon's description of the Grand Army's pathetic survivors, quoted in Caulaincourt.
7 Dunn-Pattison, R.P., *Napoleon's Marshals.*
8 Atteridge, A.H., *Joachim Murat.*
9 Palmer, Alan, *Alexander I: Tsar of War and Peace.*
10 MacDonald, Jacques Etienne, Recollections of Marshal MacDonald, Duke of Tarentum.
11 *Ibid.*
12 MacDonald, Jacques Etienne, *o;. cit.* To be fair on Yorck, he committed himself to strict neutrality and resisted all pressure actually to turn-coat.
13 Atteridge, A.H., *op. cit.*. Caroline was frequently unfaithful to Murat (she once had a notorious affair with Junot) and relished the freedom his absence on campaign afforded her. An intelligent, capable and ambitious woman, she acted as her husband's regent during the Russian expedition and managed Neapolitan affairs of state with a skill worthy of a Bonaparte.
14 *Ibid.*
15 *Ibid.*
16 Quoted in Wheeler, Harold F.B., *The Mind of Napoleon: as Revealed in His Thoughts, Speech and Actions.*
17 *Ibid.*

Bibliography

The following books were consulted in the preparation of this work and I would like to acknowledge my debt to their authors, editors and translators.

Atteridge, A. H., *Joachim Murat*, London 1911.

Barnett, Corelli, *Bonaparte*, London 1997 (reissue).

Blond, Georges, *La Grande Armée*, London 1995.

Bourgogne, Jean-Baptiste, *Memoirs of Sergeant Bourgogne*, London 1899.

Bourrienne, F. de, *Memoirs of Napoleon Bonaparte*, London 1905.

Brandt, Heinrich von, *In the Legions of Napoleon: the Memoirs of a Polish Officer in Spain and Russia 1808–1813*, London 1999 (translated and edited by Jonathan North).

Brett-James, Antony, *1812: Eyewitness Accounts of Napoleon's Defeat in Russia*, London 1967.

Bryant, Arthur, *The Age of Elegance: 1812–1822*, London 1950.

Caulaincourt, Armand de, *With Napoleon in Russia*, New York 1935.

Chandler, David G., *The Campaigns of Napoleon*, London 1966.

Chandler, David G., *Dictionary of the Napoleonic Wars*, London 1993.

Chandler, David G., *Napoleon's Marshals*, London 1987.

Chandler, David G., *On the Napoleonic Wars*, London 1994.

Chuquet, Arthur, *Human Voices from the Russian Campaign*, London 1914.

Clausewitz, General Carl von, *On War*, London 1908.

Clausewitz, General Carl von, *The Campaign of 1812 in Russia*, London 1843.

Cohen, Louis, *Napoleonic Anecdotes*, London 1925.

Coignet, Jean-Roch, *The Narrative of Captain Coignet: Soldier of the Empire*, London 1928.

Connelly, Owen, *Blundering to Glory*, Wilmington 1987.

Duffy, Christopher, *Borodino and the War of 1812*, London 1972.

Dunn-Pattison, R.P., *Napoleon's Marshals*, London 1909.

Elting, John R., *Swords Around a Throne*, London 1989.

Esposito, Vincent J., and Elting, John R., *A Military History and Atlas of the Napoleonic Wars*, London 1999 (reissue).

Faber du Faur, Christian Wilhelm von, *With Napoleon in Russia*, London 2001 (translated and edited by Jonathan North).

Foord, Edward, *Napoleon's Russian Campaign of 1812*, London 1914.

Gallaher, John G., *The Iron Marshal: A Biography of Louis N. Davout*, Edwardsville 1976.

Haffner, Sebastian, *The Rise and Fall of Prussia*, London 1980.

Handel, Michael I., *Masters of War: Classical Strategic Thought*, London 1992.

Haythornthwaite, Philip J., *Die Hard! Dramatic Actions from the Napoleonic Wars*, London 1996.

Haythornthwaite, Philip J., *Who Was Who in the Napoleonic Wars*, London 1998.

Herold, J. Christopher, *The Mind of Napoleon: a Selection from His Written and Spoken Words*, New York 1955.

Horne, Alistair, *How Far From Austerlitz?*, London 1996.

Hourtoulle, F.-G., *Borodino – the Moskova: the Battle for the Redoubts*, Paris 2000.

Johnson, David, *Napoleon's Cavalry and its Leaders*, New York 1978.

Johnson, David, *The French Cavalry, 1792–1815*, London 1989.

Jomini, Baron Antoine Henri de, *The Art of War*, London 1992 (reissue).

Knowles, Elizabeth (editor), *The Oxford Dictionary of Quotations*, London 1999.

Lachouque, Henry and Brown, Anne S.K., *The Anatomy of Glory: Napoleon and His Guard*, London 1997 (reissue).

Laffin, John, *Brassey's Battles*, London 1986.

Lejeune, Louis-François, *Memoirs of Baron Lejeune*, London 1897.

Leroy-Dupré, L.A.H., *Memoirs of Baron Larrey*, London 1862.

MacDonald, Jacques Etienne, *Recollections of Marshal MacDonald, Duke of Tarentum*, London 1893.

MacDonnell, A.G., *Napoleon and His Marshals*, London 1934.

Marbot, Jean-Baptiste de, *Memoirs of Baron de Marbot*, London 1900.

McLynn, Frank, *Napoleon*, London 1997.

Nafziger, George F., *Napoleon's Invasion of Russia*, Novato 1988.

Nicolson, Nigel, *Napoleon: 1812*, London 1985.

Palmer, Alan, *Alexander I: Tsar of War and Peace*, London 1974.

Palmer, Alan, *An Encyclopaedia of Napoleon's Europe*, London 1984.

Palmer, Alan, *Napoleon in Russia*, London 1967.

Pawly, Ronald, *The Red Lancers*, Ramsbury 1998.

Richardson, Robert, *Larrey: Surgeon to Napoleon's Imperial Guard*, London 1974.

Rogers, Colonel H.C.B., *Napoleon's Army*, London 1974.

Ségur, General Count Philippe-Paul de, *An Aide-de-Camp of Napoleon: Memoirs of General Count de Ségur*, London 1895.

Ségur, General Count Philippe-Paul de, *History of the Expedition to Russia Undertaken by the Emperor Napoleon in the Year 1812*, London 1827.

Seward, Desmond, *Napoleon and Hitler*, London 1988.

Smith, Digby, *Borodino*, London 1998.

Smith, Digby, *The Greenhill Napoleonic Wars Data Book*, London 1998.

Uexküll, Detlev von, *Arms and the Woman: the Diaries of Baron Uxkull*, London 1966.

Vossler, H.A., *With Napoleon in Russia*, London 1969.

Watson, S.J., *By Command of the Emperor: A Life of Marshal Berthier*, London 1957.

Wheeler, Harold F.B., *The Mind of Napoleon: as Revealed in His Thoughts, Speech and Actions*, London 1910.

Wilson, Sir Robert, *Brief Remarks on the Character and Composition of the Russian Army and a Sketch of the Campaigns in Poland in the Years 1806 and 1807*, London 1810.